British Institute of Archaeology at Ankara

Monograph No. 23

CANHASAN SITES 1

CANHASAN I: STRATIGRAPHY AND STRUCTURES

by

DAVID FRENCH

Published by

THE BRITISH INSTITUTE OF ARCHAEOLOGY AT ANKARA

1998

British Institute of Archaeology at Ankara
c/o British Academy, 10 Carlton House Terrace,
London SW1Y 5AH

This book is available from Oxbow Books,
Park End Place, Oxford OX1 1HN

ISBN 1 898249 09 1
ISSN 0969–9007

The front cover shows a reconstruction of the Canhasan I settlement seen from the SE (drawing by Ian James Walls). The back cover shows Canhasan I from the SW (September 1961).

Printed by Stephen Austin, Hertford

Contents

Preface

There is a mental ease to be won from nostalgia and reminiscence and in the preparation of this volume I have felt the pleasure of both emotions. At the same time I have come fully to accept the essential anachronism of the publication. Perhaps obscured in 1968, the inadequacies of approach, technique and interpretation, are today an embarrassment. In my view these inadequacies have become so magnified that the originality, such as it was, of the enterprise has mutated into an historical event of little substance and, I suspect, now of little relevance, a conclusion enforced neither by conscience nor by guilt but by reality.

Between 1962 and 1968 I published nearly one hundred pages of preliminary reports: suitably organized and reprinted they would have been recognized, in the eyes of many (if not most) archaeologists of that era, as more than enough for a final publication. The terseness of these preliminary reports has been retained. No doubt there are some who would prefer a more expansive account and a less telegraphic style. Nevertheless, in the volumes which follow, I have deliberately chosen a minimalist prose partly in order to keep close to the idiosyncrasies of the first accounts but principally to focus on the record more than on the interpretation.

In some ways, then, this and the succeeding volumes are no more than a revision, an up-date, of the preliminary reports. In a word, I have chosen, by the methods employed in the first accounts, to describe and illustrate the context of structures and objects rather than to emphasize an assumed importance for the things discovered.

If it seems that in my approach to publication I follow the spirit of an earlier generation, notably the American excavators at Troy, then I willingly acknowledge the debt, since it was Professor Blegen who at Pylos in 1958 introduced me to the rigours of that taciturn discipline which was the characteristic of his own life and work.

Acknowledgements

Amongst the many persons who have assisted me in the preparation of this volume I wish to acknowledge, first and foremost, the contribution made by Brian Williams who prepared the plans and the section-drawings. On numerous occasions he corrected my errors and disentangled the problems created by insufficient recording and inadequate notes. Without his meticulousness and clarity this, the finished publication, would have been threadbare and incoherent. Ben Claasz Coockson made the copy which appears here as Fig. 03.

The prints made from the Canhasan photographic archive are the work of Tuğrul Çakar. I am grateful for his skill.

The penultimate version of the text was read by Lisa French, Machteld Mellink, Nicholas Postgate and Geoffrey Summers. I have greatly benefited from their help, advice and constructive criticism.

To all those (listed below, Section 1.9) who participated in the Canhasan excavations and to the Ministry Representatives who guarded our interests in all circumstances and weather I owe an unpayable debt. To both I offer my grateful thanks.

The late Michael Gough, my Director, and Ferdinand de la Grange, the BIAA Secretary in Ankara until 1970 and for the preceding twelve years my guide and mentor, were my greatest support at all times. It is a pleasure to recall their trust and belief. I do so with the deepest affection.

I wish here to acknowledge the support (listed below, Section 1.8) given to the excavations by the fund-giving bodies.

The Turkish authorities always looked on the case of Canhasan, both during and after the excavation, with the utmost patience and dealt benignly with a wayward director who chose to abandon the site in favour of rescue archaeology on the River Euphrates. Certainly during my thirty-six years in Turkish archaeology I received not one word of reproach for my decisions, though I did hear the gentlest of regrets, that I had not done more at Canhasan. I respect the privilege which was given me and I honour the forebearance which the host extended to the guest. In dedicating this book to my many Turkish hosts I wish to acknowledge the hospitality, the *misafirperverlik*.

List of Figures

Unless otherwise stated, all drawings are by Brian Williams

List of Plates

Bibliography

BELKE, KL.

1984 *Tabula Imperii Byzantini* 4. *Galatien und Lykaonien*. Vienna (DenkschrWien 172)

DAVIS, E.J.

1879 *Life in Asiatic Turkey. A Journal of Travel in Cilicia (Pedias and Trachæa), Isauria, and parts of Lycaonia and Cappadocia*. London

FRENCH, D.H.

1962a Can Hasan 1961. *AnatSt* 12: 8

1962b Excavations at Can Hasan, First Preliminary Report, 1961. *AnatSt* 12: 27–40

1962c. Can Hasan, Karaman: 1961. *TürkArkDerg* 11,2: 36–37

1963a. Can Hasan 1962. *AnatSt* 13: 7–8

1963b. Excavations at Can Hasan, Second Preliminary Report, 1962. *AnatSt* 13: 29–42

1963c. Can Hasan, Karaman 1962. *TürkArkDerg* 12,1: 21–22

1964a. Can Hasan 1963. *AnatSt* 14: 9–10

1964b. Excavations at Can Hasan, Third Preliminary Report, 1963. *AnatSt* 14: 125–134

1965a. Can Hasan 1964. *AnatSt* 15: 10–11

1965b. Excavations at Can Hasan, Fourth Preliminary Report, 1964. *AnatSt* 15: 87–94

1965c. Can Hasan 1963 and 1964. *TürkArkDerg* 13,2: 27–31

1966a. Can Hasan 1965. *AnatSt* 16: 14–15

1966b. Excavations at Can Hasan, Fifth Preliminary Report, 1965. *AnatSt* 16: 113–123

1966c. Can Hasan 1965. *TürkArkDerg* 14,1/2: 147–150

1967a. Summary of the Results of the 1966 Season at Can Hasan. *AnatSt* 17: 10–11

1967b. Excavations at Can Hasan, Sixth Preliminary Report, 1966. *AnatSt* 17: 165–178

1967c. Can Hasan 1966. *TürkArkDerg* 15, 1: 69–73

1968a. Can Hasan 1967. *AnatSt* 18: 9–10

1968b. Excavations at Can Hasan, Seventh Preliminary Report, 1967. *AnatSt* 18: 45–53

1968c. Can Hasan 1967. *TürkArkDerg* 16,1: 89–94

1994 Isinda and Lagbe. In French, D.H. (ed.), *Studies in the History and Topography of Lycia and Pisidia*: 84. London (BIAA Mono. 19)

GARSTANG, J.

1953 *Prehistoric Mersin. Yümük Tepe in Southern Turkey*. Oxford

MELLAART, J.

1954 Preliminary Report on a Survey of Preclassical Remains in Southern Turkey. *AnatSt* 4: 175–240

1963 Early Cultures of the South Anatolian Plateau, 2. *AnatSt* 13: 199–236

1965 Çatal Hüyük West. *AnatSt* 15: 135–156

STERRETT, J.R.S.

1884–85 *The Wolfe Expedition to Asia Minor*. Boston (PapAmerSchClStAth. 3)

WHEELER, R.E.M.

1954 *Archaeology from the Earth*. Oxford

Canhasan mound from SW, September 1961

1. Introduction

This volume begins the publication of excavations conducted by the author between 1961 and 1967 at Canhasan, about 13 km NE of Karaman in south central Turkey. It is mainly concerned with the stratigraphy and structures of the mound known as Canhasan I, but the first section (1.1–5) presents the location of the site, the objectives of the excavation, the means and techniques employed to achieve those objectives and the developments in the work as they occurred. In a final chapter (3.1–5) there will be an attempt to evaluate the results in relation to the stated aims.

In describing the operations and procedures, together with the aims and objectives of the excavation, I wish to present an account which will assist an interpretation of the results. The excavation was not perfect and the reader, examining the remains of a thirty-year old dig, will undoubtedly discover the faults of policy (strategy and tactic) and practice (method and technique). For the imperfections and errors I alone bear responsibility. Nevertheless to me it has seemed valuable to present a description which will enable the reader, researcher or future archivist to understand the mechanics of the operation and to evaluate the strengths and weaknesses of the excavation and its results.

1.1 The location and topography of the site

There are three sites (all mounds, Turkish *höyükler*) at Canhasan: by the expedition they were numbered I, II and III, although elsewhere (Mellaart 1963: 209 site no. 67) Canhasan III was designated Canhasan II and assigned to the EBA.

Canhasan I is the largest of the three mounds and lies on the N side of the road to Suduraği (formerly known as Sidivre). In October 1958 when I accompanied James Mellaart and Alan Hall to the site and saw the mound for the first time, it lay c. 250 m. from the northern edge of the village. On all sides of the village stretched a near-treeless plain, much of which was still an uncultivated grazing land, steppic in appearance and character. In the last twenty-five years orchards have been planted all round the village and now flourish. Tractors have been acquired. The circle of cultivation has enormously widened. The mound of Canhasan III, which in 1958 was surrounded by open plain is now partly concealed by trees and no longer visible from all directions. On the edge of Alaçatı new houses have been built on the northern side of the road to Suduraği, thereby reducing the distance between village and mound I to c. 200 m.

Canhasan II, a much smaller mound (c. 100 × 5 m.), is now (1995) almost on the northeastern edge of the village, between it and Canhasan I. It is located in the eastern angle formed by the Suduraği road and the main entrance to the village. Canhasan II is no more than 150 m. SE of the Canhasan I.

Canhasan III lies c. 1 km. NW of Canhasan I.

On the Turkish 1:25,000 map (sheet Karaman—N 30, b 4) Canhasan I is named "Mezarlıhöyüğü" and Canhasan II "Küçükhöyük". Canhasan III is not indicated. The spot-height on Canhasan I is given as 1016 m.

Alaçatı ("grey roof") is the modern, official name of the village on whose territory the three mounds are situated. Formerly, however, it was called Canasun. Variants on the name include Cenasun (*Köylerimiz* [İstanbul 1933]), Canasun (1950 Census) and Canason (1955 Census). The toponym Cinasınören is found on the Turkish 1:200,000 map (Konyaereğlisi sheet 66–Iu, c. 24 km. NE of Canasun). A Byzantine church was marked by Sterrett (1884–85: map I Zeininin-ören) at this spot; when I visited the site (22.07.1962) no church could be recognized (cp. Belke 1984: 151).

The Reverend E.J.Davis crossed the plain of Karaman from E to W on 13 June, 1875. Starting from Anbar village (formerly Serpek or Anbararası) he came to the village of Kaleköy, crossed through the range of the Çakır Dağ via the defile immediately N of Cinasınören and then rode directly across the plain to Suduraği and Alaçatı and finally to Karaman. His account (1879: 286–290) is valuable for the excellent description of the Karaman plain before it was altogether lost in the rapid developments of the twentieth century:

"Here we crossed a high ridge between two marble hills, and another very extensive reach of the great plain opened before us, bounded on the south by low hills, towards which the ground trended away in long undulations of red, yellow, brown, green, and black, over which the shadows of the clouds played, like so many great bands of coloured velvet. As we advanced the vegetation became scanty, the flowers gradually ceased, till there was nothing but a little withered herbage; for there is no water whatever here, and even the heaviest rainfall

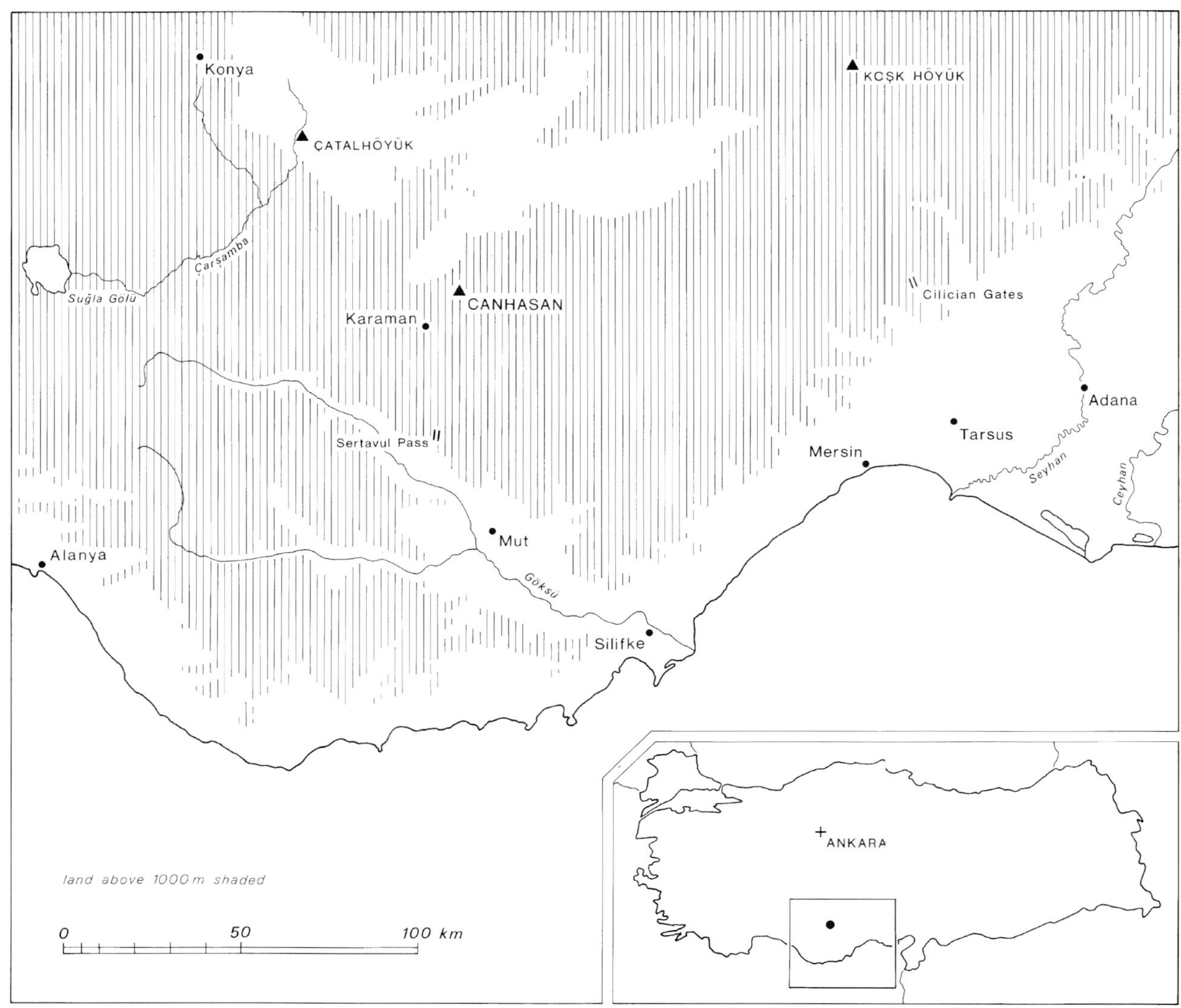

Fig. 01. Map showing location of Canhasan in Southern Turkey

disappears almost immediately, leaving the chalky soil parched and dry as before. Animal life was as scanty as vegetable. There was not a living creature, except some beetles in the path, and a few vultures soaring high overhead. Before us, and to all appearance quite close, was a green spot marking the site of Sidevre; but in reality the village was nearly four hours distant, and it looked as if rising from a lake, so complete was the mirage. ... We had now reached the level portion of the plain; it extended in front five or six hours more to Karaman, and nearly as far northwards to the very foot of Kara Dagh, which rose from it abruptly, as some rocky island from the sea. But between us and the mountain lay an immense and impassable marsh, into which all the waters of the district drain; but this could not be seen from the low ground on which we were, for the whole plain is level as a billiard table. Looking back I saw the spot where we had crossed the marble ridge. It seemed quite close, although we had been riding without a halt, and at a fast pace, for nearly five hours. Far back beyond that, and now fading in the distance, was the great snow range of Bulghar Dagh; yet so clear was the atmosphere, that I could still distinguish the deep ravines in the mountain side, in one of which was Ibreez. As we approached Sidevre, cultivation gradually reappeared. Large herds of cattle covered the plain; ... We reached Sidevre at about 2 P.M. It is a large village of mud-brick houses, faced with a plaster of clay mixed with fine straw. ... Left Sidevre at 3 P.M. In half an hour passed the pretty hamlet of Yemasoon. Just beyond Yemasoon a wolf started up before us, but speedily trotted out of sight. The green gardens, citadel and hill of Karaman, were now before us. ... We passed over an extensive marsh, and at 6.30, after having been eight and a half hours in the saddle, entered the town, which looked very pretty, being full of orchards and gardens, and surrounded by a district rich in splendid crops of grain, now ready for the sickle".

This account was still valid in September 1961, even to the presence of wolves.

Two parts of the Turkish 1:200,000 maps, sheets Konyaereğlisi and Mut have been photocopied and are included here (Figs 2 and 3) as an illustration of those geographical aspects which Davis described in 1875. The maps were, in fact, drawn c. 1895, soon after Davis' visit. They convey the most important features mentioned by Davis: the flat plain "as level as a billiard table" [the Karaman ovası], the "marble ridge" [the Çakır Dağı, which produces a hard, blue limestone], the foothills of the Toros mountains, of which the most prominent peaks are the Yalnız Dağı 1132 m., Mihail Dağı 1818 m., Oburk Tepe 1880 m. and, above Gaferiyat (now named Kazımkarabekir), Hacibaba Dağı or Pusala Dağı 2464 m., and finally, in the W, Karadağ 2271 m.

J. R. Sitlington Sterrett also travelled from E to W through the Karaman plain in 1885:

"June 3. From Sidivre we cross the plain to Karaman (2h.39m.), passing Djen Hassanüñ Tchiftligi" (1884–85: 19; and map I).

Kiepert (Karte von Kleinasien 2nd ed.1914, sheet Adana) used the spelling Canasun. The forms Can Hasan (of the Turkish 1:200,000 map) and Djen Hassan (of Sterrett) probably reflect a 19th century variant of a much older toponym to which the vernacular form Canasun may, in fact, come closest.

For the 19th century origins of the Turkish 1:200,000 map, see French (1994: 84).

Like other place-names in the Karaman region (and, of course, elsewhere in Turkey) Canasun may be derived from a Hittite or Neo-Hittite original: CAN (from the lost original) + asun from (?)DAN + assos, Turkish c (= English j as in jam) from (?)d, cp. hard g to Turkish soft ğ, Ağlasun from Sagalassos. Interestingly IA pottery (Black on Red, Phrygian Grey) has been recovered both from Canhasan I and from Canhasan III, and from other sites (such as Karaman SW: DHF survey 1964) in the Karaman region. The same formation is found in two other toponyms, both known from the Karaman area: Mandasun village (now re-named Demiryurt) and Gödelesin Hüyük (ancient Kodylēssos) near Bosala (now re-named Özyurt).

I have retained the form Canhasan for the ancient sites but in reference to the modern village I use the name Alaçatı.

The village Alaçatı is situated c. 13 km. (by direct line) NE of Karaman.

In 1958 when I visited Canhasan I with Alan Hall and James Mellaart we used a Land Rover; the approach to the village was by a dusty cart-track over the Karaman plain. As we later discovered, the track frequently became impassible after heavy rains or melting snows. In the late 1960s a new şose was built on the line of a road initiated in the 1950s by the then Prime Minister, Adnan Menderes. At the same time the Karaman-Ereğli road was completed (and later tarmac-surfaced). The approach over the plain to the village then fell into disuse. The line of the cart-track is indicated on the Turkish 1:200,000 map (sheet Konyaereğlisi 64–Iv). It passed to the S of the Çavuş mound and the marsh (Turkish *bataklık*) of the same name. Çavuş Hüyük is a low but not large site (c. 200 × 100 × 4 m.) of late date (Roman and pre-Turkish Medieval) (visited DHF 27.08.1964). This track must surely represent the route taken by Davis in 1875 and Çavuş bataklığı be his "extensive marsh" before Karaman.

Sterrett (1884–85: 19) described the settlement at Canasun (now Alaçatı) as a *çiftlik* (farmstead). In this description he was accurate. Until recently (so far as I have understood, until the 1940s or early 1950s) the çiftlik was owned by the Eren family (still resident in the village) but the land was not correctly registered nor sufficiently documented. A migration from the Toros mountains, in particular from the region of Bozkır, took place c. 1950–1960 (our dig watchman, İlyas Yörük, came from Dereiçi, formerly Gederet, shortly before 1961) and the land in the vicinity of the çiftlik was farmed as a village community. The registration of the fields, and indeed of the hüyükler, is still (in 1995) in dispute. The legal uncertainties led to unresolved problems of expropriation, which was then, and is still, a contractual obligation on the excavator (and now the sponsoring institution).

The main mound at Canhasan (mound I) is regular neither in plan nor in shape. The highest point on the mound was recorded towards the northern end of the site and it was here that the first trenches (S23a and b) were opened on the last day of September, 1961. The surface of the mound was then, and is still, covered by a thick, tough carpet of steppic vegetation, principally the strong scented artemisia. Within living memory the mound has not been ploughed. Until excavation took place over the top and sides these areas were used in autumn for the location of threshing-floors and storage clamps (grain heaps covered by straw and earth). On the surface of the mound, therefore, there were few sherds to be seen. The best collections were made on the lower western edge of the mound, in the pits which had been dug (and were still being dug even in the 1960s) for earth to spread on the roofs of the village houses. The nature and quality of the soil was deemed to be excellent for this purpose. As a consequence of this activity it was not unusual to see

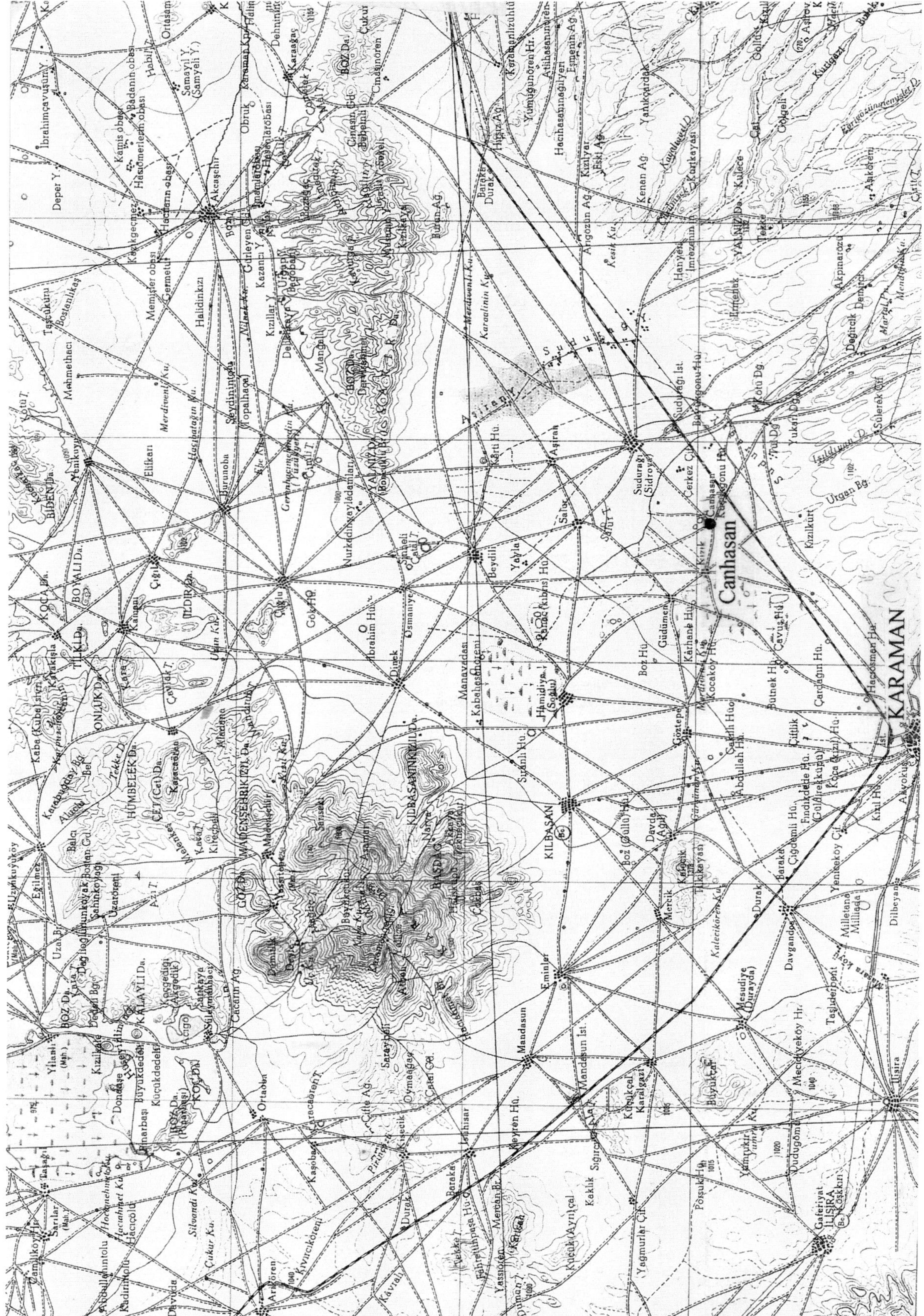

Fig. 02. The Karaman region (1:250,000)

Fig. 03. The Karaman region (1:250,000)

Fig. 04. The geographical zones of Western and Central Turkey

Chalcolithic sherds (mostly Middle and Late Chalcolithic varieties) in and around the village houses and courtyards.

There was no water on or near the site nor were there trees. In 1961 the nearest water supply (a *shadūf* or *serenli kuyu*, a pole-well) was located c. 100 m. away in the meadow. The village-cemetery, enclosed by a dry-stone wall, occupied (and still does) the southern half of the site. Before the dig-house was built (in 1964) a cart-track, later a tractor-track, running towards Beydilli crossed the western edge of the mound: it now passes the dig-house at the foot of the mound by a new track along the eastern side of the village meadow (Turkish *mera*).

For the location of Canhasan in the Konya Plain and its geographical position in relation to the coastal sites, Mersin and Tarsus, and to the inland sites, Çatal Hüyük and Köşk Hüyük, see the map, Fig. 01, drawn by Brian Williams. The map has been drawn specifically to emphasize the importance of the route through the valley of the Göksu (ancient Calycadnus) from the Mediterranean at Silifke via the Sertavul Pass to the plateau of South-Central Anatolia at Karaman; cp. the map and the comment in the 1961 report: "Geographically the importance of Karaman and its surrounding villages lies in its unique position at the end of the route (Fig. 01) through the Taurus which begins at Silifke and follows the Gök Su (Calycadnus) as far as Mut, from where there is little difficulty in crossing the watershed (today by the Sertavul beli) between the river valley and the Karaman Plain. This is one of the great routes through the Taurus and one of the easiest: there are others. All of them are used even today, when nomads [transhumants] with pack animals travel up to 300 km.

Fig. 05. Contour-survey of Canhasan I mound (1:2,500)

through the Taurus from summer to winter pastures." (French 1962: 27 and map, Fig. 01) For the location of the southern Konya Plain around Karaman and its relationship to Central Anatolia as a whole and to the geographical zones of Western and Central Turkey, see the map, Fig. 04. For a contour survey of the Canhasan I site, see the map, Fig. 05, prepared by Rory Fonseca and Ian Walls during the 1962 season.

1.2 The objectives of the excavation

The aims of the excavation were set out in the preliminary report for the first season which took place in 1961, as follows:

"Our interest in the site of Canhasan was roused by some sherds collected by Mr Mellaart in 1951–52" [published by Mellaart 1954: 185 nos 62, 68, 71–75, 80, 81] "and 1958. These clearly belonged to the range of Mersin XIX–XIII; some were, in fact, identical with examples published in Prehistoric Mersin" [Garstang 1953]. "More important was one sherd of Halaf-type" [French 1962: 29 and Fig. 2], "the only certain piece from the western plateau. Furthermore, though a few Middle Chalcolithic pieces had been found by Mr. Mellaart on other sites, only Canhasan has produced Polychrome ware; an excellent piece" [French 1962: 29 and Fig. 3] "was found in 1961 in a pre-excavation survey". "The potentialities of the site were, therefore, clear. As the new excavations planned by Mr. Mellaart at Çatal Hüyük (Çumra) were expected to produce pottery of both Neolithic and Early Chalcolithic periods and those at Canhasan to produce pottery overlapping with the latest from çatal West (the Early Chalcolithic mound), a beginning would thus be made toward the establishment of a stratigraphic sequence for the Konya Plain. Moreover, since there was no deep overlying deposit of later periods at Canhasan, area excavation would be easy. By the finding of Mersin wares, and possibly Halaf-type sherds, in contexts with Konya Plain wares, the geographical and archaeological gap between, on the one hand, the pottery culture of Hacılar and, on the other, those of Mersin and Halaf would be at least partially bridged. Halaf ware in stratified contexts on the plateau would provide a direct link between Anatolia and North Syria and Mesopotamia and would obviate much tedious comparative chronology" (French 1962: 29).

In a word, therefore, we sought two objectives: (1) a stratigraphic sequence for the Chalcolithic of the Konya Plain, (2) an area-exposure of the Chalcolithic period at Canhasan. These objectives were pursued as directly as money (and therefore time) would allow but it must be admitted that the path was not straight. No one single trench has provided a complete sequence and it is by no means certain that every occupational or structural phase has been recovered. This subject will be discussed in detail below, in Section 3.1.

1.3 The methods and techniques of excavation

In the seven seasons (1961–1967) of work at Canhasan I there was a gradual development of the techniques and methods employed in pursuit of the overall objectives. The development took place irregularly, as the excavation progressed (a term which here indicates only the passage of time) and largely in response to events, new constraints and new perceptions (see this section, below).

Throughout the seven seasons at Canhasan the preferred time of the year for excavation was always the autumn when the weather was cooler and therefore less enervating. Dust was a continuous problem. Usually the September rains came too late to provide relief. The strongest reason for an autumn rather than a summer season was archaeological: the soil in the trench dried more slowly. Freshly revealed deposits retained their moisture, and hence their texture and colour, longer in the cool, autumn months than in the hot, and excessively dry, months of summer. Colour distinctions and discontinuities, as for instance between pits and domestic surfaces, remained sharp and bright in the cooler, moister conditions of autumn.

In 1961 14 men plus one foreman were employed. Three of these (the *çavuş*, foreman, and two *ustalar*, skilled men) came from Çivril in the province of Denizli, the remainder from the village of Alaçatı. The Çivril men had worked on the BIAA excavations at Beycesultan and at Hacılar. In the early years (1961–63 and 1965) they were also employed, during the summer months, on the Çatal Hüyük excavations. They came to the Canhasan excavations for five seasons, 1961–1965. In their last full year, 1964, they built the Canhasan dig-house (Pl. 1.2). In the course of the 1965 season the Beycesultan men became unemployable and from that year onwards a varying number of men from Alaçatı village were recruited (see below, Section 1.7).

The foreman was responsible for the daily registration of the workmen and for matters of discipline. In the army he had been a sergeant (*çavuş*). The skilled men, the ustalar, were pickmen (*kazmacı*): the rest were shovel- and barrow-men (*kürekci, arabacı*). This job-demarcation was rarely disturbed.

The principal digging-tool for the ustalar was the large pick (*kazma*), one blade pointed, the other broad edged, for releasing the soil, and a long bladed, single edged knife (*bıçak*) for investigating the released soil. Two weaknesses were always apparent: (1) the soil could be released as lumps or clods and was not invariably reduced by the action of the pick to loose earth in which sherds and other materials could be easily observed, (2) one firm blow, whether from the point or from the broad edge of the usta's pick, could be (and often was) lethal to all buried objects. To avoid these and other weaknesses, smaller tools were introduced and sometimes used. These included small picks: a reduced version of the normal pick (Pl. 1.1, bottom row, right; initially acquired from the Mycenae excavations), another form (Pl. 1.1, top row, right; directly inherited from Tel Açana) and a third, single-bladed, sharp-pointed form (Pl. 1.1, top row, centre; imitated from an Iraqi exemplar). Available and handy was a combination tool, one blade in the form of a small, flat-ended pick, the other in the shape of a hoe (Pl. 1.1, bottom row, left). This object was indeed called a hoe (*çapa*). On the whole none of these supplementary tools was popular with the skilled men. The big pick and knife were their symbols of office.

The normal shovel with long handle and roughly heart-shaped blade (Turkish *kürek*, shovel-man *kürekci*) was used to remove the dug soil to a wheelbarrow (Turkish *araba*, hence *arabacı*, barrow-man) for transporting to the dump. There were variants on the normal shovel: one with a short shaft for use in a confined area (such as a pit), another with a broad, rounded head particularly well suited to the operation of scraping and cleaning a flat surface (Pl. 1.1, left). An alternative tool for this same operation was a long-bladed brick-layer's trowel (Pl. 1.1, centre row, left), very efficient in small areas.

The basic tools used in the first seasons—picks, shovels, wheelbarrows—were inherited from earlier BIAA excavations. After 1964 small tools for probing and cleaning, especially a 5–inch (12.5 cm.) or 4–inch (10 cm.) trowel, came into general use. At all times the trench kit (Turkish *takım*) (Pl. 1.1; for the photograph the tools were laid out on a woven reed-mat, Turkish *hasır*) included several forms of plaster- and dental-tool (Pl. 1.1, bottom right). "Tea-spoon archaeology"—the term applied to Canhasan in the 1960s—was critical but apt. Pins and tooth-picks (Pl. 1.1, box, bottom right) were very occasionally employed for the most delicate tasks which could not be carried out in the dig-house.

No skill was required from the shovellers. It was the pickmen on whom the responsibility for locating and investigating soil-changes and features (mud-brick, stone, hearths, floors) fell. At that time (the late 50s and early 60s) this system and job-demarcation were standard for Turkey. The pickmen had worked elsewhere (Beycesultan, Hacılar) and were considered good and reliable at their job, in the same manner and to the same degree as in other Middle Eastern countries. Indeed, in the recognition and recovery of mud-brick, the ustalar were invaluable, not least to those who were unfamiliar with the nature of ancient (and modern) mud-brick walls.

Both pick-man and shoveller were instructed and trained to recover everything that met their eye. Both groups of men were supervised by one or more trench-assistants whose general responsibilities were to ensure, within their own competence, the accuracy and discipline of the pickmen and the attention of the shovel- and barrow-men. The task of recording is outlined below (Section 1.4).

From observation it was calculated that one pickman (with a back-up team) could excavate 1 cu.m. of soil per diem when there was nothing to delay his progress. This work-rate was never achieved (and only rarely desired) in the first two seasons, even when the deposits were largely fallen mud-brick: thereafter the method and style of excavation changed somewhat fundamentally. The changes were gradually introduced after the consequences of a single event had been absorbed: the major elements of a finely incised bowl (CAN/62/415) were discovered on the dump. At the beginning of the excavation it had been intended to employ a (dry) sieve not in all but only in carefully selected conditions: (1) when there were no observed contaminants such as recognizable sherds (from above, i.e. intrusives, or from below, i.e. residuals) or observed contaminations such as rodent burrows and the like, or (2) when there was an apparent need to recover archaeobiological remains such as carbonized grain by means other than hand-recovery. The skill of the pickmen was good (but not infallible) in the tracing of walls, especially mud-brick. The eyesight of pickmen and of shovel- and barrow-men was excellent when both groups were concentrating on recovery. Sometimes there were lapses in concentration. The recovery of all pieces from a whole but broken pot *in situ* is not difficult. There was a constant problem, however, in the collection of sherds and, of course, other materials such as animal bone. Too many were needlessly lost. The workmen, despite all encouragement and instruction, collected not what they saw but what, bending down, they were inclined to pick up. When, in the days following the first recovery on site and treatment in the dig-house, the sherds of an apparently restorable pot were assembled, it was usually too late to return to the dump of excavated earth, in the hope of finding the missing pieces. In the case (mentioned at the beginning of this paragraph) of the fragments belonging to an incised bowl (CAN/62/415) chance played the leading role. The bowl had not even been isolated among the collected sherds. The major fragments, fortuitously recovered on the dump, met our eyes in the open palm of the foreman after his evening stroll around the site.

As was stated above, there was no intention, at the beginning of the excavation, to make wholesale use of dry-sieving procedures except in previously agreed conditions (outlined in the previous paragraph) and in circumstances which favoured the recovery of bio-archaeological materials, principally animal bone and carbonized seeds and fruits, namely, (1) in tightly defined stratigraphical contexts (e.g. bins) and (2) in abundant quantities. In fact, dry sieves were employed on a few occasions to recover small objects such as beads and ornaments. In 1965, however, after four seasons of excavation on Canhasan mound I, a general policy of dry sieving was introduced. Small, round, close-meshed sieves (wooden frame, wire mesh; mesh-size c. 1 mm; bought in the local market) were brought into general use and became a standard—but not entirely universal—operational tool.

The loss of materials through the non-use of sieves, whether wet or dry, cannot be calculated—unless the dumped earth were to be tested by sieving—but on the restored pottery from the early seasons at Canhasan I the number of loss-areas, i.e. areas where fragments are missing, is a qualitative and quantitative indication of technical failure for which I can offer no excuse. At Canhasan as at so many excavations in the Middle East and Eastern Mediterranean a penalty, sometimes calculable, sometimes not, has been paid for the excessive trust in the proclaimed excellence of skilled pickmen rather than on non-mechanical means of recovery.

After the incident of the missing sherds (recounted above) the use of large pick was confined to the appropriate deposits, whenever these could be safely recognized: it was replaced by the smaller hand-tools such as the 5–inch trowel.

In part the change occurred for two other reasons: (1) the replacement of the experienced pickmen from Çivril—in the first week of the 1965 season they were no longer employable—by local workmen and (2) the increasing complexity of the stratification. It was felt that neither the skills and experience of the pickmen nor the tools that were customarily used by them were sufficient to meet the needs of an excavation on which the objectives of the operation and the complexity of the soil-deposits conflicted with the traditional methods of excavation. In 1965 and thereafter there was an ever increasing reliance on the skills of the trench-supervisors and assistants for the clarification of complex soil-deposition. As a consequence the rate of soil-removal was visibly reduced but there are no quantitative calculations on which to base a comparison between earlier and later years.

Was there a loss of accuracy in the stratigraphic control? a loss which resulted from the methods and techniques of excavation? The short answer is Yes. No excavation is perfect and mistakes will always be made. I believe, however, that at Canhasan, as at other earlier and (then) contemporary excavations in Turkey and elsewhere in the Middle East and the Eastern Mediterranean the loss of stratigraphic control and the poor nature of recovery may be directly attributed to an ill-judged trust in the big (and often small) pick in the hands of the ustalar, the trusted local experts. The refusal to recognize the correlation between excavation method and archaeological interpretation has been a great stumbling block to improvement in both. Interpretation of the data can be only as good as the method of data-collection.

The consequences of poor digging-technique in the early seasons at Canhasan may be summarized as follows: (1) not all distinctions in the soil were recognized, (2) not all soil-distinctions, though recognized, were accurately excavated.

The consequence of inaccurate excavation was the mixing or conflation of different soil-deposits, a result that was clearly demonstrated by a comparison of the 'as-drawn' with the 'as-dug' sections of the same trench-profile. The 'as-drawn' sections are not a mirror image of the 'as-dug' sections (where these were recorded); in other words, the as-drawn sections are not a guarantee of accuracy in digging and therefore not a guarantee of reliability in stratigraphic control.

For 'as-dug' and 'as-drawn' sections, see below, Section 1.4.

The inadequacy of stratigraphical control thus led to unreliability in the definition of artifactual assemblages. Because the soil-depositions were not accurately defined, contexts became confused and contents accordingly mixed.

For these defects in the earlier seasons there is now—unfortunately—no remedy. Any improvement in the accuracy of stratigraphic control in the later seasons may be directly attributed to (1) the abandonment of traditional tools, methods and techniques, (2) the introduction of tools, especially the small trowel, more suited to the nature of the soil-deposits, (3) the reduced pace of excavation, (4) greater deployment of the supervisors and assistants in the crucial, 'coal-face' operations in the trench and (5) changes in methods of recording.

1.4 The methods of recording

The intention throughout the excavation was simple: to exercise the greatest control at all levels of the operation. Control was, therefore, attempted firstly on-site (excavation in the trench, and collection and recording of excavated materials) and then off-site (processing, and archival recording of excavated material, in the house). It was part of the strategy that there should be the closest integration between on-site and off-site recording. The systems were devised to meet this aim.

As in the methods and techniques of excavation, so too in the methods of recording, there was a gradual but irregular development.

(1) On-site

In September 1961, before digging began, a 10–metre grid was constructed on the highest point, i.e. at the northern end of the mound. Four 10 × 10 m. squares were laid out, an area of 400 m. The longitudinal axis was aligned, by accurate sightings on the Pole star, to true North. Selected intersections on the 10–metre axes were then established over an area 50 × 50 m. and marked by nails set in concrete blocks or in wooden pegs. The highest point on the mound and the top of the datum block was arbitrarily designated 10 m. (in reality 1016 m., see the note above, p. 1). As not infrequently happens, some pegs were lost in subsequent years, particularly during the winter months, to inquisitive minds and nimble fingers; these pegs had to be replaced. Nevertheless four concrete markers have been left at the axis between (1) R/S and 18/19 (top of block at 9.146), (2) P/Q and 28/29 (top at 9.765), (3) R/S and 28/29 (top at 9.930) and (4) T/U and 28/29 (top at 9.365).

Each 10–metre square was designated (1) by a number from North to South in sequence and (2) by a letter from West to East in alphabetical order. Both numbers and letters began on an axis well away from the present edge of the mound. The 10–metre squares were then divided into four minor squares or quadrants, each 5 × 5 m. These were designated a (= north-west), b (= north-east), c (= south-west) and d (= south-east). Each quadrant was, in fact, excavated not as a 5 × 5 m. but as a 4 × 4 m. trench. On all sides of each 4 × 4 m. trench, therefore, there was unexcavated border, 0.50 m. wide, which thus formed a clear and clean walkway, 1.00 m. wide, precisely bisecting the 10 × 10 m. squares from N to S and from E to W. Contiguous borders thus constituted a baulk measuring exactly 1.00 m. between each 4 × 4 m. quadrant and between each 10 × 10 m. square. When the profile (= trench-section) on both sides of the baulk had been drawn, the baulk was then removed. This procedure gave some measure of stratigraphic control between neighbouring trenches. The baulk could be recorded, exempli gratia, as R21a/b. For a wonderfully lucid and concise account of the 'square' method of trench-layout and excavation and for photographs of the trench-layout at Taxila, see Wheeler (1954: 64 and Pl. 5).

The descriptive unit of area for all records, whether archival (plans, sections, notebooks) or material (pottery, bone *et al.*), is the quadrant designation. The unit of vertical or horizontal separation is the batch-number. This is a unique number. In the first season, 1961, numbers were used as required, without regard to quadrant. Thereafter groups of numbers were assigned to individual quadrants. Even so not all numbers were used. There was an attempt to begin each season at a round figure, 70, 90 or similar, with a minimal lacuna. The batch-numbers refer to soil-units. There can be several batch-numbers for the same soil-unit. New numbers were assigned in the morning, i.e. at the beginning of each day, even though excavation of the same soil-unit could (and did) continue from one day to the next. Old numbers, i.e. numbers employed on the previous day or earlier, were never re-used. Batch-numbers were sometimes changed when the same soil-unit was being excavated in deliberately discrete areas within the same quadrant. Very occasionally—and confusingly—the term quadrant designates the four corner-squares (2 × 2 m.) in a 4 × 4 m. trench.

The same batch-number was given to all groups of material excavated in the same soil-unit. In the system of recording there was no sequence of numbers dedicated to different materials.

The system of batch-numbers was never changed: it remained unaltered throughout the excavation.

In the trench different materials were collected in different containers, e.g. wooden trays for sherds, paper bags for animal bone. Plastic bowls were substituted for wooden trays when the former became readily available. For labels in trays wood was used in the first seasons; later it was replaced by a light-weight alloy form ('garden label') ionized to retain the marks of a lead pencil even in rain or under water. Paper labels were employed for all other containers. Generally the paper labels were inserted into small plastic bags for protection. Later the paper labels were partly replaced by metal. Also in later seasons stamped labels were introduced in order to ensure optimal recording in the trench. A pre-prepared stamp impressed, on a card label, the outline of several 'boxes' arranged according to an agreed format, each box dedicated to a specific category of information. In the 'boxes' basic, essential data could be entered and later processed off-site, i.e. in the dig-house. The 'boxes' were printed or stamped (with indelible ink) on a thin card label of uniform size. An example is illustrated here (Fig. 06).

The pre-prepared labels were intended both for on-site and for off-site operations and procedures; they proved invaluable in the recording and later monitoring of all materials from the moment of excavation until finally transferred to the depot.

The same alloy tags, as used for labels, were chosen to mark soil-units and stratigraphic features on the trench-sections after an initial, and unsuccessful, experiment with paper tags. Employed as markers in the trench-sections, they formed the basic, visible record for the drawing of 'as-dug' sections (for a description of 'as-dug' sections, see below).

CAN HASAN I 196

TRENCH LAYER	
BATCH No:	
DESCRIPT.	
MATERIAL / OBJECT	
DATE & INITIALS	
TRENCH No.	CONTROL BK No.

Fig. 06. Example of stamped label

In 1961 the trenches were set out in 5–metre squares measured by a 25–metre cloth tape; this was replaced in later seasons by a metal version. Measurements in the trenches were made with small, 2–metre hand-tapes. A somewhat antiquated theodolite, inherited from Professor Garstang's excavations at Mersin, was used for all levelling in the first two seasons. A similarly antiquated dumpy-level took the place of the theodolite after the latter accidentally tumbled over—in a high wind—onto the only large stone visible for miles.

The draughtsmen or the trench-supervisors and I drew plans by plane-table combined with theodolite in the early seasons, later by plane-table alone. The results were subsequently—in Ankara—transferred to an overall plan drawn out on tracing paper. Draughting film was not then generally available. The trench-supervisors (or assistants) and I drew the trench-sections on squared paper ('graph-paper') in lead-pencil.

Trench plans were drawn at the scale 1:50, sections at 1:20.

Not all sections were recorded. In the first two seasons I decided not to draw every detail of fallen mud-brick debris when these deposits began immediately below the surface and ended on the floor of a structure. In these cases, only the top and bottom of the mud-brick deposit were levelled and drawn on the trench- sections.

In the early seasons only 'as-drawn' sections were prepared. 'As-drawn' sections were a record of the features (floors, surfaces, walls, pits, ash-lines, etc.) as they were observed and drawn after excavation had been completed. Owing to the minimal use of tags or markers on the trench-sections, the recording of 'as-drawn' sections did not always define the starting- and stopping-points of each operation nor did they accurately define the configuration of a soil-unit as excavated. Nor did they record the accuracy with which a soil-change (such as a floor, surface, ash-line or even a wall) had been recognized and pursued. It soon became clear (after rain, for instance, or after drying) that some soil-features (e.g. colour changes, soil textures) visible in the sections *after* excavation had not been observed *during* excavation; cp. the sections drawn for R21c/22a and Q21d and the batch-numbers as recorded (French 1963b: 32–33, Figs 3–4). In response to this defect in accuracy, metal tags were inserted into the sections as a record of each batch-number as used. From day to day, therefore, the starting and finishing points of each batch number were available for drawing. Hence the transition, as it was excavated, from one soil-unit or soil-deposition to another could be easily examined and drawn, and at any time checked. The tags or markers, as recorded on the 'as-drawn' sections, allowed a direct control on the accuracy of excavation. In the latest seasons, it became general practice to draw separate sections. These were the so-called 'as-dug sections'; on them were recorded only the points at which either the excavation of a soil-unit or soil-deposit had begun and finished or the use of a batch-number started and stopped. Usually there were several pairs of such points since more than one batch number may have been used. The 'as-dug' sections, re-drawn on tracing-paper, could then be laid over the the 'as-drawn' sections and examined for accuracy.

The Munsell Soil Color Chart (Baltimore 1954) was adopted for the notation of soil colour standards, e.g. 'Y-b' or 'Yellow-Brown' (= 2.5 YR Yellow-Brown).

(2) Off-site

As in the trench (on-site), so in the house (off-site), the primary aims were (1) to maintain the closest possible control over the processing of materials recovered on excavation and (2) to integrate the recording on-site and off-site, so that material could be united with context through the medium of the recording system. In those pre-computer days at Canhasan this task was not easy. By contrast, the numerical notation employed on the excavations at Tille was specifically designed (in 1979) for computer-processing of data. The difficulties of the Canhasan system of notation will be made clear in the next two volumes. The recording system used at Canhasan suffered from a major fault-line. Unlike the procedures devised for Tille, the off-site recording practices at Canhasan did not automatically monitor or control the day-to-day discoveries in the trench.

1.5 Procedures

All materials were taken from the trench to the dig-depot, almost always, at the end of the day. From 1961 to 1963 the dig-depot was situated in a village house, from 1964 to 1967 inside the dig-house (Pl. 1.2) located on the western foot of the mound. To the dig-house a lockable and sealable depot (constructed by the village usta, Ahmet Aral, with Mustafa Altınsoy from mud-bricks prepared in the Spring by Ramazan Kelek and Mehmet Çolak) was added in May 1967.

In the dig-house, materials were first separated and then treated by category; sherds and bones remained in the trench-containers until they were processed. Sherds (and occasionally whole pots) were water-washed and laid out to dry in small squares delimited by stones (cp. the photograph of a similar system used by Wheeler [1954: 167 and Pl. 18] at Arikamedu). At Canhasan, after the dig-house was built, the use of such grid-squares proved to be unhelpful; they were cumbersome and inaccessible. In any case they were usually too small for the amount of pottery and too dusty. This practice was abandoned in favour, at first, of reed-mats (Turkish *hasır*, illustrated Pl. 1.1), then of nylon-sheeting, on which sherds after washing could be more conveniently dried. When duplicate tags were tied to the mats there was seldom any confusion or loss. A high wind, however, was a danger if the mat had not been adequately weighted and secured. Animal bone fragments were cleaned with a dry tooth-brush or a denture-brush.

All material of other categories received appropriate treatment which included conservation where necessary.

After cleaning and drying, sherds were scrutinized, examined and selected for retention; those not selected were discarded and buried on site. All feature sherds (rims, handles *vel sim.*, bases) were kept. Sherds representing the different fabrics and treatments, as observed, were also retained. Small and very small sherds, and poorly preserved sherds, were discarded, together with most large and/or undecorated sherds and sherds with worn and unrecognizable patterns.

All artifacts made of baked clay or bone were kept and all small objects of stone. Large objects of stone (particularly querns and pounders) were washed. After examination, a selection was retained, the remainder was discarded and buried on site. Locations of buried materials are recorded in the dig notebooks, e.g. for 1964 and 1965 in vol. 2 of the Dig Notebooks for 1965. A large number of stone samples was collected on site; off site these were reduced in number by discarding. In October 1993 the worked stone and unworked stone samples were re-examined and the whole collection further reduced.

Chipped stone and obsidian were retained in toto.

Whenever possible or feasible all objects and materials were marked with indelible ink ('Indian ink', 'Encre de Chine') and the markings sealed with a weak solution of PVA in acetone. Not all materials could be marked. Some were too large in quantity, some were too small in size.

The markings give the year of excavation, the trench, the level (frequently omitted) and the batch-number, as follows: CAN67 R21b 5 2000. Where the surface was too rough or the available area too small, only the batch-number was written.

The registration number given on the dig was written as follows: CAN/67/1000. Some registered objects carry four sets of numbers: the dig batch-number etc., the dig registration number, the inventory number given first by the Ankara Museum, then by Karaman. Concordances (1) of dig and (if current) Ankara Museum registration numbers and (2) of dig and Karaman Museum registration numbers will be given in later volumes.

The numbers of calendar dates were written in Arabic for the day, miniscule Latin for the month and Arabic for the year, e.g. 30/ix/61.

1.6 Storage

All objects were divided by the Ministry Representative into two categories: (1) suitable for exhibit in a museum, (2) suitable for study purposes only. The first category (*müzelik*) was then registered on pre-prepared forms, the second (*etüdlük*) was simply listed and stored.

With a few exceptions, all registered objects (the *müzelik* or *envanterlik*) were sent, from 1961 to 1967, to the Archaeological Museum in Ankara (now the Museum of Anatolian Civilizations). In 1988 (officially 21.07.1988) most of the registered objects were returned to Karaman and only a selection retained in Ankara. Some registered objects (both from Canhasan I and from Canhasan III) were transferred in 1967 from Ankara to Konya-Ereğlisi Museum. In 1961 a few objects (the bulky, baked clay and stone objects) were officially

Fig. 07. Plan of the excavations: yearly operations (1:200)

delivered to the Konya Archaeological Museum. At the time of writing the objects in Konya and Konya-Ereğlisi have not been returned to Karaman.

With the exception of some stone artifacts all the non-registered objects and materials (the *etüdlük* is stored in the dig-house depot at Canhasan. It is arranged by category of material on metal ('Dexion') shelving, (1) the sherds in wooden boxes, (2) the animal bone in wooden boxes and in plastic bags, (3) small, light materials (such as chert and obsidian) in wooden boxes and (4) heavy materials (such as stone and clay) in wooden crates.

1.7 Year-by-year operations

The progress of the excavations was irregular and uneven. After the first seasons it became clear that deep sondages would necessarily destroy the Layer

2B structures uncovered in the area where the first trenches were dug in 1961 and 1962. Moreover in expanding outwards from these trenches in order to add to the number of Level 2B structures already revealed we were immediately confronted by an extensive area of later occupation. Trenches did not always suit objectives.

The diagrams (Fig. 07) illustrate the areas of each yearly operation:

1961 R22d, 23b&d; S22a&c, 23a–c
1962 Q21d, 22b&d, 23b&d; R21c&d, 22a–c, 23a&c, 24a&b; S21c, 22a&c, 23d, 24a&b
1963 R24c&d, 25a&b; S24c&d, 25a&b
1964 P22d; Q21c, 22a&c, 23a; R21c&d; S24c, 25c&d, 26a&b; T25a&c
1965 R21a&b; S25c, 26a
1966 Q21c&d; R21b; S25a&c, 26a
1967 Q22a; R21a&b, 24c&d; S24c

Included here for ease of reference is a list of all trench numbers, layers and the figures (if any) on which the plans and sections are illustrated:

Trench	*Year(s)*	*Layer(s)*	*Fig(s):Plan(s)*	*Fig(s):Section(s)*
P22d	1964	1	26,27	35
Q21c	1964,1966	2B&A,1	11,12,23,24,26,27	35,49,51,54
Q21d	1962,1966	2B&A	11,12,16,21,23,24, 26,27	35,49
Q22a	1964,1967	2A,1	23,24,26,27	51,54
Q22b	1962	2B&A	11,12,16,21,23,24	
Q22c	1964	1	26,27	35,53
Q22d	1962	2A	23,24	35
Q23a	1964	1	26,27	53
Q23b	1962	2A	23,24,26,27	
Q23d	1962	2B&A,1	11,12,14,21,23,24,26–7	
R21a	1965,1967	4,3,2B&A,Byz	09–11,12,19,21,23, 24,32	34,37,39,40,44
R21b	1965–67	7–3,2B&A,Byz	08–11,12,19,21,32	38,41–43
R21c	1962,1964	2B	11,12,16,19,21	34,35,50,52
R21d	1962,1964	2B	11,12,16,21	35,50
R22a	1962	2B	11,12,16,21	34
R22b	1962	2B	11,12,16–18,21	
R22c	1962	2B	11,12,15,16,21	34,35
R22d	1961	2B	11,12,15–18,21	35
R23a	1962	2B	11,12–15,21	34
R23b	1961	2B	11,12,15,21	
R23c	1962	2B	11,12,14,21	34
R23d	1961	2B	11,12,14,21	
R24a	1962	2B	11,12,14,20–21	34
R24b	1962	2B	11,12,14,20–21	
R24c	1963,1967	2B,1	11,12,20–21,26,34,28–31	34,36,51,55,57
R24d	1963,1967	2B,1	11,12,20–21,26,28–31	36,51,56,58
R25a	1963	2B,1	11,12,20–21,26,28–31	34,55,57
R25b	1963	2B,1	11,12,20–21,26,28–31	56,58
S21c	1962	2B	11,12,18,21,23	35,50,53,54
S22a	1961–2	2B	11,12,17,18,21	
S22c	1961–2	2B	11,12,13,15,17,18,21	35
S23a	1961	2B	11,12,13,15,21	
S23b	1961	2B&A	11,12,13,21,23	35
S23c	1961	2B	11,12–14,21	
S23d	1962	2B	11,12,13,21	
S24a	1962	2B	11,12,13,21	
S24b	1962	2B&A	11,12,13,21,23	
S24c	1963–4,1967	2B&A,1	11,12,20–21,23,25,26,28–31	34,36,45,52,58
S24d	1963	2B,1	11,12,21,26,28–31	36,52
S25a	1963,1966	2A,1	25,26,28–31	34,46,58
S25b	1963	1	26,28–31	
S25c	1964–66	1	26,30,31	34,36,47,55,57
S25d	1964	1	26,30,31	36,55,57
S26a	1964–66	1	26,30,31	34,48,56–58
S26b	1964	1	26,30,31	56–58
T25a	1964	1	26,28–31	36,52
T25c	1964	1	26,28–31	36

1.8 Finances and Remunerations

	1	*2*	*3*	*4*	*5*	*6*
1961	113.32	214.25	57.61	21.58	11.87	418.63
1962	143.11	301.83	47.11	43.83	4.68	540.46
1963	87.71	203.24	46.40	14.29	33.59	385.23
1964	254.09	434.81	92.26	55.18	40.43	876.77
1965	156.88	311.34	50.06	60.03	13.16	591.47
1966	160.15	411.15	45.55	32.60	5.99	655.44
1967	273.31	601.86	36.08	142.56	5.52	1059.33
	1188.57	2478.48	375.07	370.07	115.24	4527.43

1. = Food and Living; 2. = Wages and Remunerations; 3. = Transport; 4. = Equipment; 5. = Miscellaneous; 6. = Total.

Exchange Rates: 1961–1967 £1 = TL25.20.

Wages and Remunerations

	1961	*1962*	*1963*	*1964*	*1965*	*1966*	*1967*
1.	17.50	17.50	17.50	25	—	—	—
2.	15	15	15	20	—	—	—
3.	10	10	10	10	10	12.50	15
4.	12	14	14	14	400*	400*	600*
5.	10	10	50*	10	10	12.50	15
6.	500*	500*	500*	500*	600*	600*	600*

1. = Foreman (çavuş); 2. = Skilled pickman (usta); 3. = Workman (işçi); 4. = Cook (aşçı); 5. = Watchman (bekçi); 6. = Ministry Representative (Bakanlık Temsilcisi; earlier komiser).

** Monthly figure.*

Working-days (Trench)

1961	3 men	(3 × 42)	= 126	
	12 men		= 135	15 men for 261 working-days
1962	3 men	(3 × 46)	= 138	
	12 men		= 307	15 men for 445 working-days
1963	3 men	(3 × 25)	= 75	
	10 men		= 173	13 men for 248 working-days
1964	4 men		= 141	
	8 men		= 321	12 men for 462 working-days
1965	4 men		= 60	
	10 men		= 237	14 men for 297 working-days
1966				8 men for 289 working-days
1967				10 men for 417 working-days
			Total	87 men for 2419 working-days

Working-days (Sieving)

1965	4 women	= 82 working-days
1966	7 women	= 233 working-days
1967	7 women	= 309 working-days
Total	18 women	= 624 working-days

Grants

	1961	*1962*	*1963*	*1964*	*1965*	*1966*	*1967*	*Total*
1.	—	200	—	250	200	—	—	650
2.	125	150	250	—	150	200	500	1375
3.	100	100	—	100	100	100	100	600
4.	—	—	—	250	150	—	200	600
5.	50	—	—	—	—	—	—	50
6.	—	—	—	—	—	39.68	—	39.68
7.	145	100	135	277	—	315.76	260	1232.76
				*500				
	420	550	385	1377	600	655.44	1060	5047.44

% of total grants	
1. British Academy	12.88
2. British Institute of Archaeology at Ankara	27.24
3. Mediterranean Archaeological Trust	11.88
4. Edinburgh University, Munro Fund	11.88
5. Professor Max Mallowan	1.00
6. Anon.	0.79
7. EBF and DHF	34.33

* *The dig-house: the construction costs of the Canhasan dig-house (built, in 1964, by the Çivril men, i.e. by the foreman and the skilled pickmen, before excavation began) were paid by EBF and DHF. The sum was approximately £500.*

1.9 List of dig participants and Ministry representatives

Team			
BA	Behin Aksoy	house asst	1967
MMB	Maureen Barry	house asst	1961
MB	Margaret Bell	conservator	1966
CB	Charmian Biernoff	house asst	1964
DCB	David Biernoff	field asst	1964, 1966
DJB	David Blackman	field asst	1963
ALB	Anne Blackman	house asst	1963
ACC	Carol Cruikshank	house asst	1962
AÇ	Altan Çilingiroğlu	field asst	1967
MCCD	Mark Davie	house asst	1963
EAD	Elizabeth Dowman	conservator	1965
RWD	Roderick Dutton	field asst and surveyor	1964
RF	Rory Fonseca	surveyor	1962
DHF	David French	director	1961–1967
EBF	Elizabeth French	house manager	1961–2, 1964–5, 1967
ÜG	Ülge Göker	house asst	1967
TH-S	Teresa Harrington-Smith	house asst	1966
SWH	Svend Helms	field asst	1967
ACH	Ann Hird	house asst	1965
RJH	Roger Howell	field asst	1967
NHSK	Nicholas Kindersley	field asst	1961–4
MM	Margaret MacGregor	conservator	1961
CM	Catherine MacLucas	house asst	1961–2
TM	Tessa Martin	conservator	1964
REO	Robin Oakley	field asst	1961–2
SMP	Stephanie Page	house asst	1965

SP	Sebastian Payne	field asst	1964–6
VP-P	Viola Pemberton-Piggott	conservator	1964
JNP	Nicholas Postgate	field asst	1965–7
CP	Carolyn Prater	house asst	1966–7
PMTP	Pamela Pratt	conservator	1964
JER	Julian Reade	house and field asst	1963–4
HCR	Cressida Ridley	house asst	1967
AS	Ann Searight	house asst and conservator	1962
CS	Colin Slack	conservator	1966
IJW	Ian Walls	surveyor	1962, 1964
MAW	Margaret White	conservator	1964
RJW	Rosemary Worth	house asst	1964–5
		house manager	1966
MZ	Monica van der Zwann	house asst	1967

Ministry Representatives

	Ziya Ceran		1961
	Behçet Erdal		1963
	Cengiz Karadağ		1967
	Hayrettin Solmaz		1962, 1964–5
	Bedri Yalman		1966–7

1.10 List of published reports and summaries

1961 Season

a. Can Hasan 1961. *AnatSt* 12: 8 (= French 1962a)
b. Excavations at Can Hasan, First Preliminary Report, 1961. *AnatSt* 12: 27–40 and Pls 1–2 (= French 1962b)
c. Can Hasan, Karaman: 1961. *TürkArkDerg* 11,2: 36–37 and Pl. 25 (= French 1962c)

1962 Season

a. Can Hasan 1962. *AnatSt* 13: 7–8
b. Excavations at Can Hasan, Second Preliminary Report, 1962. *AnatSt* 13: 29–42 and Pls 1–2 (= French 1963b)
c. Can Hasan, Karaman 1962. *TürkArkDerg* 12,1: 21–22 and Pls 20–22 (= French 1963c)

1963 Season

a. Can Hasan 1963. *AnatSt* 14: 9–10 (= French 1964a)
b. Excavations at Can Hasan, Third Preliminary Report, 1963. *AnatSt* 14: 125–134 (= French 1964b)

1964 Season

a. Can Hasan 1964. *AnatSt* 15: 10–11 (= French 1965a)
b. Excavations at Can Hasan, Fourth Preliminary Report, 1964. *AnatSt* 15: 87–94 (= French 1965b)
c. Can Hasan 1963 and 1964. *TürkArkDerg* 13,2: 27–31 (= French 1964c)

1965 Season

a. Can Hasan 1965. *AnatSt* 16: 14–15 (= French 1966a)
b. Excavations at Can Hasan, Fifth Preliminary Report, 1965. *AnatSt* 16: 113–123 (= French 1966b)
c. Can Hasan 1965. *TürkArkDerg* 14,1/2: 147–150 (= French 1966c)

1966 Season

a. Summary of the Results of the 1966 Season at Can Hasan. *AnatSt* 17: 10–11 (= French 1967a)
b. Excavations at Can Hasan, Sixth Preliminary Report, 1966. *AnatSt* 17: 165–178 (= French 1967b)
c. Can Hasan 1966. *TürkArkDerg* 15, 1: 69–73 (= French 1967c)

1967 Season

a. Can Hasan 1967. *AnatSt* 18: 9–10 (= French 1968a)
b. Excavations at Can Hasan, Seventh Preliminary Report, 1967. *AnatSt* 18: 45–53 (= French 1968b)
c. Can Hasan 1967. *TürkArkDerg* 16,1: 89–94 (= French 1968c)

Can Hasan. In *The Dictionary of Art* (forthcoming)
Can Hasan. In Sams, G.K. (ed.), *The Archaeology of Anatolia: An Encyclopedia* (forthcoming)

2. Stratigraphy and Structures

2.1 Introductory

In the preliminary reports the word 'level', as defined below, was subsumed under the term 'layer'. The latter possesses a wider significance. It may include one or more 'levels' (or, as defined below, 'structural levels'): it may also include soil-deposits or activities, e.g. pit-digging, which are not directly associated with any of the structural levels as recognized on site.

Layers were designated by number, in a simple, straightforward sequence from top to bottom. There are eight layers of which Layer 7 is the earliest, Layer 1 the latest. In the first season, 1961, two layers, though stratigraphically distinct, were given the same number: 2. The earlier layer, clearly substantial and well preserved, was designated 2B. The later layer was numbered 2A, since it was seen to be a re-occupation within and over the earlier walls. In pottery terms both are interpreted as transitional between Early and Middle Chalcolithic.

The descriptions, Early and Middle Chalcolithic, have been retained, since they were used in the preliminary reports. These and other, similar terms (Late Chalcolithic, Early Bronze Age and so on) have found, to some degree, an acceptance among archaeologists working in Turkey. A change here, in this report, would create confusion. Until an alternative system of descriptive terms has been proposed and accepted, it seems wiser to maintain the traditional phraseology.

In this, the final publication, as in the preliminary reports, the descriptive terms are applied only to pottery. In practice they serve as shorthand. The phrase 'Layer 2B, Early Chalcolithic' means 'Layer 2B (in which pottery described as) Early Chalcolithic (has been found)'.

The word 'level', as used here, means a structural level, i.e. a constructional operation, the results of which can be defined as one or more recognizable buildings or structures preserved wholly or in part. A more expanded term would be 'building-level' or 'structural level'.

A 'phase' indicates a sub-level, a division of 'layer'. 'Phases' are designated by letter, from top to bottom.

'Period' signifies a length of time or a number of calendar years. Both length and number may undergo constant revision.

These and other terms, as used at Canhasan, may be set out in tabular form as follows:

PERIOD	Chalcolithic	defined by pottery but composed of one or more layers.
LAYER	numbered 1, 2 etc.	a layer can be composed of one or more structural levels or of one or more major soil-deposits without structural levels.
LEVEL		a level (or 'structural level') is composed of one or more contemporary buildings (= inhabited structures, units).
PHASE	lettered a b etc.	a sub-level; minor external or internal modification(s) or additions to the plan of an existing structure but the main walls are retained intact or nearly intact.
FEATURE		a non-structural feature (not an inhabited building or structure) resulting from a human act, e.g. tomb, pit, ditch, oven, hearth, stair.
FLOOR		a prepared surface on which occupation takes place *inside* a structure; a deliberate artifact, e.g. a coating of mud, coloured clay-plaster, pebbles; sometimes described as a 'living surface'.
SURFACE		surface on which occupation or activity takes place *outside* a structure; not prepared; an accidental artifact; trodden, worn; loosely used for any surface on which occupation takes place inside or outside a structure.
LINE		a horizontal boundary or division between soil-deposits; frequently used for an interface, i.e. a thin soil-deposit which separates two major soil-deposits.
DEPOSIT		soil-deposits or soil-layers, resulting from human or natural activities.
FILL		frequently used to mean soil-deposit.

At Canhasan the periods, layers and levels may also be set down in tabular form, as follows:

Period	*Layer*	*Level*
Byzantine	Post-Chalco. 1	1 level plus pits and sherds; coin recovered from the dump
Roman	Post-Chalco. 2	sherds, reported coin
Hellenistic	Post-Chalco. 3	sherds
Classical	Post-Chalco. 4	sherds
Iron Age	Post-Chalco. 5	pits, sherds
Chalcolithic, Late	1	5 levels
Chalcolithic, Middle	2A	(?)3 levels plus phases & deposits
Transitional	2B	1 level
Chalcolithic, Early	3	1 level
Neolithic (latest)	4	1 level
Neolithic	5	1 level plus phases
Neolithic	6	1 level plus phases
Neolithic	7	1 level

The ceramic finds will be published in Part 2, the remaining categories of material in Part 3.

As indicated above (p. 10) the highest point of the two trenches (S23a and b) where excavation was started on the mound in 1961 was taken to be 10 m. All vertical measurements as given refer to this notional height. According to the measurements, taken in 1962 for the production of the contour plan, there is a difference in height between the eastern and western sides of the mound. The meadow (Turkish *mera*) on the W is 1 m. higher than the fields on the E. The lowest depth reached in the trenches is approximately midway between the two or c. 0.5 m. below the height of the meadow.

2.2 Layers 7–4

In 1966 a small test trench was excavated in the SW quadrant of R21b. Excavation was halted at 4 m., i.e. at c. 0.50 m. below the surface of the meadow on the W of the mound. At this point ground water began to fill the bottom of the trench. The muddy nature of the deposits reduced the work to uncertainty. No attempt was made to test the lower deposits. In 1967 the Dachnowsky corer was not available. On the basis of measurements taken in the pits (dug by us for the disposal of rubbish) on the edge of the meadow it was estimated that settlement deposits continued to c. 3 m. absolute, i.e. to c. 1 m. below the layer at which excavation in R21b was halted in 1966.

In 1967 the small test trench, opened in R21b in 1966, was expanded and the whole square (4 × 4 m. = 16 sq.m.) taken down to the base of Layer 5 as identified. In parallel, Square R21a was excavated to the base of Layer 4 as identified.

Given the structural sequence from Layer 7 to Layer 4 and the form of the buildings in those layers, it can be conjectured with some probability that the structures preceding Layer 7 were similar in size and shape.

The structures of Layers 7–4 were small, when compared in width of wall and area of room with those of Layer 2B. Walls were built without stone foundation. For the most part they rested on a wall of the immediately preceding level. The effect of this structural continuity was to confer an identical orientation on each successive structure. Although large-scale excavation could not be made in Layers 7–4, it may be accepted on the available evidence that the orientation of each layer had been imposed by the structures of the preceding level. Probably in Layer 3 but certainly in Layer 2B the orientation of the settlement follows that of the earliest layers.

All structures were built from roughly shaped but not mould-made mud-brick and, as noted above, without stone foundations. During the Neolithic period at Canhasan the use of stone in walls and doors was exceedingly rare. Building techniques were entirely founded in a mud-brick tradition. Walls were built in consistent, regular courses of mud-brick laid on, and held together by, a thick matrix of clay (into which chaff or straw had not been puddled). The colours of this clay, as do the mud-bricks themselves, vary. The surface of the walls was covered with a thick mud-plaster (?chaff-tempered). There is evidence for the use of a red (?)ochre colouring over the mud-plaster.

The thickness of walls was dependent on the thickness of the mud-bricks from which the walls were constructed. The method of headers-and-stretchers (for the purpose of thickening, while at the same time strengthening, walls) has not been noted at Canhasan before Layer 2B, although double lines of bricks, i.e. laid in parallel, have been recorded in Layer 3.

In the modern village of Alaçatı (and, indeed, throughout Turkey) the inherent weakness of narrow walls is overcome by the employment of two brick sizes, one square, the other rectangular i.e. half the size of the square brick. At Alaçatı mud-bricks are made—still—in a wooden mould. There are two forms of mould, a new (Pl. 2.1) and an old. Both are used: dimensions 0.815 × 0.545 × 0.15 m. (old form) or 0.12 m. (new form). The resulting brick sizes are, approximately, 0.25 × 0.25 × 0.15 m. (old form) or 0.12 m. (new form). In general there are 3 bricks in one mould, i.e. 1 square (Turkish name *anna*) and 2 rectangular (Turkish name *kuzu*) but frequently 6 bricks are made from one mould, 2 square and 4 rectangular. In late eighteenth century buildings in Karaman the following sizes have been recorded: 0.27 × 0.27 × 0.10 m. and 0.14 × 0.27 × 0.10 m. (information from the Karaman Museum).

In Layers 7–4 at Canhasan there is no recorded evidence of differing brick sizes. Mud-brick sizes in Layers 7–4 (0.50 × 0.30 × 0.08 m.) are smaller than those in Layers 3 and 2B (pp. 25, 27, below: approximately 0.80 × 0.40 × 0.10 m.). The bricks of Layers 7–4 appear to have been regularly shaped (? by hand-held boards) and the surfaces seem to be flat, though now distorted. In general they do not give the appearance of a precisely formed, uniformly sized, mould-made mud-brick, although in size they do not vary beyond 20% of the dimensions as calculated on site and indicated above.

The significant change to a more regular size (approximately 0.80 × 0.40 × 0.10 m. in Layer 2B) takes place, on present evidence at Canhasan, between Layers 4 and 3.

The colour of the clay varies, presumably according to source: red, yellow-brown, yellow speckled, grey, grey-green. Chaff or chopped straw was invariably mixed into the clay.

Kiln fired bricks are unknown.

Similarly the use of a partly concealed, wooden frame (horizontal, diagonal and vertical timbers) for the purpose of strengthening and re-inforcing a wall is not known at Canhasan, although some thin, horizontal branches or small beams, laid along (or slightly above) the base of the wall and at right-angles through the wall from face to face, are known from Layers 5 and 4 (cp. Layer 2A, below). Free-standing, vertical timbers (for the support of a ceiling or roof) and horizontal timbers (for ceiling or roof construction) have been recorded only in Layer 2B.

On the other hand, the smallness of the rooms and the use of timbers for the roof no doubt gave to each structure a certain horizontal strength, although not the overall, tensile cohesion of a timber frame. By the coherent use of timber and differential brick-courses the modern village of Alaçatı is able to construct two-storey houses. It is interesting to note that precisely in Layer 2B, when extensive free-standing and part-enclosed vertical timbers combined with the technique of mud-brick arrangement known as 'headers-and-stretchers' was consistently employed, it is possible to observe the material remains of two-storied buildings. Although it is assumed here that this innovation, the introduction of a two-storied building, took place in Layer 3 or 2B, the proposition that the structures of Layers 7–4 were single storied cannot be demonstrated without positive evidence from observable remains.

The orthodox view, that the roofs of prehistoric, and indeed later, mud-brick buildings in Anatolia were flat, is corroborated by the finds at Canhasan, namely, fragments, admittedly broken and not in-situ, of reeds and thin branches embedded in earth or clay (now hardened or baked in the destruction fire). These fragments are typically the remains of roofing materials. The modern successors of the roofing-system in which reeds, twigs or thin branches were laid over horizontal roof-beams and sealed with straw or chaff and finally with rolled soil can still be seen in modern Alaçatı. On the fragments from Layers 7–4 the imprint of the reeds or thin branches are clearly evident.

Hearths have been noted. Partitions, representing the walls of bins, were recorded in a structure of Layer 5. These bins contained grain and seeds in considerable quantity. Grinders, querns and mortars were found nearby. Floors and walls were mud-plastered (brownish, yellow-brown, yellowish) and occasionally coloured with a thin coat of white clay or of red (?)ochre. It is possible that the choice of surface for white plaster was significant, e.g. for the sake of cleanliness in storage containers such as bins. There is no indication of a ritual significance in the use of red colouring.

Layer 7

Excavated in 1967 (trench R21b).

Illustration: section, Fig. 43.

In R21b, in the SW quadrant: a single wall. Thin, low bricks. No foundation stones. A single floor. It is conjectured here that in the northern half of the trench lay a structure on the same alignment as a later building of Layer 5 (see below) and that the sole surviving wall of Layer 7 was part of this conjectured building.

The Layer 7 wall went out of use and the top of the wall was partly buried beneath a thin deposit of loose earth.

Colour of mud-brick: yellow.

Dimensions of mud-brick: (?), probable max. c. 0.50 × 0.30 × 0.08 m.

Layer 6

Excavated in 1967 (trench R21b).

Illustration: section, Fig. 43.

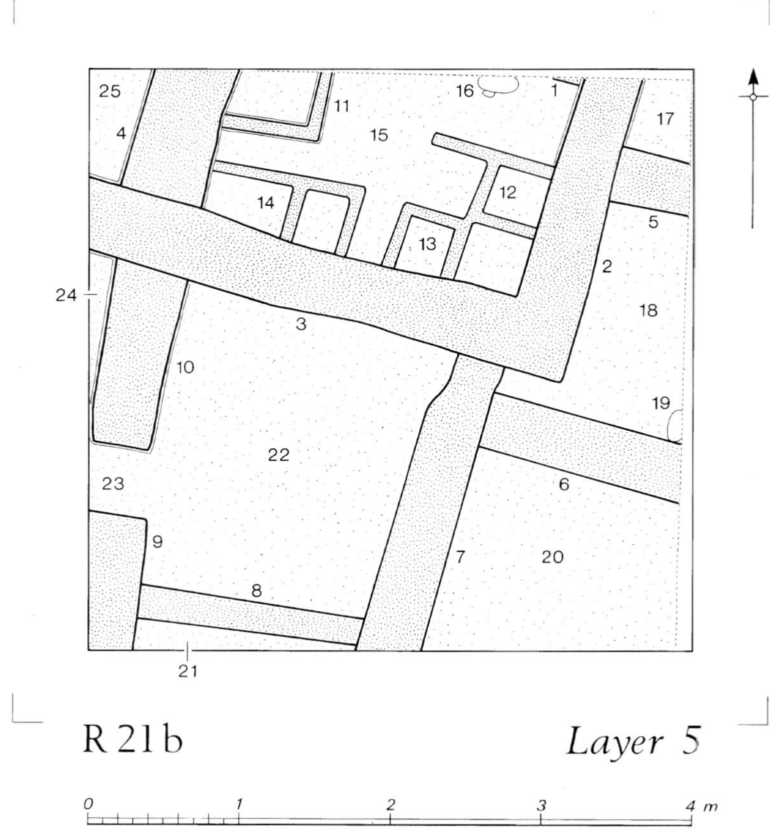

Fig. 08. Plan of Layer 5: R21b (1:50)

Note: In the keys to all plans the figures in brackets identify the same features in the relevant sections.

Cf. Sections, Figs 38, 41–43

1 (7) Wall: E–W; white plaster on S face
2 (8) Wall: N–S; white plaster on W face and on N end of E face
3 (9) Wall: E–W; white plaster on N face
4 (10) Wall: N–S; white plaster on E and W faces
5 (11) Wall: E–W; white plaster on N face
6 (12) Wall: E–W
7 (13) Wall: N–S
8 (14) Wall: E–W; inserted between Walls 7 and 9
9 (15) Wall: N–S
10 (16) Wall: N–S; white plaster on all three faces
11 (17) Partition: for bin(s); on Floor 15; against Wall 4; white-clay plaster
12 Bin: on Floor 15; against Wall 2; white-clay plaster
13 Bin: same; against Wall 3; white-clay plaster
14 Bins: side-by-side; on Floor 15; against Wall 3; white-clay plaster
15 (18) Floor: white-clay; against Walls 1–4
16 (19) Quern (stone): on Floor 15
17 Floor: against Walls 2 & 5; imperfectly excavated
18 (20) Floor: against Walls 2, 5 & 6
19 (21) Quern (stone): on Floor 18
20 (22) Floor: white-clay; against Walls 6 & 7
21 (23) Floor and burnt Hearth: against S face of Wall 8
22 Floor: against Walls 3, 7–10
23 Door: Walls 9 & 10
24 (24) Floor: white-clay; against Walls 3 & 10; imperfectly excavated
25 (25) Floor: white-clay; against Walls 3 & 4; imperfectly excavated

In R21b, in the SW quadrant: a single wall.

At some point after the abandonment of the Layer 7 wall a new wall was built over the top of the Layer 7 wall and on the same alignment. It can be assumed that as in Layer 7 the new wall was part of a structure which retained the orientation of the preceding layer.

Colour of mud-bricks: red.

Dimensions of mud-brick: (?), probable max. 0.50 × 0.30 × 0.08 m.

Layer 5

Excavated in 1967 (trench R21b).

In R21b, over the whole of the trench: several modifications = phases G (the earliest) to A (the latest).

Illustrations: plan, Fig. 08; sections, Figs 38, 41–3; photograph Pl. 2.2. A plan has been published (French 1968b: 50 and Fig. 3); repeated here (Fig. 08). It illustrates only one phase, G (the earliest). Succeeding phases are defined as modifications of the earliest plan.

A new structure is built on the alignment of the Layer 6 wall and stratigraphically above the older, pre-existing building in the southwestern corner of the trench. The Layer 5 structure is represented by two main walls (nos 2 and 3 on the plan, Fig. 08) in the northern half of the trench. A third wall (no. 4 on the plan) is probably part of the original construction. The division between Wall 3 and Wall 4 may represent only a line or interstice between the mud-bricks, not an abutment. The building thus formed is here termed the main structure. It had at least two rooms, an eastern and a western. To these three walls (nos 2, 3 and 4) were added, it seems, three other walls (nos 5, 7 and 9–10), which appear to abut the three main walls.

There is evidence for the use of twigs and/or branches in the construction of the main E–W Wall (Wall 3). The twigs/branches were laid both through the wall, i.e. at right-angles to the face, and parallel with the face (Pl. 3.1, 2).

In addition, two walls, (nos 6 and 8) further subdivide the space S of the main structure. One (no. 6) abuts the eastern side of the N–S wall (no. 7), the other (no. 8) abuts the western side of the same N–S wall (no. 7) and the eastern face of the N–S wall (no. 9).

The internal walls of the structures were plastered with a coating of white clay. The plaster has not always survived.

Floors were given a mud-plaster surface. The floors of the northwestern and northeastern rooms were not totally excavated, owing to the awkwardness of the location.

The eastern room of the main structure was used as a store. The greater part of the floor was occupied by bins containing considerable quantities of grain and seed. It is possible that the wall in the N section (no. 1 on the plan) is the S face of yet another bin. Grinders, querns and mortars were found nearby, in the room-fill. One quern in-situ is indicated on the plan (Fig. 08); the others, not located on the floor, were clearly displaced, (?)fallen from the top of the bins or from a niche. Another quern in-situ is located on the plastered floor of the room added on the E (no. 19 on the plan, Fig. 08).

Dimensions: existing internal lengths (main structure) 2.15 (E–W) × 1.50 m. (N–S); thickness (Wall 2) 0.40–45 m., (Walls 6 and 7) 0.40 m., (Wall 8) 0.20 m.; width of door (Walls 9–10) 0.45 m.

Phases F and E

In Phase F the grain-bins in the main structure go out of use and the area is covered by a plaster-floor which is then renewed at least five times.

On the W or internal face of the N–S Wall (no. 7) a semi-circular hearth was built. This feature disappears in Phase E and is replaced by a square hearth in front of the opposing N–S wall (Walls 9–10).

The E–W wall (no. 5) attached to the eastern wall (no. 2) of the main structure disappears in Phase F. In Phase E the second additional wall (no. 6) also disappears, and the whole of the eastern area is then covered by ash-lines.

Floor and walls: no observable traces of white plaster or red colouring.

Dimensions: square hearth 0.50 × 0.50 m.

Phase D

The main structure continues as before but the enclosed area on the S is now given an additional door, through the eastern wall (no. 7). Several plaster floors; large stones (set into the floors of the enclosed area).

Floors and walls: no observable traces of white plaster or red colouring. Dimensions: (width of door in Wall 7) 0.45 m.

Phase C

The walls and doors of the enclosed area S of the main structure are retained. The E wall (no. 2) of the main structure itself is re-built and then re-inforced by the addition of a mud-brick skin to the inner face. A thick mortar of mud was used to provide both bedding and packing for the new wall. The E–W dimension of the S wall was thereby reduced from 0.40 to 0.35 m. There are 6+ floors (a red, 'bricky' material) to this room. In the southern area the walls and doors of the previous phase are retained. The floor, however, is now a white plaster. A white plastered step or threshold is set in front of the door (in Walls 9–10). A second step, one brick high, was constructed between the two N–S walls (Walls 7 and 9–10) on the alignment of the earlier bench (no. 8 on the plan).

Phase B

The walls of the previous phase (Phase C) are retained but the door through the N–S wall of the S area (Walls 9–10 on the plan) is now closed by bricks. The door in the E wall of the S area (Wall 7) is partly blocked by bricks and replaced by a narrow opening. The external surface of the wall at this point was plastered.

Dimensions: width (narrow opening) 0.20 m.

Fig. 09. Plan of Layer 4: R21a and b (1:50)

Cf. Sections, Figs 37–44

1 (41) Wall: E–W; white plaster on S face
2 (49, 50) Wall: N–S; white plaster on E and W faces
3 (51) Wall: N–S; white plaster on E face
4 Wall: N–S; white plaster on all three faces
5 Wall: N–S; indeterminate at S end
6 Wall: N–S
7 (42) Wall: N–S
8 Wall: E–W; indeterminate at W end
9 (43) Wall: N–S; white plaster on E face
10 Wall: E–W; corner with Wall 11; white plaster on S face
11 (44) Wall: N–S; corner with Wall 10; white plaster on S and W faces
12 (47) Wall: E–W; perhaps a buttress or a wall divided by a door; white plaster on N face
13 (48) Wall: N–S; white plaster on E face
14 (45, 46) Facing: Mud-brick against W face of Walls 10 & 11
15 (54) Floor: surface against W face of Wall 9 and N face of Wall 1
16 (65) Floor: surface against Walls 1, 9–11 (with facing [no. 14])
17 (70) Floor: white-clay; against Walls 2, 10 & 12
18 (72) Floor: surface against the base of Walls 12 & 13
19 (73) Floor: surface against the base of Walls 12 & 13
20 (74) Floor: surface against the base of Walls 1–4
21 Door: Walls 3 & 4
22 Floor: against Walls 1 (W end), 3–6
23 Door: Walls 5 & 6
24 Floor: white-clay; against Walls 5–8
25 Partitions: white-clay; low dividers
26 (62) Floor: surface of brown clay against the S end of Wall 7
27 Layer 3 cut

Phase A

The narrow opening in the N–S wall (no. 7) is blocked and, at floor layer, bridged to form a 'cat-door' or 'cat-hole'. The internal wall-surfaces are re-plastered. The external face of the wall (no. 7) is coated with a thick mud mortar which also covers both the earlier, narrow opening.

No evidence for white plaster or red colouring.

Dimensions: width ('cat-hole') 0.10 m.

Colour of mud-bricks: yellow, yellow-brown, yellow-grey, grey, brown, red.

Dimensions of mud-bricks: irregular; (max.) 0.85–80 × 0.65–42 × 0.10–08 m.

Layer 4

Excavated in 1966–67 (trench R21b) and 1967 (trench R21a).

In R21a and b, over the whole of the two trenches: one phase.

Illustrations: plan, Fig. 09; sections, Figs 34, 37–44.

Insofar as it is possible to reconstruct the plan, there is in Layer 4 a re-shaping of the whole structural complex. The basic plan of the structures in trenches R21a and b (N: Wall 1, E: Wall 2, W; Walls 5 & 6) resemble the internally buttressed houses typical of Layer 2B. The massiveness of the Layer 2B walls, however, is not found in the buildings of Layer 4. The basic structural traditions of Layer 4 are still those of the preceding layers.

The main room of Layer 5 Phase A (the latest phase) is retained. but the two N–S walls (Walls 7 and 10 on the plan, Fig. 08) in the S area were re-built. No S wall has been discovered. As in Layer 5, wooden beams were laid against, i.e. parallel to, the western face of the new W wall (Layer 4, nos 3 & 4 on the plan, Fig. 09). Beams were also laid under the wall, at right-angles to it, and under the floor. A thick, yellowish mud-plaster covered both the wall and the floor, cp. Walls 1 and 11, below. The internal faces of the walls and the floor were also coated with a fine, yellowish mud-plaster.

A short wall (no. 12 on the plan) was added to the eastern face of the E wall (no. 2). A (?)buttress (no. 13 on the plan) attached to the S face of the short wall (no. 12) creates a small alcove. Most faces of these additional walls were coated with a fine white clay-plaster.

The packing of the floor (no. 16 on the plan) in the N room was composed of wooden beams, now rotted, set in clay. In the same manner as described above (Walls 3 and 4), the beams lay parallel, and at right angles, to the walls (Pl. 4.1; N face of Wall 1). The purpose of these arrangements is not clear.

After the construction of the walls in the NE quadrant of R21b (Walls nos 10 and 11 on the plan) a narrow 'skin' (Wall no. 14 on the plan) was added to the inner face.

Excavation in R21a revealed the western extension of the complex. Both the NE and the SW corners of the structure came to light. Beyond the W wall (nos 5–6 on the plan), in the NW quadrant of the trench, the area is divided by partitions (no. 25 on the plan) into four unequally sized compartments. The purpose of these divisions is not apparent. The partitions are narrow; the surfaces are coated with a fine, yellowish mud-plaster. Dimensions: thickness of wall c. 0.50 m. (N), c. 0.45 m. (W), c. 0.40 m. (E), c. 0.10 m. (partitions), c. 0.70 m. (door in Wall 5–6, no. 23 on the plan).

Below the threshold of the door (no. 23 on the plan) were found the skeletons of two dogs, laid head to tail (Pl. 4.2, 5.1).

Colour of mud-brick: yellow, grey-green, brown, brown-red

Dimensions of mud-bricks: irregular; (max.) 0.80 × 0.38 × 0.10 m.

2.3 Layer 3

Excavated in 1965 (trench R21a) and 1966 (R21b), thus creating an area of 45 sq.m. over the two trenches, including the baulks R21a/b and R21a/c.

Illustrations: plan, Fig. 10; sections, Figs 34, 37–44, 50, 52.

The structure in S24c, published (French 1968b: 47 and plan, Fig. 1) as Layer 3, has been re-assigned to Layer 2B (see below, p. 42, Structure 10).

It was evident during excavation and later observable in section that the walls of Layer 3 had been deliberately constructed on the top of Layer 4 walls (?for stability). Certainly the orientation of Layer 3 houses was influenced by Layer 4. The origins of the internally buttressed house, typical of Layer 2B, are clearly exhibited by the structures of Layer 3. It can be proposed, therefore, on the basis of the existing evidence from Layer 3, that this layer represents a turning-point of some importance in the sequence of Neolithic and Chalcolithic settlement- and house-plans.

Five aspects are noteworthy:

(1) the introduction of mud-bricks (presumably mould-made) of a near-standard size larger than the sizes of mud-bricks in the preceding layers (see above, p. 21),
(2) the increased width,
(3) and hence the massive size, of the Layer 3 walls,
(4) the dimensions, and
(5) the regularity—approaching symmetry—of the Layer 3 structure.

All five aspects anticipate the characteristics of the Layer 2B settlement.

No structure of Layer 3 has been excavated *in toto*. The attempt to preserve, in the state in which they were found, the houses of Layer 2B led to the abandonment of that part of our programme which concerned the structures below Layer 2B. Without serious destruction to the Layer 2B settlement it was possible to excavate below Layer 2B only in R21a and b, an area of 36 m. after the removal of the baulk intervening between the two trenches.

The orientation of the walls both in trenches R21a and b is nearly exactly that of Layer 4. This orientation was subsequently transmitted to the houses of Layer 2B.

In trenches R21a and b the surviving walls are massive and substantial. In plan the walls approach the regularity of Layer 2B structures. The surviving remains are sufficient to permit a reconstruction of

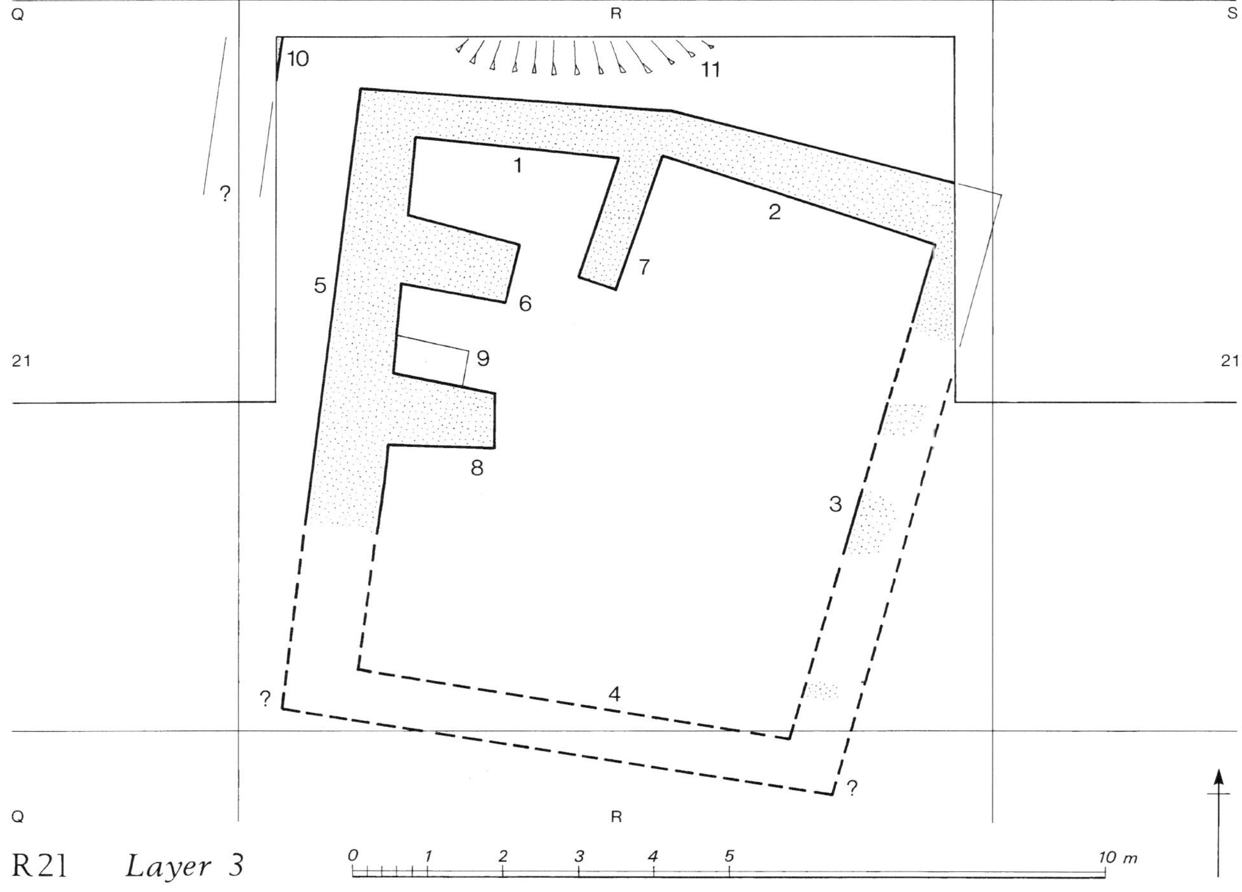

Fig. 10. Plan of Layer 3: R21 (1:100)

Cf. Sections, Figs 34, 37–44, 50, 52
1 (80) Wall: E–W
2 (80) Wall: E–W
3 (8) Wall: N–S; re-use of Layer 4 wall-stump at N end
4 Wall: E–W (restored)
5 (84) Wall: N–S
6 Buttress: E–W; on E Face of Wall 5; white-clay plaster on E Face
7 (81) Buttress: N–S; on S Face of Wall 1
8 (1) Buttress: S of Buttress 7; white clay plaster on E Face
9 (85) (?)Bench: against N Face of Buttress 8; not recorded in trench
10 (86) Wall: N–S; fill of Mud-brick debris between E face and W face of Wall 5
11 (79) Cut

the building. The type of structure appears to be an internally buttressed house nearly square in plan. It is possible that internal buttresses—now lost—once existed on the E and S walls.

There are no stone foundations. The mud-brick was arranged in header-and-stretcher technique, bonded with a thick mud mortar and laid in even, regular courses, although there appears to have been considerable lateral movement in the Layer 3 walls in trenches R21a and b. The present narrowness of the buttress against the northern wall is probably due to deterioration at the end of, or immediately after, the lifetime of the structure. The walls and floors were plastered with a red clay and in the SW corner there are traces of a white clay plaster (? suggesting a two-coloured decoration).

There is no evidence of destruction by fire. The structure appears to have collapsed inwards (the walls have moved in this direction). When the Layer 2B settlement was created, the Layer 3 house in R21a and b was filled in, the tops of walls (to judge from the straightness of the surviving line) cleanly sliced off, the area filled in and levelled. The settlement of Layer 2B was then built on top.

Dimensions: surviving wall lengths 6.00 (N–S) × 8.50 m. (W–E); width of walls 0.80 m. (average 0.75); length of buttresses 1.40 m. (on W wall), 1.90 m. (on N wall).

Colours of mud brick: red, yellow, yellow-green, grey-green

Dimensions of mud brick: 0.80 × 0.40 × 0.10 m.

2.4 Layer 2B

Excavated in 1961 (trenches R22d, and 23b&d; S22a&c, and 23a–c); in 1962 (trenches Q21d, 22d, and 23b&d; R21c&d, 22a-c, 23d, 24a&b; S21c, 22a&b, 23d, and 24a&b); in 1964 (trenches R21c&d); in 1965 (trenches R21a&b); in 1966 (trenches R21b; Q21d); in 1967 (trenches R24c&d; S24c); an approximate area of 650 sq.m.

Illustrations: plans (general), Figs 11,12; sections, 37, 38, 40–44; 45; 49.2; 50.1–3; 51.1,2; 52.1, 2; 53.1; 54.1; 55.2; 56.2; 57.3; 58.1, 3; for large-scale plans, relevant sections and photographs, see lists under individual structures.

The Layer 2B plan published after the 1962 season (French 1963b: Fig. 1) is no longer valid. It has been extensively revised. The structures located on the W side of the site have been re-assigned to Layer 2A, as follows:

Trench Q21d, N end	=	Layer 2A Structure 1
House 8	=	Layer 2A Structure 2
Q22d,Q23b	=	Layer 2A Structure 3
Q23d	=	Layer 2A Structure 4

The structure in S24c, published (French 1968b: 47 and plan, Fig. 1) as Layer 3, has been re-assigned to Layer 2B, Structure 10 (plan, Fig. 20).

Our first trenches in S23a and b came upon well-preserved, heavily burnt mud-brick walls immediately below the surface. When the trenches were expanded, it was seen that the walls belonged not to one but to several substantial buildings destroyed by a very severe fire. On the plans (Figs 11–20) all these buildings have been called structures—'houses' in the preliminary reports—and numbered 1–10. Although several pits of the Roman or Early Byzantine period have cut into walls and associated burnt debris, comparatively little damage was done and it was found that in many places the walls were still standing to a height of c. 3 m.

The floor levels vary between structures, e.g. 7.40 absolute in Structure 3 to 5.20 absolute in the eastern half of Structure 10. Structure 3 thus stood at the highest point of the Layer 2B settlement. Undoubtedly the configuration of the underlying layer (Layer 3) had influenced the vertical relationships of the later, Layer 2B structures (see the composite sections, Figs 34–36), as also it had affected their orientation (see the comments, p. 66).

Each structure was independent of its neighbours; no use was made of party-walls. There is no evidence that walls such as the western wall of Structure 1 and the eastern wall of Structure 3 were in any way bonded. Similarly, no two walls are exactly parallel, though very closely juxtaposed. Stone foundations are absent. The mud-brick was laid directly on soil or on the wall-tops or wall-stumps of earlier (Layer 3) buildings. There is great regularity in the construction of the walls, no doubt the result of (1) the uniformity in the size of the bricks and (2) the skill of the builders. The mud-bricks were laid in even and regular courses, end-to-end in parallel rows. At each corner the courses of mud-brick were bonded, i.e. in alternate rows the corner bricks were set crosswise i.e. at right-angles. This same technique was used for the construction of the buttresses.

A mud-brick of a standard size, c. 0.80 × 0.40 × 0.10 m., was used throughout, and a tough grey-green clay employed as mortar, c. 0.02–03 m. thick and untrimmed. That the mud-bricks were mould-made is evident (1) from the informity of size and (2) from the smoothness of the sides (the smoothness of the surfaces is visible in the photographs, Pls 2 and 3).

The buttresses protrude into the interior of the houses for a distance of c. 0.80 m., i.e. the length of one mud-brick. Sometimes, as in Structure 5, extra bricks have been added to the end of the buttresses. The depth of the buttresses in Structure 5 is irregular, unlike those in Structure 3.

In the building of the Layer 2B structures there is no evidence for the use of a timber frame or timber re-inforcement. The employment of timber was prominent only in the support of the roof or ceiling which also functioned as the floor of the upper storey. For wooden posts used to support a roof/ceiling, see the plans, Figs 14 (Structure 2) and 15 (Structure 3). For the use of horizontal timbers to take the weight of ceiling/roof beams, see the remarks (on modern building practise) immediately below and the evidence from Structure 10 (p. 38).

In the first notes and in the on-site summaries it was thought that the vertical and horizontal passages or holes in and through the mud-brick walls represented the remains of timber beam-slots. Subsequently these passages were seen to have resulted from the activities of the industrious (and captivating) gopher.

In the first reports it was noted that the structures of Layer 2B were probably two-storied and that the roofs and/or ceilings were constructed in the manner practised in the modern village (French 1962b: 31):

"Roofing or ceiling material was found at a height of c. 2 m. above the floor in the debris of each house, particularly in Houses 2, 3" [and 10. Wooden columns were used, as necessary, to span a ceiling and to support an upper storey. Evidence for timber posts was found in Structures 2 and 3. The posts are set in the floor (without a stone pad) either free-standing or semi-engaged (Pl. 3.2)].

Fig. 11. Layer 2B: General plan (1:250)

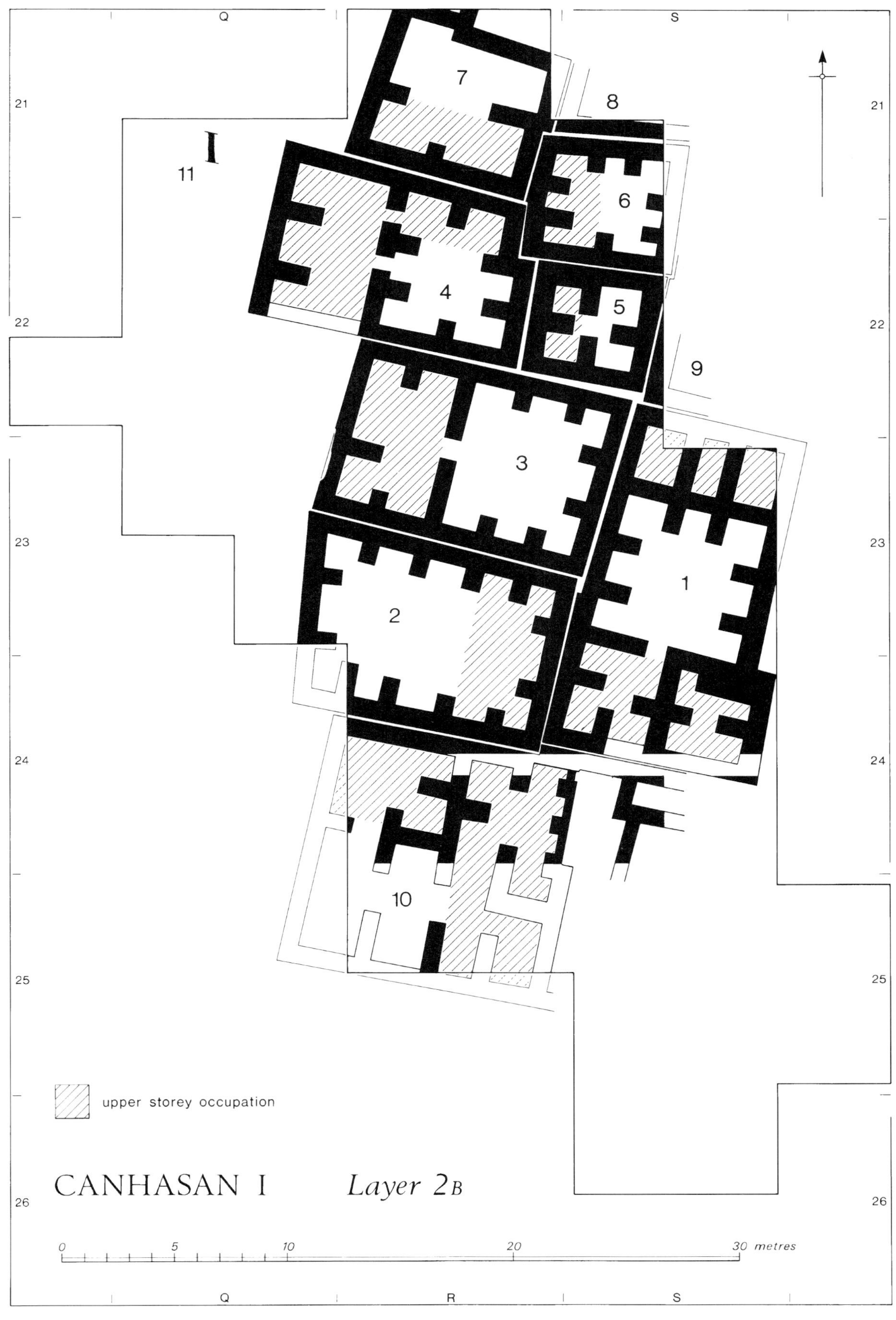

Fig. 12. Layer 2B: Area of occupation on upper stories, hypothetically reconstructed (1:250)

Fig. 13. Plan of Layer 2B, Structure 1 (1:100)

"As far as one can judge on present results, there is no difference between the technique employed for roof construction today in modern Alaçatı and that used in the prehistoric settlement. The modern roofs are built in the following stages": [firstly, long, thick beams supported along the interior and exterior edges of the wall by horizontal beams; if the span is too wide for the main beams, additional support is given by posts; sometimes additional posts are set against the interior (but not the exterior) face of the wall; secondly, narrow beams or branches, planks or a reed mat (Turkish *hasır*) laid crosswise on the main beams; thirdly, branches, twigs or reeds; finally, loose soil which is then tamped or rolled. Salt is usually added to the surface in order to provide additional cohesion to the soil, especially in rainy conditions. A reconstruction of the roofing/ceiling technique is illustrated here (Fig. 22)]. For detailed evidence on the construction of an upper storey, see below, Structure 10.

For a hypothetical reconstruction of the occupation area on the upper stories of Structures 1–6, 7 and 10, see the plan, Fig. 12, and the comments, below p. 68.

Structure 1

Excavated in 1961 (trenches S22c, 23a–c) and 1962 (trenches R24b, S23d and S24a and b).

Illustrations: plans, Figs 11–13; section, Fig. 35.

The plan displays a certain symmetry. Structure 1 consists of three parts or sections: N, centre and S. Before excavation began in 1961 the tops of the walls on the E side of the N section reached to the surface of the mound but in the S section the tops of the walls, as discovered, had been cut off at c. 0.60–0.70 m. below the ground surface.

In 1961 an occupation deposit of Layer 2A was discovered over the tops of walls in S23b, i.e. over the NW rooms of the N section of Structure 1. There is a surface of occupation (S24b, Layer 2A; excavated in 1962) and a hearth over the SE corner of the S section.

The central section is almost square and almost symmetrical. Opposing buttresses are built on the W and E walls. The N section is arranged in three rooms (one narrow between two square). The S section is divided into two unequally sized rooms. There is no visible means of entry into any room of the N section nor into the E half of the S section.

The N section: an irregularly formed bench occupies the base of the W and S walls in the NW room and symmetrically the E and S walls in the NE room.

The central section: the walls are plastered on all surfaces. The walls were presumably not timbered but the evidence is concealed beneath the plaster. The length of the buttresses varies according to the number of bricks used: 1.20 m. = 1½ bricks, 1.60 m. = 2 bricks. A low bench (not shown on the plan, Fig. 13) runs along the wall between the two buttresses (nos 1.12, 1.13) in the NE corner. Between the ends of the two buttresses (nos 1.23, 1.24) on the E wall there are narrow partitions, thickness 0.25 m. (on N) = 2 bricks plus plaster and 0.14 m. = 1 brick plus plaster (on S), forming bins. Heavy burning occurs on the S side and in the bins on the E wall; the burning reaches to the mid-point of the walls as preserved. No clear, hard floor was reached in 1961. Excavation stopped at a burnt surface of softish earth.

The S section was entered from the central section by a narrow opening, set in the wall c. 0.93 m. above the burnt surface in the central section, and was divided into two unequal rooms. The surface of the N wall with its buttresses was plastered; presumably the surfaces, now bare, of the other walls were also plastered. No timber reinforcement visible. A partition wall (no. 1.25) (0.15 m. thick = 1 brick + plaster) at the end of the N buttress (no. 1.20) on the W wall forms a bin; there is a fine mud plaster on the partition wall and on the face of the wall and buttress inside the bin. An alcove has been formed in the N wall of the E room where the thickness (c. 1.60 m.) is twice the normal dimension (c. 0.80 m.). It is possible that the extra thickness is the result of repair or shoring/strengthening.

No clear, hard floor; in the NW corner a line of burning. There are traces of heavy burning on the W and S sides of the S section.

There is some displacement of the W wall (no. 1.5) of the central section and of the two facing buttresses (nos 1.16, 1.17) in the eastern half of the S section. The explanation for this displacement is probably to be sought in the fire and the subsequent collapse of the building. It is interesting to note, however, that the western wall (no. 1.5) is narrower in the upper courses than in the lower and that the narrow, upper courses are an integral part of the northerly buttress (no. 1.22) on the W wall but not of the southerly (no. 1.21) with which the wall does not bond. The narrowness of the upper courses is matched by the width of the western wall (no. 1.5) at its northern end. An explanation for this anomaly is not easy: (?)a repair, or possibly the surviving courses of an upper storey, cp. the walls (nos 10.2, 10.3 and 10.7) and the buttresses (nos 10.19 and 20) of Structure 10 (plan, Fig. 20).

Colour of mud-brick: yellow, burnt to red in places.

Dimensions: the width of the walls and buttresses, in almost all cases, is a multiple of the standard brick length, 0.80 m., e.g. × 1½ (= 1.20 m.), × 2 (= 1.60 m.).

Area of ground-plan: c. 140 sq.m.

Structure 2

Excavated in 1961 (trenches R23d) and in 1962 (trenches R23c, R24a and b and Q23d).

Illustrations: plans, Figs 11, 12, 14; section, Fig. 34; published photograph, French 1963b: 35 and Pl. 1.a.

The tops of the walls lay immediately below the surface dust. No traces of Layer 2A over the top of the structure. Roofing or ceiling material was found in the uppermost fill. Burning was visible on all four sides but, on the inside face, could be followed only down to c. 2.00 m. below the tops of the walls (at their highest point). At this level the traces of burning stopped. The structure, as excavated, had been completely filled with mud-bricks, neatly stacked over the whole area occupied by the interior of the structure. The plan of the building was traced from the outline of the scorched wall-faces, inside and out. Similarly the posts or roof-supports were detected

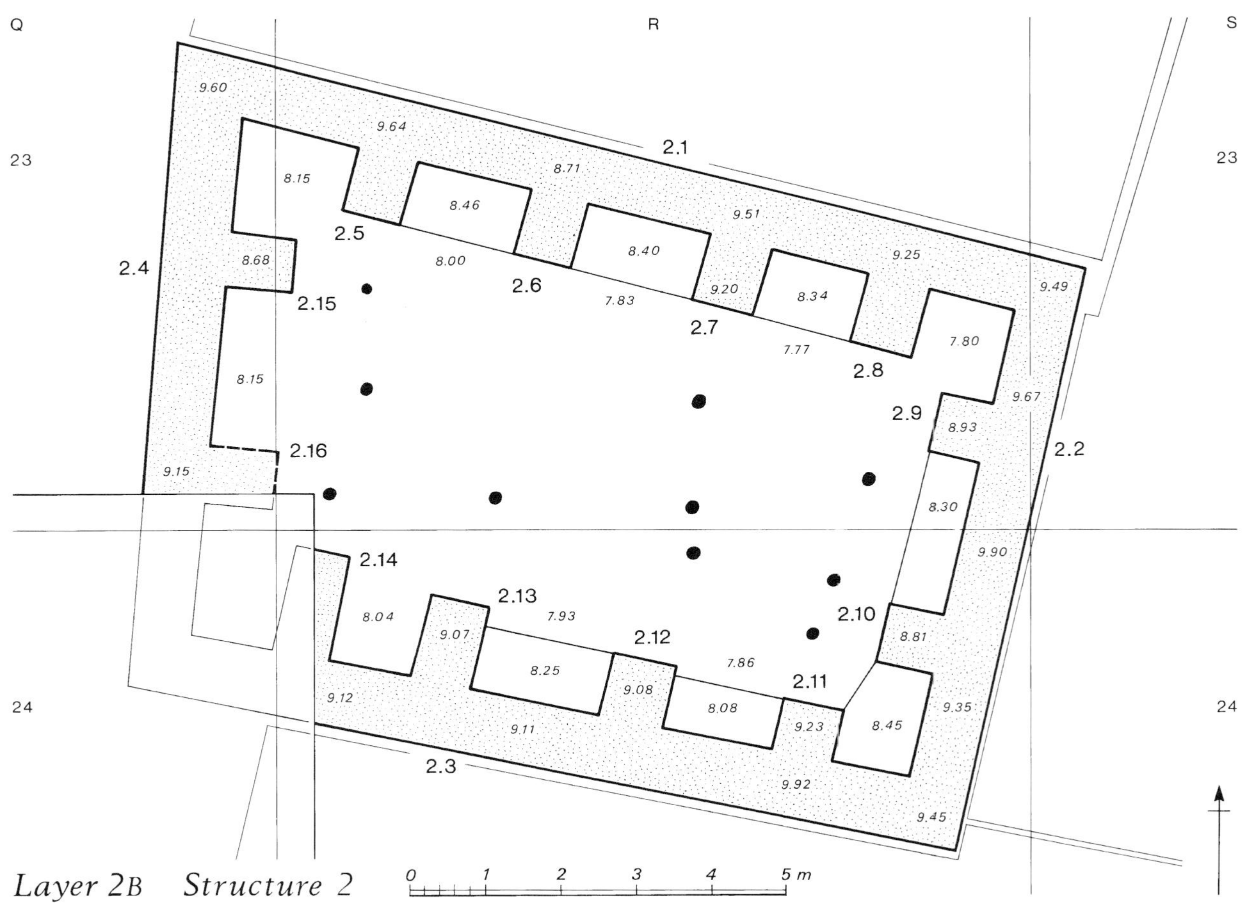

Fig. 14. Plan of Layer 2B, Structure 2 (1:100)

by the presence of burnt circles visible in the layers of the mud-brick stacked inside the structure. The floor was not sought; there is no evidence, therefore, for partitions or bins. A burnt mud-brick face (shown on the plan, Fig. 14) was observed between the buttresses on the N, E and S walls. The burnt face probably represents the presence of benches. On the inside faces of the walls there is no trace of plaster nor, in the walls, of timbering.

As excavated the walls show a tilting towards the S, as if the structure had begun to collapse southwards before the process of collapse was halted by the solid in-fill of mud-brick, (?)intended to prevent damage to the structure (no. 10) in the path of the collapsing walls.

The burning of the walls and stacked mud-brick was undoubtedly caused by the intense fire in Structure 3.

Colour of mud-brick: yellow and, where burned, bright red.

Dimensions: the thickness and width of walls and buttresses are multiples of the length and width of the standard-sized mud-brick, 0.80 m.

Area of ground-plan: c. 97 sq.m.

Structure 3

Excavated in 1961 (trenches R22d, S22c, R23b and S23a) and in 1962 (trenches R22c and 23a). Structure 3 was named the 'Plaster Room' in the 1962 report (French 1963b: 29).

Illustrations: plans, Figs 11–12, 15; section, Fig. 34; photographs, Pl. 5.2 and 6.1; published photographs, French 1962b: 30 and Pl. 1.a, and French 1963b: 35 and Pl. 1.b.

The tops of the walls were visible immediately below the surface layer of soft dust. There are some patchy later, 2A deposits over the area of the E room but no later re-occupation of the room nor re-use of the walls. Some late pits (of Roman or Early Byzantine date) have been dug down into the walls and the associated debris.

The walls stand to a maximum height of 3 m. There are no stone foundations. The floor was a simple layer of hard earth over small pebbles.

Originally, no doubt, the interior face of the walls was coated over-all with a mud/clay plaster but this facing has survived only in a few areas. The vertical and horizontal surfaces of the benches were not, it seems, coated with a mud/clay plaster.

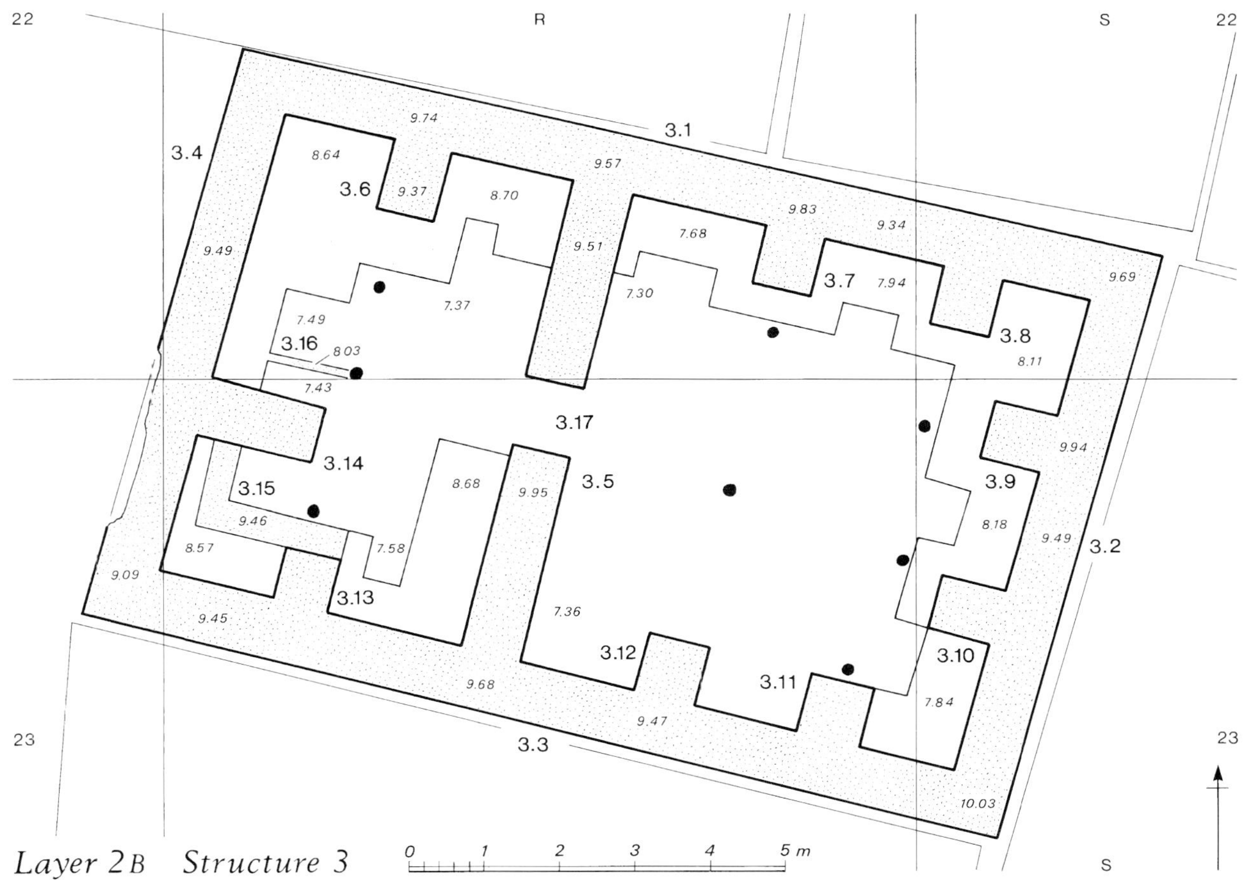

Fig. 15. Plan of Layer 2B, Structure 3 (1:100)

There is evidence for only one layer of plaster.

Structure 3 was divided by a substantial wall (no. 3.5) into two sections of which the western is the smaller. The two sections are linked by means of a door (no. 3.17; photograph, French 1963b: 35 and Pl. 1a) built in the dividing wall (no. 3.5). The door was constructed, it seems, without the help of wooden beams. The width (0.75 m. at the base, 0.66 m. at the top) is approximately the length of one mud-brick, i.e. 0.80 m. The ceiling of the door was constructed on a simple bridging technique. The gap was spanned by two mud-bricks which met at the middle; one half projected to the centre of the door, the other half, firmly embedded on two sides and weighted from above, remained in the wall. The corners of the door were rounded and then plastered.

In the western section the mud/clay plaster (a single coat only) is well preserved on the N, S and E walls but not on the W. The mud/clay plaster is white. On this surface there is a single coating of a grey or perhaps blue wash. As indicated above, the preserved height of the walls of Structure 3 was c. 3 m. above the floor. At the highest point of the walls the number of identifiable courses was 18 above the bench. There were seven courses of bricks in the bench itself (ht of bench c. 0.80 m.; thickness of clay mortar between each course c. 0.015 m.). The bricks were laid in irregular formations of courses, arranged (1) in parallel lines and (2) in headers-and- stretchers, between a thick layer of clay mortar, sometimes c. 0.03 m. thick. Corners were fashioned by means of brick-courses laid in alternating directions. Buttresses were attached to the main walls by the use of header-bricks in alternate courses. Benches occupy the area at the foot of the N and E walls of the E room and of the N, W, S and SW walls in the W room. The height of the benches against the E wall is c. 0.80 m. above the floor but only 0.45 m. at the NW corner. The plan of the benches in the W room is somewhat irregular. There is a bin (no. 3.15) in the SW corner.

Support for the roof (and upper storey) is most clearly demonstrated by 5 post-holes in the E room and 3 in the W room. The diameter of the holes is c. 0.20 m. One post was carefully set in plaster, traces of which are visible on the face of the buttress (the middle of the three posts on the E side of the E room; photo. French 1962b: Pl. 1a). Within the area enclosed by the walls of the W room there was a fill compris-

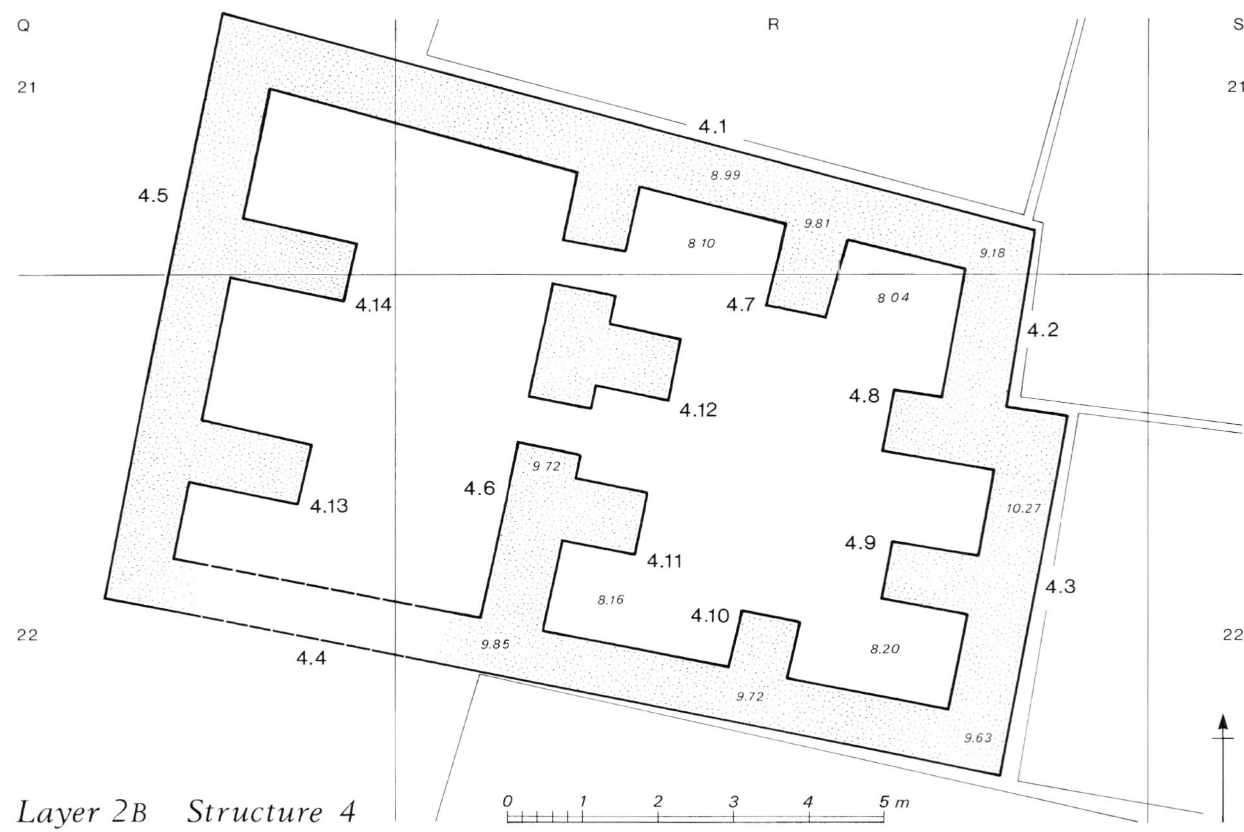

Fig. 16. Plan of Layer 2B, Structure 4 (1:100)

ing roof/floor debris, decorated plaster fragments (red on white; grey/blue monochrome) and pots. The association of these materials provides the clearest evidence for the existence of a second storey above the existing walls of Structure 3. The concentration of the materials in the W room suggests that the upper storey was, in fact, located only over the W room, cp. a similar concentration of roof/floor debris and patterned plaster in the W half of Structure 10, W part.

The gap between the walls of Structure 4 and Structure 3 is never more than 0.10.

Dimensions: door (3.17 on the plan, Fig. 15) c. 1.36 m. (ht), c. 0.76 m. (base) and 0.66 m. (top) (wi.), c. 0.80 m. (depth).

Colour of the mud-brick: burnt red, frequently black; traces of straw temper; some bricks are now extremely crumbly and friable.

Area of Structure 3: 103.75 sq.m., 44 sq.m. (W section).

Structure 4

Excavated in 1961 (trenches R22d), 1962 (trenches Q21d, Q22b, R21c–d, R22b–c) and 1966 (trench Q21d). In the dig-notes for 1961 and 1962 Structure 4 was designated the 'Red House' on account of the striking redness of the mud-brick used in the construction of the walls.

Illustrations: plans, Figs 11–12, 16; sections, Figs 34, 49.2, 50.3, 52.1.

There was no evidence of re-use or re-occupation of Structure 4, although in the soil above the walls and associated debris there were sherds assignable to Layer 2A.

A large and deep pit which penetrated as far as the floor did considerable damage to the walls at the NE corner of the structure. Only the SE corner of Structure 4 was excavated in 1961 (in the SE quadrant of trench R22d) but not to the level of the floor. Total excavation of Structure 4 took place in the following year, 1962. The tops of the walls in trench R22d lay c. 0.60 m. below the ground-surface.

The plan of Structure 4, as first revealed in 1962, was thought to be square. Re-interpreted, however, the shape of the structure is now seen to be rectangular, the whole being divided into two unequal sections, an Eastern and a Western.

The Eastern section is almost square. The NE corner is irregular, owing to the adjustment for the SW corner of Structure 6. As discovered, the W wall of the eastern section (Wall 4.6 on the plan, Fig. 16) appeared originally to have been built with two 'niches' which ran directly into the wall. These 'niches' were blocked by the E wall of another struc-

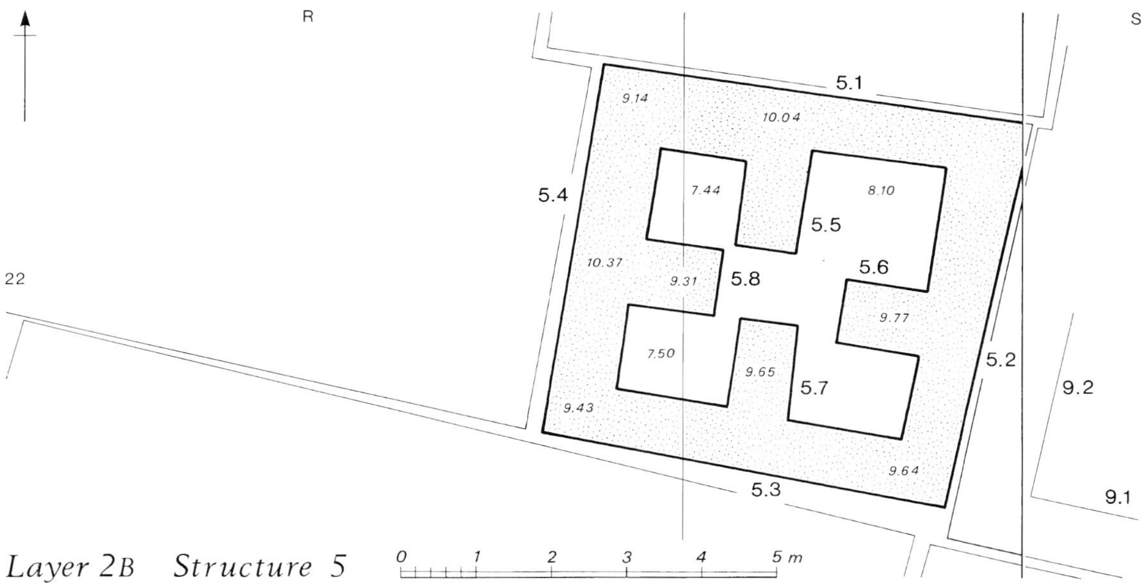

Fig. 17. Plan of Layer 2B, Structures 5, 9 (1:100)

ture (in 1962 designated 'House 8'). It is now clear, however, that this E wall (here no. 2.2 on the plan, Fig. 24) is a later, Layer 2A construction and, consequently, that the 'niches' are, in all probability, doors, measuring c. 0.68 m. wide, 0.89 m. high. It was too dangerous to excavate them completely without first removing the 'E wall' of 'House 8'. Structure 4 thus emerges as a two-roomed building similar to Structure 3.

The walls (Wall 4.5 and buttresses 4.13 and 4.14) revealed in trench Q21d below the structure which in 1962 was designated 'House 8' (now seen to belong to Layer 2A; numbered 2 on the plan, Fig. 24) survive only for a few courses of mud-brick. The colour of these mud-bricks is a bright yellow (similar to those used for Structure 7). The external surface-lines associated with the base of the W wall slope downwards towards the W. There is some evidence (mud-bricks, apparently in situ) for the presence of another structure (no. 11 on the plan, Fig. 11) beyond, i.e. W of, the W wall (4.5 on the plan) of Structure 4 (see the E profile of trench Q21c, Fig. 51.1, Walls 1 and 2).

No evidence for post-holes was discovered in the E room of Structure 4. The floor of the Western section was not found. In the Eastern section there is a simple, earth floor. There was no substantial evidence of roofing-material fallen from an upper storey. It is possible that this absence of debris may be significant (see below, Structure 5) but it is also possible that any debris associated with the W room (in 1962 designated 'House 8') was dug out at the time when Layer 2A Structure 2 was inserted over the basal courses of Layer 2B Structure 4.

A mud/clay wall-plaster was probably used on all interior faces but it is extensively preserved only on the N wall.

The size of the mud-bricks used in the walls and buttresses is the standard 0.80 × 0.40 × 0.10 m. There was clearly an attempt to accommodate the plan to the available space. The construction of Structure 4 and Structure 6 appears to be contemporary, since the NE corner of Structure 4 and the SW corner of Structure 6 are adjusted to take account of each other. The walls were constructed in regular courses of mud-bricks laid in parallel. The technique of headers and stretchers was a standard feature in the corners and in the buttresses where it was used to bond buttress to wall. The length and width of the buttresses are multiples of the standard mud-brick dimensions: 1 mud-brick = 0.80, 1½ mud-bricks = 1.20 etc.

There were no benches, partitions or bins.

Colour of mud-brick: red; crumbly and friable (described as 'chicken-feed' in the dig-notes).

Area of Structure 4 including the W room (= 'House 8' in the preliminary reports; see French 1963b: 30 and facing Plan, and 1967b: 169 and Plan, Fig. 2): 88 sq.m.

Structure 5

Excavated in 1961 (trenches R22d and S22a and c) and in 1962 (trenches R22b, S22a and c). In the dig-notes for 1961 the structure is called the 'Yellow House' from the predominant colour-tone of the mud-bricks used in the construction of the walls.

Illustrations: plans, Figs 11, 12, 17; section, Fig. 36.

There was no re-use or re-occupation of Structure 5.

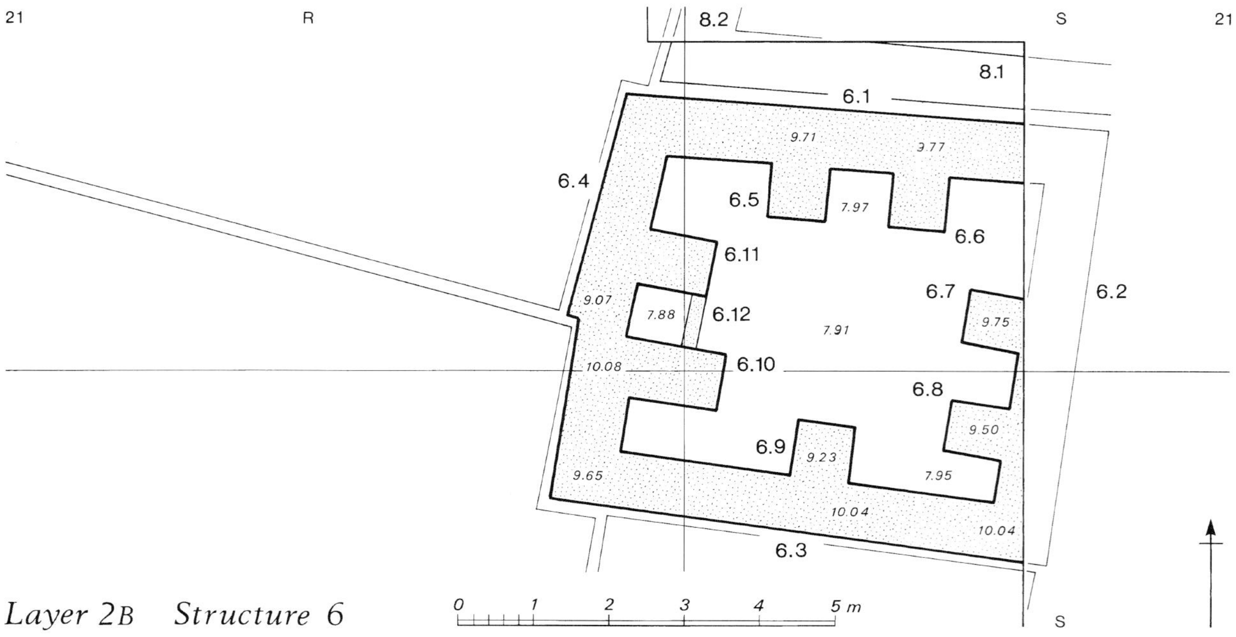

Fig. 18. Plan of Layer 2B, Structures 6, 8 (1:100)

The structure is well preserved. The W wall appeared just below the surface. The maximum height (as it exists) of the walls is 2.93 m. above the floor-surface.

The mud-bricks are standard (0.80 × 0.40 × 0.10 m.) and the thickness of the walls and the depth and width of the buttresses are, therefore, multiples of the brick size. The mud/clay mortar is c. 0.02–3 m. thick.

The walls were faced with a white-clay wash laid on a mud/clay plaster, straw tempered and c. 0.02 thick.

There are no benches nor any post-supports, presumably because of the narrowness of the enclosed space.

There were no indisputable indications of an upper storey, cp. the narrow walls and white plaster of the upper storey in Structure 10. The absence of such evidence is probably fortuitous. On the other hand a large deposit of sherds and broken pots lay against the S and E walls (5.2 and 5.3 on the plan); roofing/ceiling material was found below the pottery which presumably had been sitting on the floor of the roof/ceiling, cf. the remarks on similar roofing/ceiling in Structures 6 and 10 (see below).

Colour of the mud-brick: predominantly yellow. Grey clay mortar.

Area of Structure 5: c. 35 sq.m.

Structure 6

Excavated in 1962 (trenches R21d and 22a, and S21c and 22a).

Illustrations: plans, Figs 11, 12, 18; sections, Figs 53.1, 54.1.

It was reported after the second season (French 1963b: 30) that a substantial and well defined deposit associated with this re-occupation (Layer 2A) was found inside and over the stumps of the walls in trench S21c (see the plan, Fig. 23) and that the burning which was observed on the interior face of the wall-stumps is to be associated with a later, Layer 2A, re-use. There are no valid grounds for a revision of this statement although fragments which could be interpreted as roofing/ceiling material were found below the pottery, cp. the remarks on the stratigraphic association of roofing/ceiling material in Structures 5 (see above) and Structure 10 (see below). In Structure 6, however, this material can be assigned to the top of the Layer 2B deposit (mud-brick debris) which lies below the ash and fill (of Layer 2A) running over the top of the Structure 6 walls (see the section, Fig. 53.1, S21c, W Face). The date of the deposit will be considered in a discussion of the pottery from the area of Structure 6.

Structure 6 was not well preserved. Three pits destroyed much of the N wall (6.1). As excavated, the buttresses (6.7–11) on the W, S and E walls now lean towards the N; the surface became worn and damaged during the period of Layer 2A when rubbish and fill was deposited in the original structure.

Otherwise the plan of the structure is perfectly clear: an irregular square. The walls are constructed with mud-bricks of the standard size, 0.80 × 0.40 × 0.10 m., and, if one allows for the distortion affecting the position of the bricks, the dimensions of the walls and buttresses are multiples of these figures.

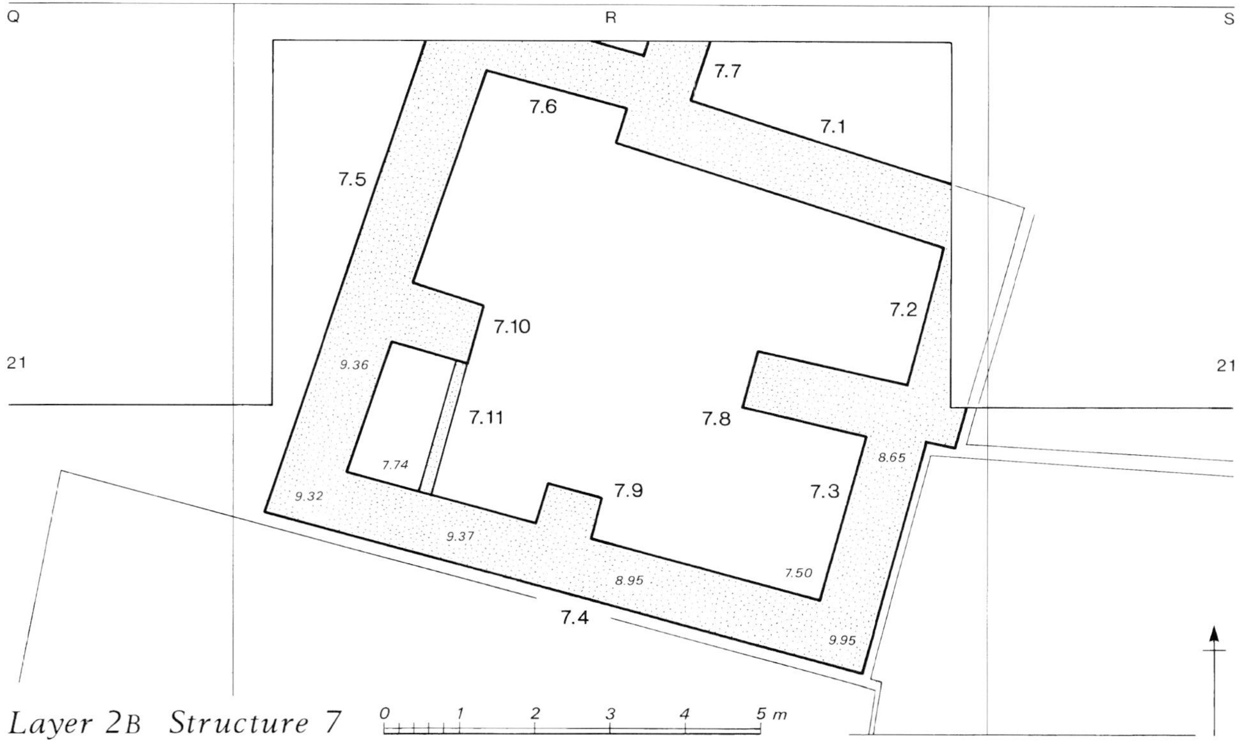

Fig. 19. Plan of Layer 2B, Structure 7 (1:100)

There is no evidence for a mud/clay plaster on the interior face of the walls, nor is there evidence for posts supporting a roof or second storey. The floor is a simple, trodden earth-surface.

There is a partition (6.12) between the two buttresses (6.10, 6.11) on the W wall (6.4).

Colour of the mud-brick: yellow and red.

Area occupied by Structure 6: c. 39 sq.m.

Structure 7

Excavated in 1962 (trenches R21c and d), 1964 (trenches R21c and d), 1965 (trenches R21a-d) and 1966 (trench R21b).

Illustrations: plans, Figs 11, 12, 19; sections Figs 37, 38, 40–44, 50.1,2, 52.1

There was no structural presence of the Late Chalcolithic period (Layer 1) but a small quantity of sherds definable as Late Chalcolithic were discovered in the upper soil-units. On the other hand considerable deposits of Layer 2A were found, especially on the N and W sides of the trench, in the NW and SW quadrants. No Layer 2A structure, associated with the deposits of rubbish and fill, came to light.

The plan of Structure 7 is somewhat irregular but the construction of the walls and buttresses follows the pattern established in other structures: the use of standard-sized mud-bricks (0.80 × 0.40 × 0.10 m.), the courses of parallel bricks, the technique of headers-and-stretchers to provide bonding (especially at buttresses and corners). The lay-out of the buttresses is asymmetrical but total symmetry is not usual in other structures.

The function of the N wall (7.1 on the plan), however, is difficult to explain. It is perhaps not the N limit of Structure 7, since on the external side, i.e. on the N side, there are frequent renovations to the face and to the floor. Thick layers of mud/clay plaster were added to both surfaces; to the plaster were applied thin coats of red (?)clay.

The cross-wall (no. 7.6 on the plan, between Walls 7.5 and 7.7) is demonstrably a late insertion (see the N profile of R21a, Fig. 37). It has been assigned to Structure 7 and thereby to Layer 2B. On the other hand the consistent use of stones below the lowest course of mud-brick could perhaps suggest a later, Layer 2A, context (see also below, p. 43) but a precise stratigraphic association could not be made, largely owing to the massive disturbance created by a deep pit in the NE corner of R21a (see the sections, Figs 37, 38, 40).

There is some evidence that Structure 7 fell into disrepair, perhaps gradually: (1) firstly the insertion of an internal, support wall (7.6), then (2) the collapse of the S wall (7.4). The structure (and subsequently the gap between Structures 7 and 4: section, Fig. 34, R21c, E Face) was filled by rubbish, firstly of Layer 2B, then of Layer 2A (section, Fig. 38, R21b, N Face). Where the underlying, Layer 3 walls coincided with the walls of Structure 7, they provided a firm base for the later walls. Otherwise, as is normal at Canhasan in all the Chalcolithic layers, the walls were constructed without foundations. There is no evidence for the employment of timber in the construction of the walls and buttresses.

No posts for the support of a roof or an upper storey were found nor any materials which could be identified with occupation.

There was a simple, earth floor.

Colour of mud-brick: mostly yellow, (as in the walls of Structure 5), some yellow-brown, some grey-green. The brick is clean, without large stones and sherds.

Area of Structure 7: c. 61 sq.m. (minimum).

Structure 8

Excavated in 1962 (trench S21c).

Illustrations: plans, Figs 11, 12, 18; sections, Figs 50.2, 53.1.

Only the line of the walls (W and S) was determined.

Brick sizes: standard, i.e. 0.80 × 0.40 m.

Structure 9

Excavated in 1962 (trench S22c).

Illustrations: plans, Figs 11, 12, 17.

Only the line of the W wall was determined.

Structure 10

Excavated in 1962 (trenches R24a and b) and in 1967 (trenches R24 c and d, and S24a).

Illustrations: plans, Figs 11, 12, 20, 21; sections, Figs 45, 51.2, 52.2, 55.2, 56.2, 57.3, 58.1,3; photographs Pl. 6.2 and 7.1.

This structure is divided into two parts: an Eastern and a Western. The Eastern part (in trench S25a) is poorly preserved. In fact, only a few mud-brick courses survive. On the other hand, the Western part is well preserved. It is divided into two halves, eastern and western.

Structure 10 appears to have been burned in the same fire which affected other structures, especially Structures 2 and 3, on the N side of Structure 10.

There are two storeys in Structure 10, an upper and a lower (plans of the upper and lower storeys, Figs 20, 21).

The walls of the lower storey were built in the standard fashion, i.e. courses of mud-brick laid in parallel rows. The buttresses were constructed, as in other structures, i.e. alternate courses were laid as headers and stretchers in order to provide a secure bond between the wall and the buttress. There are no stone foundations.

The mud-brick was of standard size, 0.80 × 0.40 × 0.10 m., with the result that the thickness of the walls and the length and width of the buttresses are multiples of the brick-size. There is no visible evidence for the use of timber-reinforcement in the construction of the walls. The mud/clay mortar between the bricks is c. 0.03–4 m. thick. No attempt was made to trim the excess mortar which protruded from the face of the wall. All the walls of Structure 10 in trench R24c were plastered. The top layer of plaster was a fine white clay, c. 0.02 m. thick. At least two coats are visible above a thick under-layer of a fine, yellow mud/clay which was strongly tempered with chaff or chopped straw. The mud/clay under-plaster was probably applied with the fingers and faced with chaff or chopped straw. There is no evidence that the plaster, either the top or the under layers, continued over the floor. The plaster curves outwards from the wall and then stops. There was only a simple, very uneven, earth floor.

No plaster was observed on the lower face of the walls in R24d.

The absolute height of the floor in R24c varies from 6.50 m. (on the W profile) to 6.30 m. (in front of the N face of the S buttress [10.16 on the plan, Fig. 20]). By comparison the absolute height of the floor in R24d varies from 7.30 m. to 7.00 m.

The corners of the walls and the corners between buttress and wall were carefully rounded.

On the whole the mud-bricks of the walls were severely burned to a bright-red colour but interestingly the bricks behind the white top-plaster, in reducing rather than in oxydising conditions, became black. The top-plaster remained white. The walls in the S half of Trench R24d are by no means as severely burned as in the N half. The lower parts of the walls in the S half are yellow and green. Some of the most important evidence concerning the nature of the structures in Layer 2B was found in Trenches R24c and d and in the Baulk R24d/S24c. This evidence shed considerable light particularly on the construction of the ceiling and of the upper storey.

There were no support-posts in Structure 10. The ceiling of the lower storey (= the floor of the upper storey) was composed of earth laid on straw, reeds or brushwood (cp. the illustration of modern practise, Fig. 22). The impressions of all three materials have been found together in large lumps preserved by the burning. In R24c, along the top of the wall (10.7), there is some evidence for the use of horizontal beams, c. 0.10 high and c. 0.20 wide, running along the face of the wall and on the top of the buttresses (both in the E and in the W parts of Structure 10). The purpose of these beams is undoubtedly reflected in modern practise: (1) to support the cross-room beams and (2) to spread the weight of the cross-room beams and thereby to prevent the crushing of the mud-brick below the cross-room beams.

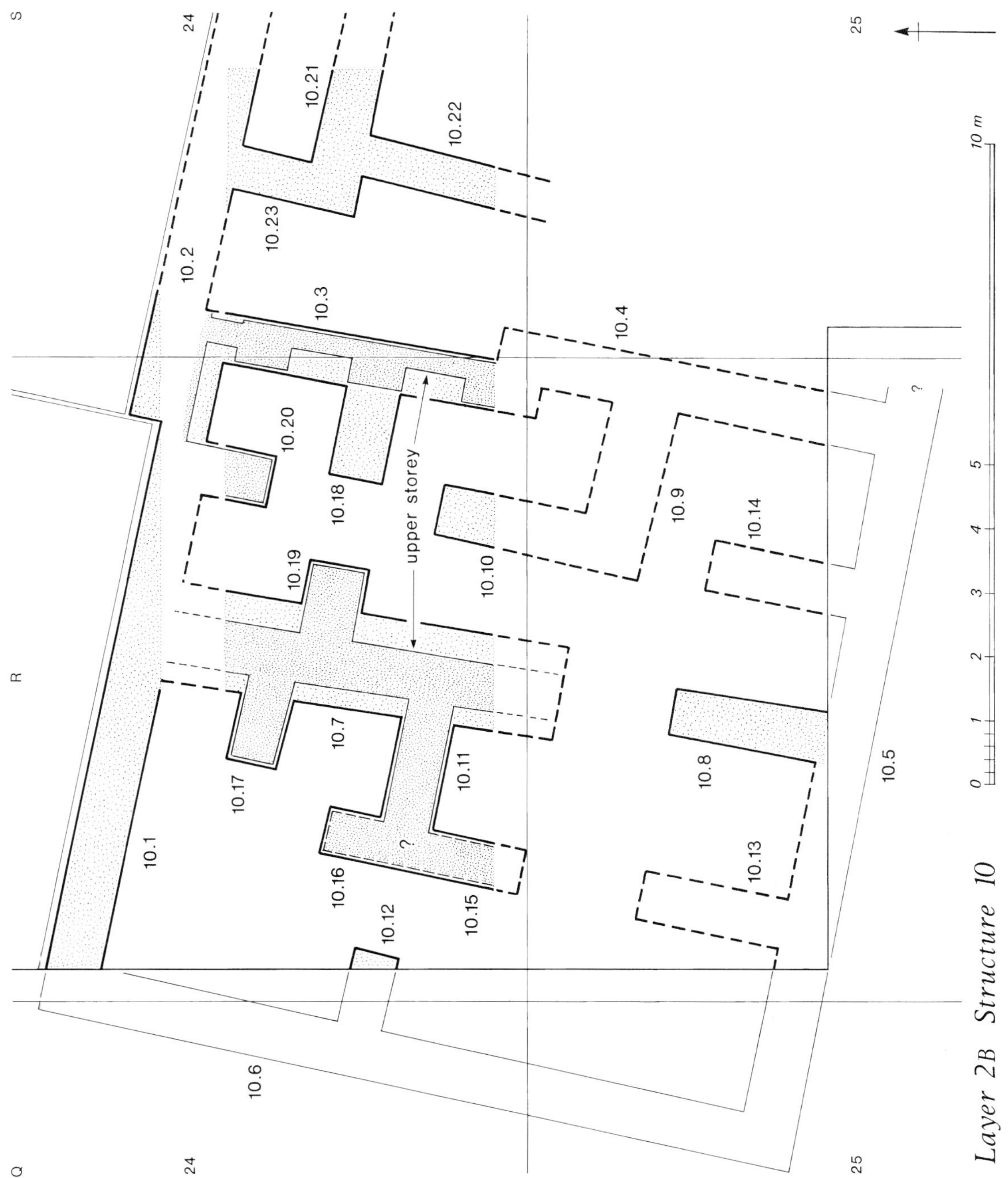

Fig. 20. Plan of Layer 2B, Structure 10 (ground level and surviving upper storey) (1:100)

In R24c, in the western section of Structure 10, the top coat of fine, white plaster reached a maximum height of 2.75 m. (= 8.95 m. absolute) above the floor on the W face of the wall (10.7 on the plan, Fig. 20), and 2.60 m. (= 8.90 m. absolute) above the floor on the N face of the S buttress (10.16) and the wall (10.11). The faces of all the walls and buttresses in R24c were coated with clay plaster.

The upper extent of the plaster on the lower face of the walls in R24c certainly marks the beginning of the ceiling construction.

In R24d, a narrow band of plaster, now broken and poorly preserved, was visible along the top of the W face of the E wall (10.3 on the plan, Fig. 20). The plaster has not survived on the wall surface below the top of the wall. As in R24c the end of the plaster defines the ceiling of the lower storey. The height of this line above the floor is c. 2.00 m. (= 9.00 absolute).

In the baulk R24c/d, in trench R24d and in the baulk R24d/S24c (Pl. 6.2 and 7.1) the traces of an upper storey were well preserved. In R24c, on the W face of the wall (10.7 on the plan, Fig. 20), the lower wall stops at c. 2.70 m. (= 9.00 m. absolute) above the floor (= 6.30 m. absolute on the E profile, Fig. 57.3, and 6.50 m. absolute on the W profile, Fig. 55.2). The core of the wall continues. The ledge thus formed must certainly have been part of a ceiling system for the lower storey and the flooring system of the upper storey. Traces of wooden beams or other material which can be associated with the construction of a ceiling or roof were observed after excavation had been completed. On the W face of the wall (10.7) the lower surface was given a thick under-layer or under-coating of yellow clay. A thick layer of white clay covers the ledge on top of the wall and curls upwards onto the face of the upper, narrow wall. The interval or gap (c. 0.20 m.) between the top of the yellow under-coat (at c. 9.00 m. absolute) on the lower surface of the wall (10.7) and the bottom edge of the white plaster on the ledge (at c. 9.20 m. absolute) defines the position of the ceiling/roof beams.

The height of the ledge thus marks the level of the upper floor. The horizontal surface of the ledge and the vertical surface of the wall core were coated with at least five layers of a white, fine clay plaster (total thickness c. 0.020–25 m.) strongly admixed with chaff. The white, clay plaster did not continue below the ledge (at c. 9.20 m. absolute) and for a depth of c. 0.20 (to c. 9.00 m. absolute), there is no trace of plaster. At this point (c. 9.00–9.20 m.) there are traces of horizontal beams running N–S below the ledge and along (but not under) the face of the upper wall (10.7); see above, p. 38. There are also impressions of branches or twigs, running E–W, on the top (at c. 9.00 m. absolute) of the buttress (10.17).

A similar arrangement was observed at the top of the wall (10.3 on the plan, Fig. 20) which divided the two halves of the western part. The wall was constructed with standard bricks, 0.80 × 0.40 × 0.10 m., laid in two parallel rows. The thickness of the wall was, therefore, 0.80 m. At the top of the wall, at a point c. 0.20 m. above the narrow band of broken plaster on the W face, only one mud-brick was used and the wall thus narrows to thickness of one mud-brick. Consequently the thickness of the upper wall became 0.40 m. A ledge was thus formed (at c. 9.20 m. absolute). There are impressions of beams/branches, running N–S, on the top of the E and W buttresses (10.18 and 19 on the plan, Fig. 20) approximately at the same height (c. 9.00 m. absolute) above the floor. Over the buttress (10.18) the position of the beams/branches was fixed at c. 0.20 m. below the line of white-clay plaster. The height of the ledge along the top of the E wall (10.3) coincides with the ledge formed on the top of the N wall buttress (10.20). The floor of the ledge and the W face of the upper, narrow wall (10.3) were plastered with a white, fine clay. There are at least two layers of plaster.

The white plaster is visible eastwards from the buttress (10.20) on the N wall (10.1) (at 9.20 m. absolute) at c. 2.00 m. above the floor (which varies between 7.00 m. and 7.30 m. absolute). The plaster is continuously preserved on all the faces of the wall forming the upper storey, including all three faces of the insets (10.24–26 on the plan, Fig. 21).

In R24c numerous fragments of carbonized beams were recovered from the burnt debris (earth and mud-brick) filling the space enclosed by the walls (10.1, 11, 7 and 6), cp. the concentration of roof/floor materials and patterned plaster, together with pottery, in Structure 3, W room. The fragments have been submitted for dendrochronological examination.

Also in R24c broken fragments of painted, i.e. red-on-white patterned, plaster were found c. 1.50 m. above the basal floor, i.e. below the level (at 9.20 m. absolute) of the upper floor. Some pieces exhibit the same shaping (right-angle corners and inward sloping surface) noted in the examples from Structure 3. It may be assumed that the Structure 10 fragments, like those of Structure 3, had fallen from the upper storey and that some internal feature (door, window, inset?) of the upper storey had been decorated.

It was reported in 1967 (French 1968b: 47) that the walls of the upper storey were thinner than those of the lower. The evidence for this statement is now presented on the plan (Fig. 20) drawn to illustrate the relationship between the thick, lower walls and the narrow, upper walls. In addition to the combined plan of the two (Fig. 20) a reconstruction of the upper storey alone is also given here (Fig. 21).

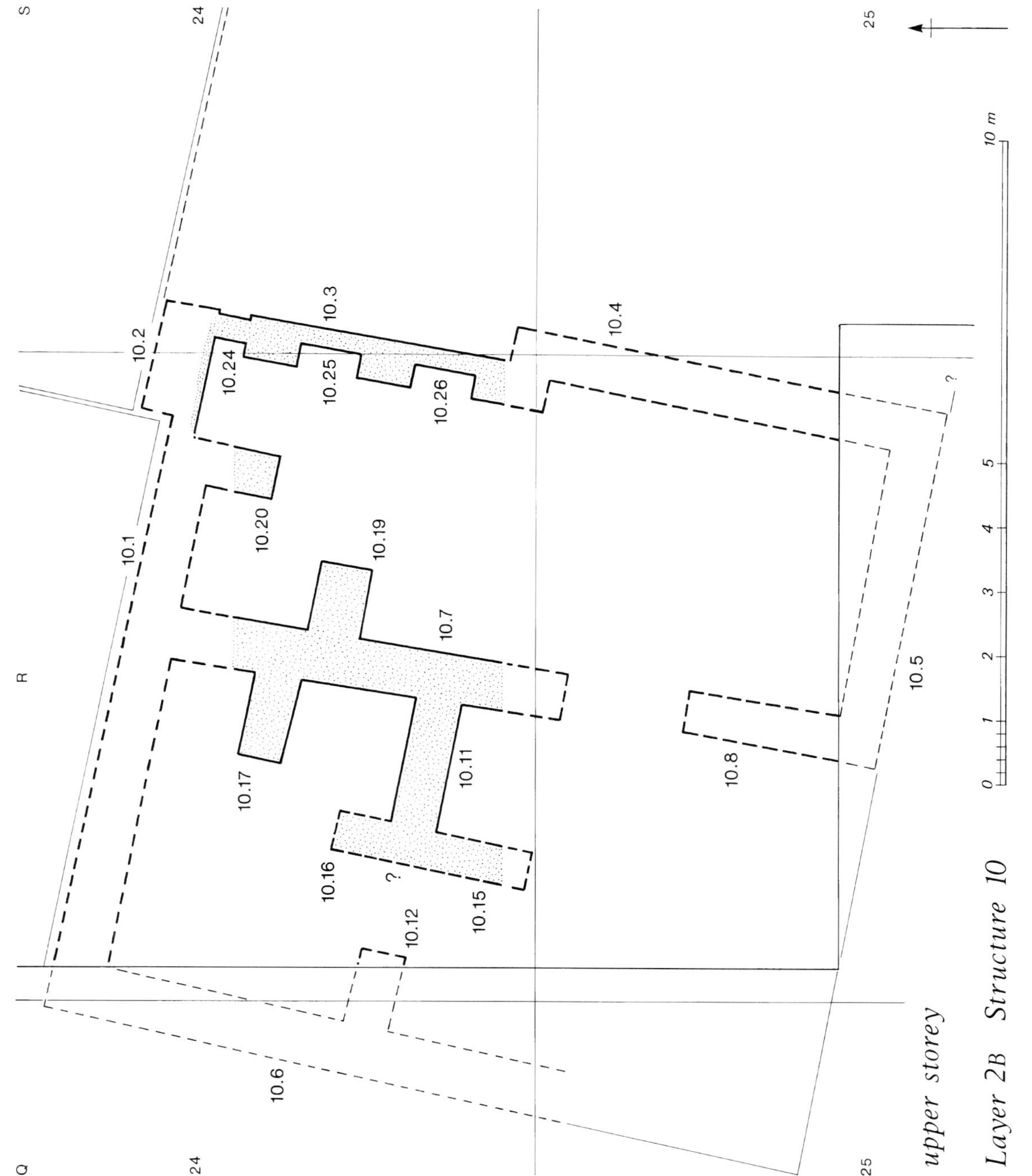

Fig. 21. Plan of Layer 2B, Structure 10 (upper storey, hypothetically reconstructed) (1:100)

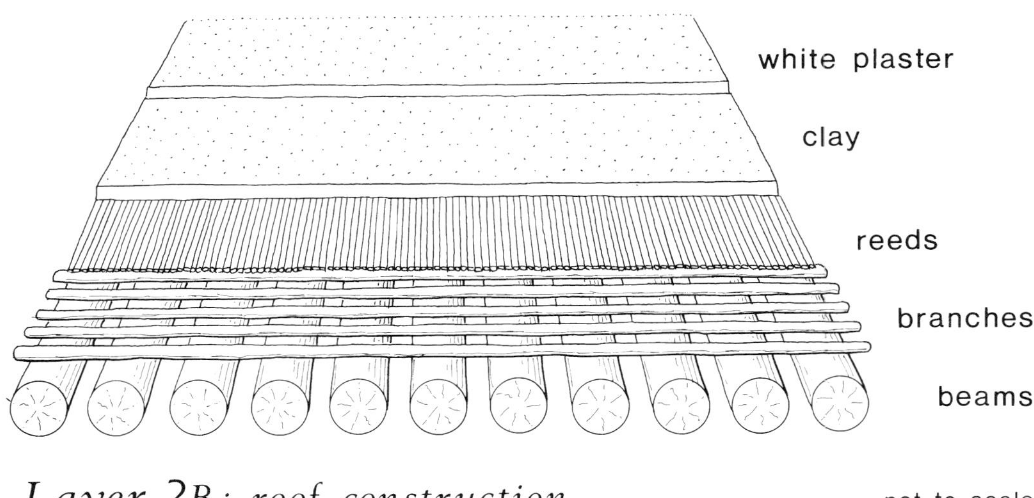

Fig. 22. Layer 2B: Diagram showing roof construction

Although the Eastern half of Structure 10 was largely destroyed in the construction of Layer 2A Structure 5, it is possible to estimate the area of roof-occupation over the western part: approximately 67 sq.m. out of 138 sq.m. = 48.5%. This figure may be compared with the calculation for Structure 3: 44 sq.m. (W section) out of 103.75 sq.m. = 42.4%.

In trench S24c the walls of Layer 2B had been largely obliterated by later (Layer 2A) activity. The structure which emerged in the E half of the trench was built from mud-brick regularly arranged, in header-and-stretcher technique, in evenly laid courses bonded with a fine mud-mortar c. 0.02–0.03 m. thick. There are no stone foundations. A fine, grey-green mud-plaster, 0.01–0.02 m. thick, covered the walls and floors (not indicated on the plan, Fig. 20). Interestingly the N–S wall (10.23 on the plan, Fig. 20), appears to abut against but not to bond with the main E–W wall (10.2). An original layer of plaster is concealed within the wall. A new layer of mud-plaster was applied, thereby concealing the gap between the two walls.

The Layer 2B walls in trench S24c have previously been published under Layer 3 (French 1968b: 47 and Fig. 1) (see above, p. 25): the stratigraphic context is hereby revised.

Colour of mud-brick: the bottom four courses in R24d are yellow and unburnt, even in the N wall. The same observation was made on parts of the E wall. Colours in trench S24c: red, reddish brown, yellow-brown, grey.

Area of Structure 10: 164 sq.m. (minimum), 138 sq.m. (W part)

Structure 11

Excavated in 1964 (trench Q21c).

Illustration: plan, Fig. 11; section, Fig. 51.1.

Only 4 courses of mud-brick survive. The orientation of the wall could not be accurately determined.

Colour of mud-brick: yellowish.

Dimensions of mud-brick: (ht) c. 0.10 m.

Structure in Q21b

It is not known whether there was a structure on the W of Structure 7 and on the N of Structure 4 (? and 11). If this space was indeed occupied, the walls have been completely removed (? by terracing against Layer 2B Structure 7 and then) by the 'insertion' of a Layer 2A structure (consult the section, Fig. 39, R21a, W Face, Wall 118 [= Layer 2A, Wall 1.1]). For 'insertion', see the description below (p. 000).

2.5 Layer 2A

Excavated in 1962 (trenches Q21d, Q22b&d, Q23b&d), in 1964 (trenches Q21c, Q22a), in 1965 (trench R21a) and in 1967 (trench S24c).

Illustrations: plan, Figs 23–25; sections, Figs 37–44, 45–47, 49.1,2, 50.1–3, 51.1, 53.1, 54.1,2, 55.1, 57.1, 58.1 ; photographs, Pl. 7.2, 8.1.

Since the publication of the plan in the first report (French 1963b: Fig. 1) the structures on the W side of the site have been re-assigned from Layer 2B to Layer 2A (see above, pp. 27, 34), as follows:

Trench Q21d, N end	=	Layer 2A Structure 1
House 8	=	Layer 2A Structure 2
House in Q22d,Q23b	=	Layer 2A Structure 3
House in Q23d	=	Layer 2A Structure 4

The stratigraphic re-assessment of structures previously thought to belong to Layer 2B is discussed below (p. 46, Structure 2), with particular reference to 'insertion' and 'insertion' combined with terracing.

In number and state of preservation the buildings of Layer 2A are poor in comparison with those of Layer 2B. Nevertheless the structural sequence between Layers 2B and 2A is significant for 2 reasons: between the two layers (1) there are points of contrast in building techniques and (2) there are clear areas of continuity.

Contrast between the two layers exists in (1) the size of mud-brick (in Layer 2A sometimes smaller than the standard Layer 2B brick, e.g. Structure 6 in Trench Q22a), (2) the plan and wall-alignment (generally right-angled corners and straight walls in Layer 2B, irregular corners and mis-shapen walls in Layer 2A).

The areas of continuity are to be found in (1) the use of internal buttresses, (2) the adoption of the Layer 2B wall-orientation and (3) the non-use of stone for foundation courses. The best evidence for the introduction of stone, as a foundation course, in the Chalcolithic period at Canhasan is, unfortunately, limited to two occurrences, one dubious. Flat stone occurs in the foundations (1) of a single, short wall in Structure 7 (Wall 7.5: plan Fig. 19 and section Figs 37–38) in R21a and b (see the remarks above, p. 37; the wall may be dated to Layer 2A rather than to Layer 2B) and (2) of a wall in Structure 2 (Wall 2.5: plan Fig. 24 and section Fig. 49.2) in Q21d. If so, the introduction of stone foundations may be as early as the Middle Chalcolithic period in clear contrast with earlier building practices, especially in Layer 2B.

Throughout the Neolithic and Chalcolithic periods at Canhasan, with these two exceptions, stone was never used for the foundation-course of mud-brick walls.

The recognition of a stratigraphic difference between Layer 2B and Layer 2A was made in the first season, 1961, when soil-deposits, stratigraphically separate from Layer 2B, were found lying within the line of, and over, the burnt walls of Layer 2B House 6 (French 1962b: 34). In 1962 it was observed that scattered patches of Layer 2A occupation occurred in almost all the squares (excavated in 1961 and 1962) except those in the area of the W room of House 3 (French 1962b: 30).

Two deposits of Layer 2A were noted in the first reports:

(1) Trench S23b (excavated in 1961): "Only in the north-east corner of S23b did we come upon layers of this period (Can Hasan layer 2A)." (French 1962b: 29) The deposits are indicated on the plan (Fig. 23) over walls of Structure 1. They consisted of burning, clay fill, and ashy lines full of rubbish, particularly sherds and fragments of animal bone.

(2) Trench S21c (excavated in 1962): "In S21c there is a well-defined but shallower" (sc. than in Q21d and Q22b) 'deposit of 2A inside and over the stumps of House 6.' (French 1963b: 30) From this deposit came an important group of objects and associated pottery. For the stratigraphic position of the deposit, see above, p. 37 (Layer 2B, Structure 6).

Both deposits are indicated on the plan (Fig. 23).

A shallow deposit—a surface or a line of occupation, and a hearth—of Layer 2A was found in trench S24a over the SW corner of Structure 1.

In the first preliminary report the suggestion was made (French 1962b: 29), that "it seems possible that the Middle Chalcolithic layers lie further out, towards the north and north-east" (sc. of the 1961 trenches) "perhaps as a result of erosion or from a deliberate shifting of the inhabited area." This suggestion is now revised (see above, the introductory remarks of this section).

In general the character of Layer 2A was apparent from the earliest seasons: "The sections of the main deposits of 2 A material showed a wealth of minor or secondary layers, the minutiae of soil stratification but almost wholly without associated features (e.g. floors). As far as possible we excavated the deposit according to these secondary layers so that the pottery batches show the details of the pottery sequence. The results of this are shown in the actual and diagrammatic sections ... of baulk Q21d/22b and in the pottery illustrations ... In general, however, it was extremely difficult to excavate these 2 A deposits with absolute accuracy and precision." (French 1963b: 30)

Structure 1

Excavated in 1965 and 1967 (Trenches R21a and Q21d).

Illustrations: plans, Figs 21, 22; sections, Figs 35, 37, 42.

In 1965 no buildings of Layer 2A, it was thought, had come to light "although it is clear that structures of the previous period, Layer 2B, were in part re-used during the early phases of the Middle Chalcolithic period." (French 1966b: 115)

Further, it was noted that "the deposits consisted, as before, of brick debris, dust, sand, gravel and ash lines; since there is a large quantity of bones and sherds in these thin lines, it is clear that they are the refuse or rubbish from a settlement of the Middle Chalcolithic period." (French 1966b: 115)

After the 1965 season it was noted that "House 7 was probably not re-used as a structure or dwelling. It is clearer to say that the stumps of the walls of House 7 were still visible in the earlier phases of the Middle Chalcolithic period." (French 1966b: 116)

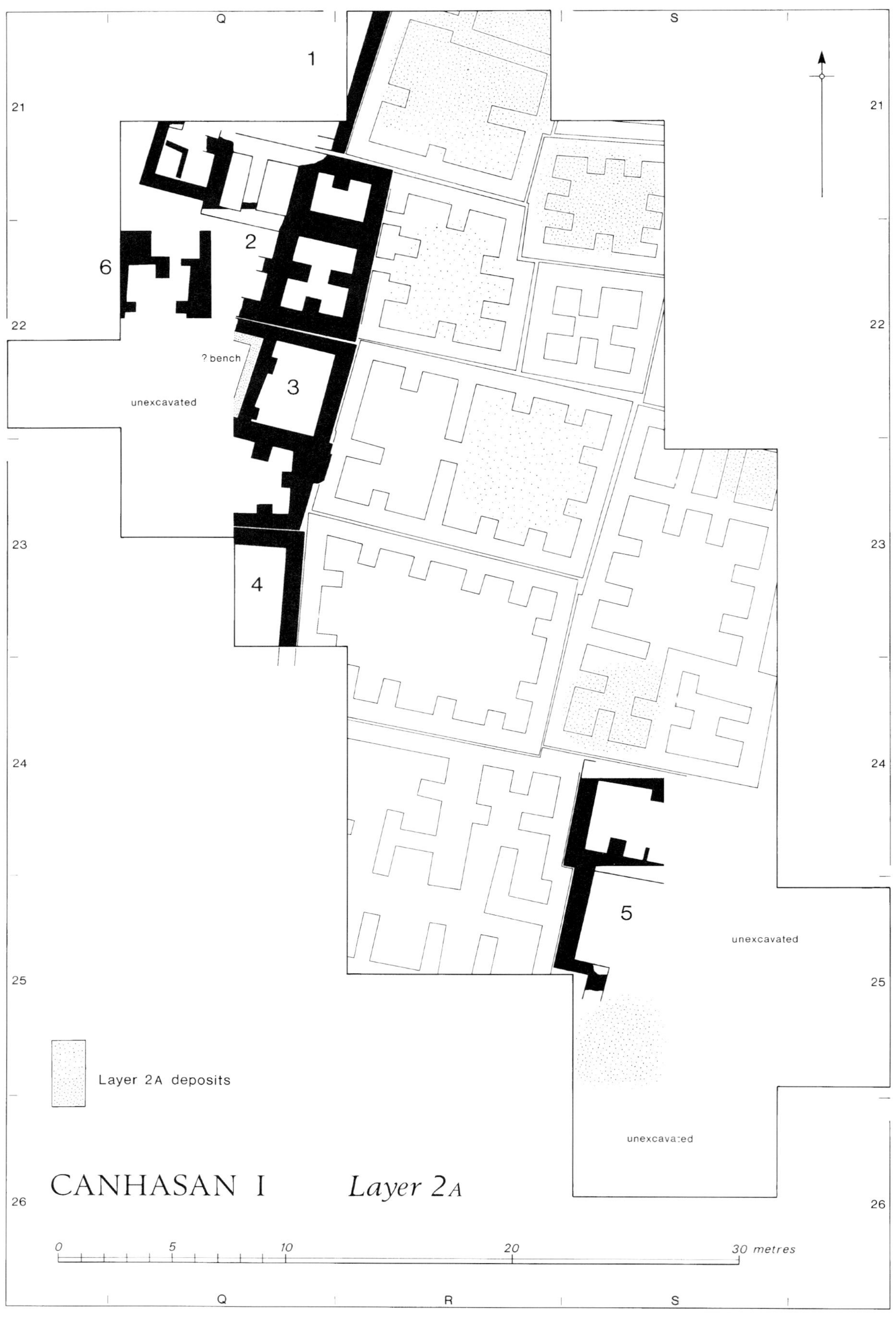

Fig. 23. Plan of Layer 2A (1:250)

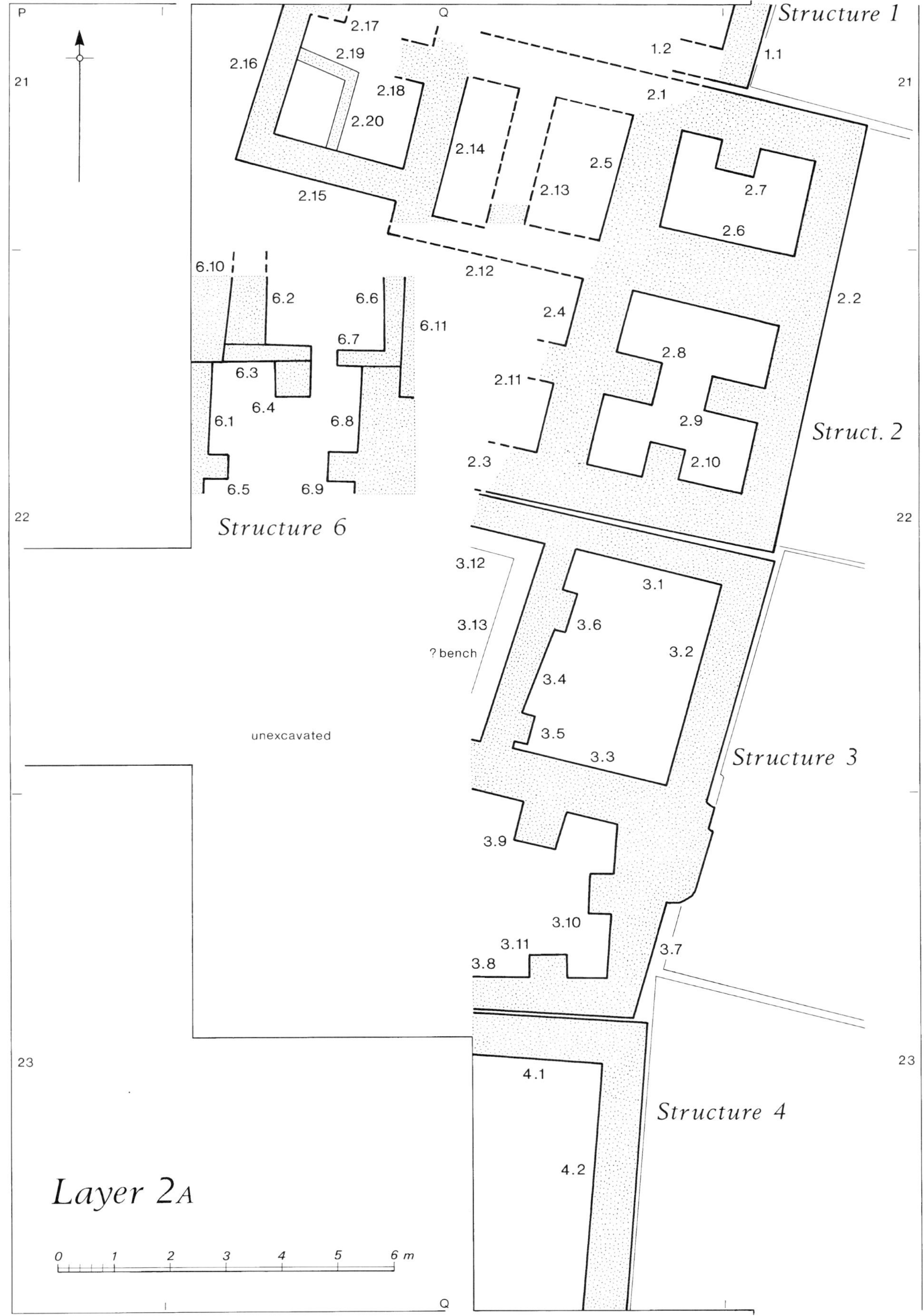

Fig. 24. Plan of Layer 2A: NW trenches (1:100)

These views can now be revised after a re-examination of the plans and profiles of trenches R21a and b. The wall (no. 1.1 on the plan, Fig. 24), adjacent to the W wall (7.5 on the plan, Fig. 19) of Layer 2B Structure 7, has been re-assigned to Layer 2A on the grounds that the western continuation of Wall 1.1 (no. 1.2 on the plan, Fig. 24) is stratigraphically associated with Structure 2 which is definitively assigned to Layer 2A.

Coincidently it is possible that the stratigraphic status of the cross-wall on the N side Structure 7 (7.6 on the plan, Fig. 19) should also be re-assessed and perhaps assigned to Layer 2A rather than to Layer 2B (see above, pp. 37, 43).

It is probable that Structure 1 was constructed, on the same alignment or orientation, over a pre-existing Layer 2B structure, either by 'insertion' wholly into structures of Layer 2B or by terracing against the 2B walls followed by partial 'insertion' into the earlier structures (for these terms, see the remarks on Structure 2, below).

Structure 1 exists, therefore, as a poorly preserved and poorly recorded building of Layer 2A. There were no internal features in Structure 1 as excavated.

Colour of mud-brick: yellowish green, greyish green; crumbly and friable; the consistency of the clay was called 'chicken-feed' in the dig note-books.

Dimensions of mud-brick: 0.80 × 0.40 × 0.10 m., i.e. the standard size in Layer 2B.

Structure 2

Excavated in 1962 (Trenches Q21d and Q22b) and 1966 (Trench Q21d).

Illustrations: plans, Figs 23, 24; sections, Figs 49.1, 2; 50.3; 51.1; photograph, Pl. 7.2.

"In Q21d and Q22b the 2A deposit is 2 m. deep, lying inside and over the walls of House 8." (French 1963b: 30) Later it became clear that Layer 2B House 8 was entirely a structure of Layer 2A. "This area had been excavated to (or nearly to) what was thought to be a floor level of a Layer 2 B house, no. 8" [numbered 8 in 1962, plan, French 1963b: Fig. 1]. "Although the pottery from this house had been entirely of Layer 2A types, this was not (in 1962) thought to be strange since re-occupation of Layer 2B structures in the 2A period was known from other trenches. Both alignment and construction exactly followed that of the 2B settlement. In 1966, however, it soon became clear that House 8 was a structure which belonged entirely to Layer 2A and was only one of a series of structures and superimposed walls, all belonging to Layer 2A." (French 1967b: 169)

This later view of 'House 8' is not a complete explanation. The structure had, in part, been 'inserted' within the existing structures (Layer 2B nos 4 and 7) on each side. The N wall of 'House 8' overlies the N and W walls (4.1 and 4.5) of Structure 4 and abuts the centre wall (4.6) of Structure 4 and the SW corner (Walls 7.4 and 7.5) of Structure 7. On the S 'House 8' abuts the N wall of Layer 2A Structure 3 (plans, Figs 23, 24). Before Layer 2A Structure 2 was built, the W wall (4.5) of Layer 2B Structure 4 was taken down to its lowest courses, as was the wall of Structure 11 (indicated on the plan, Fig. 11).

The phenomenon of 'insertion' whereby a structure of one period was inserted inside, and/or on top of, the walls of an earlier structure in juxtaposition, but without damage, to the surrounding buildings is known at Çatal Hüyük (personal observation of exposed sections on site, 03.10.1990; I have been unable to find an exact reference to the phenomenon in the Çatal Hüyük reports; for 'remodelling', see Mellaart [1963: 47]).

It is also possible, as perhaps here in the case of Structure 2, that an earlier structure was wholly or partly removed by terracing. On the terrace and over the stumps of the earlier walls a new structure was erected: this was built directly against (i.e. touching or close to) the walls of neighbouring structures. The inner side of the terrace would be deep, the outer shallow. The result could be described as 'part-insertion'. The technique of terrace and part-insertion against earlier structures can be seen in the N and S profiles of Trench R21c (N section, Fig. 50.1, Layer 2A Wall 30 [= Wall 1.1 on plan, Fig. 24] and Layer 2B Wall 9 [= Wall 7.5 on plan, Fig. 19] and S section, Fig. 50.3, Layer 2A Wall 3 [= Wall 2.2 on plan, Fig. 24] and Layer 2B Wall 1 [= Wall 4.5 on plan, Fig. 16]); cp. also Structures 3 and 4 (plan, Fig. 24) against Layer 2B structures and Structure 5 (plan. Figs 24, 25) against Layer 2B Structure 10.

'House 8', as designated in 1962, has been re-numbered and the plan revised. It is now (Layer 2A) Structure 2 (plans, Figs 23, 24). In trenches Q21c and Q22b the walls do not extend westwards as first thought (cf. the restorations on the plan of Layer 2B, French 1963b: Fig. 1). An extension, if it existed, is represented by a wall-fragment only (2.18 on the plan, Fig. 24). On the other hand, it now seems clear that there was a later re-building on the W of Wall 2.14. The re-build is indicated in the plan (Fig. 24) by Walls 2.15–17, 19 and 20. Visible in the W and S profiles of Q21c there are mud-bricks, possibly representing other wall fragments; these have not been drawn on the plan (Fig. 24).

The size of the mud-bricks used for the walls (nos 2.15 and 16) is slightly smaller than the standard dimensions of Layer 2B mud-brick (0.80 × 0.40 × 0.10 m.). The mud-brick employed for the partition (Wall 2.19 and 20) is visibly smaller: c. 0.66 × 0.20 × 0.10 m.

There appears to be no stratigraphic association between Walls 2.15 and 16 and Structure 6 in Q22a.

Over the top of the walls (2.1 and 2.13) in Q21d there was a jumble of bricks and surfaces (photograph, Pl. 7.2; the trench is seen from the N). Although it is difficult to interpret these fragments, one must nevertheless accept that they represent a phase of Layer 2A which is later than Structure 2.

The building techniques recorded in Structure 2 are not different, with one exception, from those of Layer 2B: (1) large, standard-size mud-bricks, (2) the use of headers and stretchers, (3) bonded corners and angles and (4) internal buttresses. The exception occurs in the use of stones as foundation for the mud-brick of Wall 2.5 (S face of Trench Q21d, Fig. 49.2). In the same profile there is evidence, in Wall 2.5, for the presence of a large, horizontal wooden beam.

Trench Q21c, excavated in 1964, did not amplify or elucidate the results in Q21d nor complete the plan of Layer 2A Structure 2, although the nature and character of Layer 2A deposits, isolated in 1961 and 1962 elsewhere on the site, was confirmed in 1964 in trench Q21c and enlarged in 1966: "The character of the Middle Chalcolithic (Layer 2A) deposit that was excavated in 1964 at the NW corner of the excavation area in square Q21c was similar to that of the deposits excavated in 1962. It consisted of a succession of thin soil strata and ash lines. These were excavated individually. Between two of these ash lines an extensive and close-packed deposit of animal bone and sherds was discovered." (French 1965a: 89)

"Square Q21c, the excavation of which was begun but not completed in 1964, was re-opened in 1966. From this square ... , architecture of Layer 2A came to light. The combination of the results from these two squares, Q21c and d, provides much-needed evidence on Middle chalcolithic architecture. The structures in these two squares are not as well preserved as the buildings of Layer 2 B and the line of some walls can now be reconstructed only on paper. Nevertheless there is good evidence of frequent rebuilding and remodelling ..." (French 1967b: 169)

In fact, in Trench Q21c, as in the adjacent trenches, Q21d and Q22c, the walls and stratigraphy were both confused and confusing.

The W wall of Structure 2 was recorded in trench Q21d (excavated in 1962): "In Q21d, on the west face, there is the corner of a wall showing in section." (French 1963b: 30) The wall is numbered 2.14 on the plan (Fig. 24).

In the SE corner of Structure 2 the E face of Wall 2.5 and the W face of Buttress 2.9 were plastered with white clay.

There was a hearth in the SE corner.

Colour of mud-bricks: red, yellow.

Dimensions: the standard dimensions, 0.80 × 0.40 × 0.10 m., of Layer 2B mud-brick, except for Walls 2.15 and 2.16, and the partition wall, 2.19 and 2.20.

Structure 3

Excavated in 1962 (trenches Q22d and Q23b).

Illustrations: plans, Figs 23, 24.

In the report for the 1962 season the substantial walls in Q22d and Q23b were assigned to Layer 2B (French 1963b: 35 and plan, Fig. 1) on the grounds of its juxtaposition with Layer 2B Structure 3. The stratigraphic association between Layer 2B Structure 3 and Layer 2A Structure 3, however, was never clarified. A re-examination of the evidence, however, now suggests that Layer 2A Structure 3 was built, according to the existing orientation of the Layer 2B settlement, alongside the W room of Structure 3, either by terracing or, in a manner similar to the construction of Layer 2A Structure 2 (and 5, see below), by partial 'insertion'. The former explanation is, perhaps, the more likely.

The later date also allows for an explanation of wall (3.7 on the plan, Fig. 24) which overlaps and partly covers the W wall of Layer 2B Structure 3 (shown thus on the plan, French 1963b: Fig. 1).

Layer 2A Structure 3, as excavated, has two rooms but no connecting door was found. The western extension of the three E–W walls (3.5, 6, 9–11) is conjectural only.

There is a possible bench (3.12 and 13 on the plan) alongside Walls 3.1 and 3.4.

The walls and internal features of Structure 3 are irregular but the presence of buttresses (3.1, 3 and 8 on the plan) and (?)benches (3.12 and 13) indicate a structural continuity between Layer 2B and Layer 2A.

From the presence of a hearth in front of the buttress (3.9) on the E–W Wall (3.3), possibly on the ground floor, the structure may have been single storied.

There is evidence for the use of red colouring ('red wash' in French 1963b: 35) on a white clay plaster on the walls and floor.

The excavation of trench Q22d was briefly reported in 1963: "In Q22d, on the west side of the square, walls of Layer 2 B have been cut away and a 2 A wall built across them." (French 1963b: 30) (= LCh Wall 11 on the plan, Fig. 27)

Colour of mud-bricks: red.

Dimensions: the size of the mud-bricks is not regular, cp. the remarks (below p. 49) on Structure 6 in Trench Q22a.

Structure 4

Excavated in 1962 (trench Q23d).

Illustration: plans, Figs 23, 24.

Layer 2A Structure 5

Fig. 25. Plan of Layer 2A: S trenches (1:100)

As Structure 3 in trenches Q22d and Q23b, the Structure in trench Q23d was assigned to Layer 2B (French 1963b: plan, Fig. 1).

The plan consists of two walls only. They form an irregular angle. No internal features were recorded.

Colour of mud-brick: red

Dimensions of mud-bricks: the size is not regular.

Structure 5

Excavated in 1967 (trench S24c) and 1966 (S25a).

Illustrations: plans, Figs 23, 25; sections, Figs 45, 52.2, 55.1, 58.1.

The excavation of Structure 5 and the stratigraphically related deposits was piecemeal, disjointed and mis-understood ("The stratigraphy was complex." French 1968b: 46) A re-examination, however, has now resolved most of the problems. South of the Structure 5—in trenches S25a and S25c—are located the deep deposits (of Layer 2A) noted in the first reports (French 1966b:115, and 1967b: 165).

Trenches S25c (excavated in 1965 and 1966) and S25a (excavated in 1966): "In square S25c we found a deposit of pottery which was quite unlike the pottery groups of Layer 2A pottery of previous seasons. No architectural remains were found associated with it." (French 1966b: 115)

"Work continued in square S25c on the south side of the excavation area. In the 1965 season this square produced a large quantity of pottery (and animal bones) from a deposit immediately below the earliest phase (phase f) of Layer 1. This deposit was taken to represent the latest of several which, grouped together, make up Layer 2A. The layers of the 2A period, known from S25c, were traced in S25a. This square, immediately to the north of S25c, had been excavated in 1963 to a floor of phase d of Layer 1." (French 1967b: 165)

"In square S25c no architecture was found. A series of surfaces and burnt hearth-areas began below the 2A deposit found in 1965. These surfaces continued downwards to a depth of 5.50 m. at which point excavation stopped. They may perhaps be called 'living-surfaces'; this interpretation became clear when a series of mud-brick walls came to light in square S25a, the next square to the north. The surfaces and hearths were seen in section to be in clear association with the structures in S25a. These mud-brick walls, four in number and built more or less one above the other, are not well preserved and survive only for a few courses. There are no apparent 'living-surfaces' on the north side of these walls but only an accumulation of rubbish and soil, featureless except for wash-lines (i.e. water-laid bands of fine-textured clay). The phenomenon may be explained by the discovery of a steep slope which begins at the north side of square S25a and falls abruptly southwards at a very sharp angle. The slope may represent the line of a terrace cut out of the older (Layer 2B) mound by the later inhabitants (of Layer 2A). The north wall of the mud-brick structure may therefore have served as a retaining wall. Behind (i.e. to the north of) one of these walls was found a large deposit of pottery and further north up the slope two infant skeletons." (French 1967b: 167, 169; one is illustrated here, Pl. 8.1)

One mud-brick wall is illustrated (no. 35 on the E profile of S25a, Fig. 44).

The stratigraphy and the structural remains in trenches S24c, S25a and b have been re-examined:

1. The 'Layer 3' structure in S24c (French 1968b: 47 and plan, Fig. 1; see the remarks above, pp. 27, 42) has been re-assigned to Layer 2B, Structure 10.
2. The Layer 2B walls in Baulk R24b/S24a are now divided into two separate entities, the first Layer 2B, the second Layer 2A: (1) a western wall = E Wall (10.3 and 4) of Layer 2B Structure 10, (2) an eastern wall = W Wall (5.3 and 7) of Layer 2A Structure 5.
3. Layer 2A Structure 5 is aligned according to Layer 2B Structure 10. From a study of the remains it is evident that the Layer 2B walls (?and room-fill) of Structure 10 had been dug away (at least in part) or terraced and the Layer 2A walls had been either superimposed ('inserted') or juxtaposed on the same orientation as the Layer 2B walls. As in the case of Layer 2A Structure 2, the two juxtaposed walls, the earlier (10.3 and 4) and the later (5.3 and 7), were set side-by-side without a significant gap.

Structure 5 continues the features of Layer 2B: (1) standard-size mud-brick, (2) internal buttresses and partitions.

Colour of mud-brick: pale grey, grey, brown, red.

Dimensions of mud-brick: 0.80 × 0.40 × 0.10 m.

Structure 6

Excavated in 1967 (trench Q22a).

Illustrations: plans, Figs 23,24; section, Fig. 54.2.

"In square Q22a a single small but substantially built structure was cleared. The walls which were preserved to a height of approx. 1.50 m. were faced with mud plaster and contained reinforcement of wood beams. These walls had been frequently reconstructed; consequently at least five building phases or levels could be counted. The size of the bricks used in Layer 2 A is smaller than that used in Layer 2 B." (French 1968b: 45)

Re-examination of the stratigraphic evidence suggests that, if the features, previously thought to be separate, are combined, the five phases can be reduced to three:

(1) (the earliest) Walls 6.1–3 and Buttresses 4 and 5, and Wall 6.8 and Buttress 6.9; mud-brick with white inclusions,
(2) Wall 6.3 and Buttress 6.4 (both re-modelled), and Walls 6.6 and 7; mud-brick of greenish clay; red clay mortar,
(3) (the latest) Walls 6.10 and 11.

In the post-excavation trench-summary for Q22a the following observations were made (02.11.1967):

(1) Floors: irregular; rarely hard and findable, i.e. traceable; in the uppermost levels there are good yellow clay surfaces with red plaster.
(2) Bricks: also irregular; poorly laid; the clay of the earliest phase bricks has a strong white colouring but still made with straw and pebbles; sizes: (earliest phase, mud-brick with white inclusions) 0.60 × 0.30 × 0.08 m., (middle phase, green clay mud-brick and red clay mortar) 0.65 × 0.30 × 0.08 m.
(3) Beams: (earliest phase) laid parallel with the wall face; well, (?)c. 0.70 m., above the floor; size of beams: width 0.10 m., height 0.05 m.

The plan and section (plan, Fig. 24; section, Fig. 54.2) record the stratification in this trench. There is no clear stratigraphic association between Structure 6 and Structure 2. It is possible that Structure 6 was constructed on a terrace which had been cut through the walls of S and W of Structure 2.

Summary

The location of the Layer 2A deposits and structures is illustrated in the composite plan (Fig. 23) indicating the underlying Layer 2B structure plans and the overlying Layer 2A occupation.

While the nature of the Layer 2A deposits can be understood in some detail, the form of the Layer 2A settlement is a subject more for conjecture on meagre data than for explanation from abundant evidence. In general one may summarize the existing remains as follows:

(1) in the earliest Layer 2A occupation, at least three structures (1, 2 and 5) were partly 'inserted' into the space previously occupied by a Layer 2B structure which had been cut away in order to form a deep terrace,

(2) subsequent Layer 2A occupation took place over the terraced structures, thereby raising the level of deposits above the original terrace cuts,

(3) the later occupation (Structure 6) took place without regard for the earlier Layer 2A alignment (Structures 2–4),

(4) it seems that large areas of the Layer 2B settlement became open spaces used only patchily for domestic purposes or for the dumping of rubbish,

(5) the extent of the Layer 2A occupation in the areas around the surviving core of the Layer 2B settlement is not known and cannot be estimated.

In brief, there is evidence for 3 structural levels in Layer 2A:

1. Structures 1–5, built in close relation to structures of Layer 2B, perhaps soon after the destruction of Layer 2B; there are probably 2 sub-levels or building-phases in Structure 2.
2. Structure 6, built without relation either to Layer 2B or to Layer 2A Structures 1–5; there are 3 building-phases in this structure.
3. Scrappy and insubstantial walls over Structure 2; seemingly not related to Structure 6.

The end of Layer 2A occupation on the Canhasan site is not clear from the stratigraphic sequence. It is apparent, however, from the pottery evidence that occupation later than the recorded Layer 2A structures and soil-deposits took place somewhere on the mound since Middle Chalcolithic sherds not otherwise found on the site have found their way into the mud-bricks used in structures of the Late Chalcolithic period, i.e. Layer 1. The evidence is cited in the year report for 1965 (French 1966b: 115).

It is possible that the Layer 2A site was gradually abandoned and petered out after a patchy occupation similar to the small areas or pockets of early Layer 2A occupation which lie over the Layer 2B structures (cp, the remarks above, p. 43, and the plan of Layer 2A, Fig. 23). The presence of a dark, structureless soil-deposit lying over the Layer 2A occupation-deposits and below the floors and structures of Layer 1 in Trench S25c may be significant (no. 39 on the E profile of S25a and c, Figs 46, 47; no. 3 on the W profile of S25c, Fig. 57.1; no. 11 on the N profile of S25c, Fig. 55.1). Does it represent a soil accumulating and developing (?by action of wind and water) in hollows above the abandoned Layer 2A site which was later levelled, as is clearly visible on the trench profiles, in the Late Chalcolithic period by the inhabitants of Layer 1?

2.6 Layer 1

Excavated in 1961 (trench S23a pit), in 1962 (trenches Q21d pit, Q22d pit, Q23b,d, R22b pit, S24b pit), in 1963 (trenches R24c,d, R25a,b, S24c,d, S25a,b), in 1964 P22d, Q21c, Q22a,c, Q23a, R24c,d, R25a,b, S25c,d, S26a,b, T25a,c), in 1965 (trenches R12a pit, S25c, S26a), and in 1966 (trench S25c).

Illustrations: plans, Figs 26–31; sections, Figs 45–48, 49.1,2, 51.1,2, 52.2, 53.2,3, 54.2, 55.1,2, 56.1,2, 57.1–3, 58.1–3; photographs Pls 8.2 and 9.1,2.

Essentially this layer is the so-called 'Canhasan Late Chalcolithic' but in the preliminary reports it included the Post-Chalcolithic periods. "The buildings of this period were made of comparatively small mud bricks. There are no signs of timbering or of stone foundations. The inside face of the walls was covered with thick white plaster. Floors were given a coating of hard white clay. This was frequently relaid. There is no evidence for the methods of roofing. A certain amount of space was also given to courtyards. In these courtyards were built ovens and small enclosures or bins with thin narrow walls. All these structures were constantly changed and adapted. Walls were strengthened. In some cases old walls were broken down and new ones built either above or on a different line (see plan, Fig. 1). It is not clear yet what the reasons for this constant change were, but it is possible that the open lay-out of the settlement made it easier to rebuild and replan the structures. Possibly too the lay-out was influenced by the very steep slope (from north to south) which we know to have existed in this area at the beginning of the Late Chalcolithic period." (French 1965b: 88 and plan, Fig. 1 and sections, Fig. 2)

Trench S23c (excavated in 1961) "The Late Chalcolithic material that we found came from a shallow pit in S23c (layer 1)." (French 1962b: 30)

Trenches Q23b and Q23d (excavated in 1962); "Except in squares Q22d" [corrigendum: Q23b] "and Q23d no architectural remains were found. In these, however, we found the corner (right-angled) of a structure, mud-bricks which had been used internally and externally as paving, floors, a hearth and two pits which also belonged to the complex ... a hearth, floored with Late Chalcolithic sherds, underlies the corner of the Late Chalcolithic structure mentioned above." (French 1963b: 29–30 and plan of Q23b and d, Fig. 2)

The corner is part of a structure (located in squares P22d, Q22a and c, and Q23a) illustrated on the plan of Layer 1 (Fig. 27, Walls 5, 6 and 7) and on the sections (Figs 53.2 and 54.2).

Fig. 26. Plan of Layer 1 (1:250)

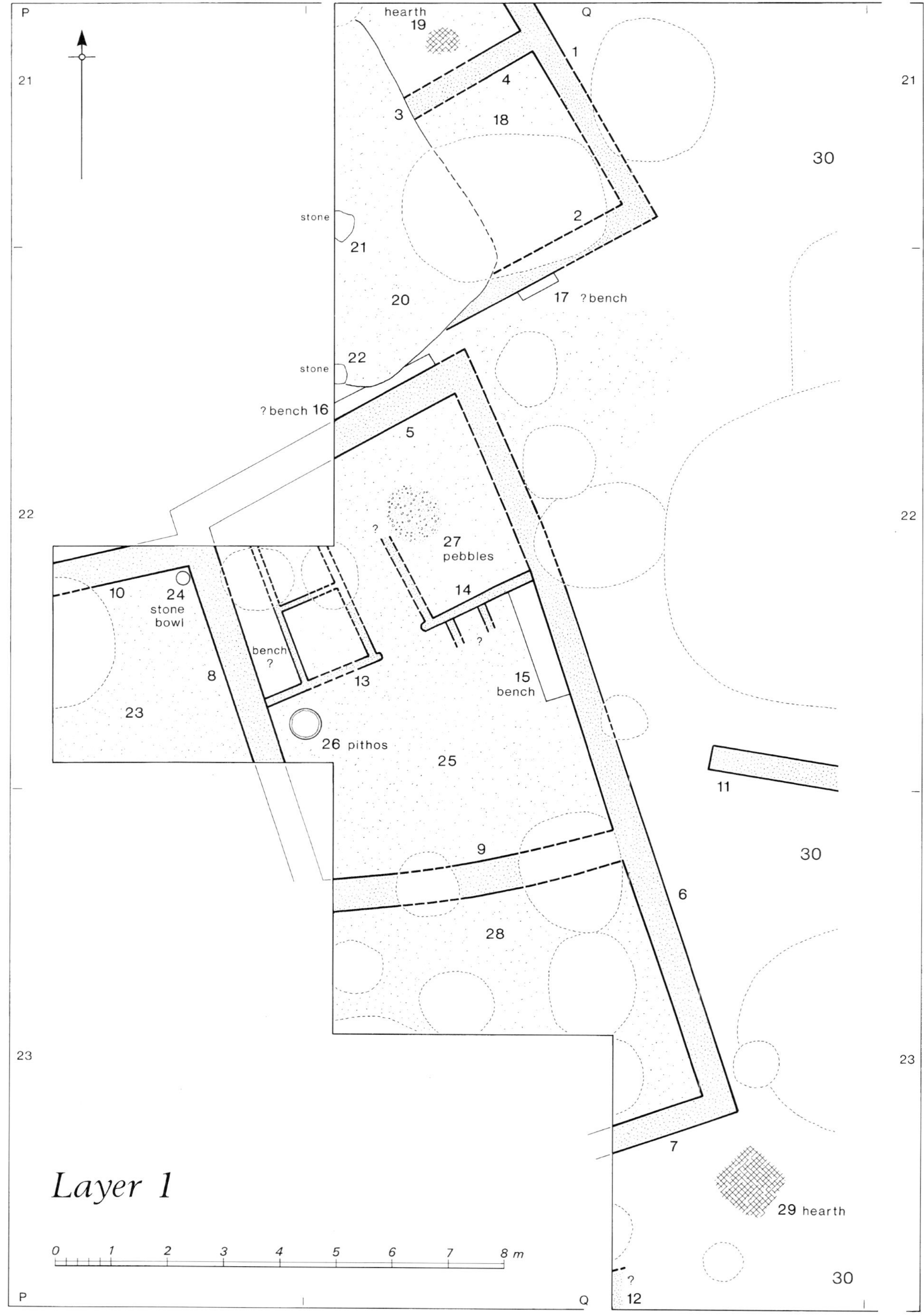

Fig. 27. Plan of Layer 1, NW trenches (1:100); key on p. 53

Trenches P22d, Q22a and c, Q23a (excavated in 1964): "... in square Q22a and the adjacent squares a relatively complete building (the continuation of one discovered in 1962, see below Corrigenda p. 91) with well preserved white clay plaster on floors and walls was cleared." (French 1965b: 88)

The complete building is illustrated on the plan of these trenches (Fig. 27). In the excavation note-books this structure is numbered I.

Trench Q21c (excavated in 1964): "A floor and a hearth overlay the Middle Chalcolithic deposit in square Q21c." (French 1965b: 88)

The floor and the hearth are indicated on the plan (Fig. 27, nos 18 and 19) and on the section (Fig. 49.1, Q21c, N Face).

Trenches R24c and d, R25a and b, S24c and d, S25a and b (excavated in 1963): "So far we have found only two structures, one (Structure II) in square S25b, the other (Structure III) in square R25a. The greater part of the area excavated is taken up by what we assume for the moment to be partition walls and courtyards outside the two structures. Walls, even the external walls of the structures, are thin; the size of brick used is ca. 0.30 by 0.18 by 0.12 m. There is, so far, no evidence of stone foundations nor of timbering. A thick grey-green clay was used as binder for the bricks. The inner wall faces were given a thick coat of white clay plaster. Floors inside the structures were of clay, although in the south-east corner of Structure III there is a patch of pebble floor. Outside the structures there are the 'courtyards'. These, usually, have a hard floor of white clay. At various times new floors were made; associated with them were 'partitions' and 'bins'. The successive phases of building can be seen on the plans ... and sections ... , the earliest phase being 'phase d', the latest 'phase a'." (French 1964: 126 and plans, Figs 1–4, and sections, Figs 5, 6)

The plans published in the preliminary reports have been redrawn here (Figs 28–31). The walls of Layer 1 Phase d has been added to the overall plan (Fig. 26) of the Layer 1 structures in the NW and S trenches. Structure III in the preliminary report (square R25a) = Walls 31–40, Structure II (square S25b) = Walls 43 and 47 with 46 and 75, on the plans (Figs 26–29).

Trench S25a (excavated in 1966): "The only Late Chalcolithic to be excavated this year was the earliest phase (phase f) of Layer 1. A surface of white clay, known from the previous season in square S25c, was cleaned and explored in square S25a." (French 1967b: 165)

Trenches P22d, Q22c, Q23a, S25c and d, S26a and b, T25a and c (excavated in 1964): "The Late Chalcolithic buildings and other structures found in 1963 were, on the whole, poorly preserved. In 1964, on the other hand, the walls belonging to this period were not so badly destroyed by the late pits. In one building (in square S26a) the walls were preserved in

Key to Fig. 27: Plan of Layer 1 (Late Chalcolithic)

Cf. Sections, Figs 49.1, 51.1, 53.2 & 3, 54.2

1 (15, 16) Wall: N–S
2 Wall: E–W
3 Wall: N–S
4 Wall: E–W; tentative presence; exposed by the brushing of the surface-dust
5 (25) Wall: E–W
6 Wall: N–S
7 Wall: E–W
8 Wall: N–S
9 (2) Wall: E–W; (?)internal
10 Wall: E–W
11 Wall: E–W; fragmentary; not certainly LCh
12 (?)Wall: fragmentary; appears only in the sections
13 (3) Partitions for bins: Mud-brick, laid on edge and plastered with white clay
14 Partitions: same
15 Bench: Mud-brick; against an internal face and on a white clay Floor (no. 25)
16 (26) (?)Bench: Mud-brick; perhaps an external buttress
17 (?)Bench: same
18 Floor: white clay
19 Hearth
20 Floor: white clay plaster
21 Stone (?post-pad)
22 Cut: stone edging; cuts through Wall 2 (first [= earliest] phase)
23 Floor: white clay
24 Stone bowl
25 (5)(27) Floor: white clay
26 Pithos
27 Pebbles: perhaps a hearth
28 (4) Floor: white clay
29 Hearth
30 Lines: ash-lines sloping downwards from E to W

some places to a height of over 1 metre. Because of the depth of fill inside these walls, the amount of material which could be recovered was greater than elsewhere on the site. The condition of the soil was soft and full of ash (but not much charcoal). The total fill inside the walls was, therefore, sieved." (French 1965b: 87 and plan, Fig. 1, and sections, Fig. 2)

"On the southern side of the excavated area, where well preserved structures of this phase had been discovered in 1963 and 1964, further work was done below the floors at which we had stopped work in previous seasons. In squares S25c and S26a, where the walls and floors of the Layer 1 structures were still in good condition even after the winter rains, it was possible to distinguish at least two more building phases. Provisionally these phases are lettered e–f. It is clear that in these squares (S25c and S26a) the earliest building to be constructed had frequently been altered and often rebuilt. There are a number of alterations to the plan and lay-out, and probably also to the function of certain areas of the complex. No new discoveries were made in building method and technique but the difference of colour and texture (but not of size) in the mud-brick made it easier to detect the sequence of alterations and reconstructions." (French 1966b: 113 and 115, and section, Fig. 1)

Key to Figs 28–31: Plan of Layer 1, Phases a–f (Late Chalcolithic)

Cf. Sections, Figs 51.2, 52.2&3, 55.1&2, 56–58

31 (10) Wall: E–W
32 (6) Wall: N–S
33 Wall: E–W
34 (5) Wall: N–S
35 (9) Wall: E–W; visible in the bottom of pit
36 Wall : E–W
37 (8) Wall: N–S
38 Floor: white clay
39 Wall: N–S; only the corner is preserved
40 (7) Wall: E–W; partly destroyed by a pit
41 Wall: E–W
42 (7) Wall: N–S
43 (9) Wall: E–W
44 (3) Wall: N–S
45 Wall: E–W
46 Wall: E–W
47 (15) Wall: N–S
48 Wall: E–W
49 (13, 14) (6) (18) (24) (15) Wall: N–S
50 (2) Wall: N–S
51 Wall: E–W; originally phase e
52 Wall: N–S; same
53 (1)(1) Wall: N–S; originally phase f
54 (17) Wall: E–W; originally phase e
55 (4)(3) Wall: N–S
56 (5)(18) Wall: E–W
57 (20) Wall: E–W
58 (1) Wall: E–W
59 Wall: N–S
60 (19) Partition: N–S
61 (22) Partitions: E–W
62 (27) Partitions: E–W
63 (?)Bench: E–W; perhaps an external buttress
64 Floor: white clay
65 Floor: same
66 (?)Floor: white clay
67 Floor: White clay
68 (?)
69 Oven
70 Oven
71 (25) Pot
72 (4) Wall: NE–SW; (?)phase f
73 (2) Wall: NW–SE; (?)phase f
74 Wall: E–W
75 (2) Wall: N–S
76 (22)(13) Wall: E–W
77 (2, 5) Wall: E–W
78 Wall: N–S
79 (7) Wall: N–S
80 Wall: E–W
81 (18) Floor: red-clay; on top of Wall 48 and against Walls 47, 49, 77, 78
82 Floor
83 (25) Partition: E–W
84 Partitions: E–W
85 Partitions: N–S
86 Partitions: N–S
87 Partitions: N–S
88 Oven
89 Hearth
90 (3) Partition
91 Partition and Oven
92 Wall: N–S; (?)phase a or b
93 (29)(14) Wall: E–W
94 Partition: E–W
95 Wall: N–S
96 Wall: N–S
97 Wall: E–W
98 Wall: N–S
99 Wall: N–S
100 Wall: E–W
101 Hearth
102 Hearth

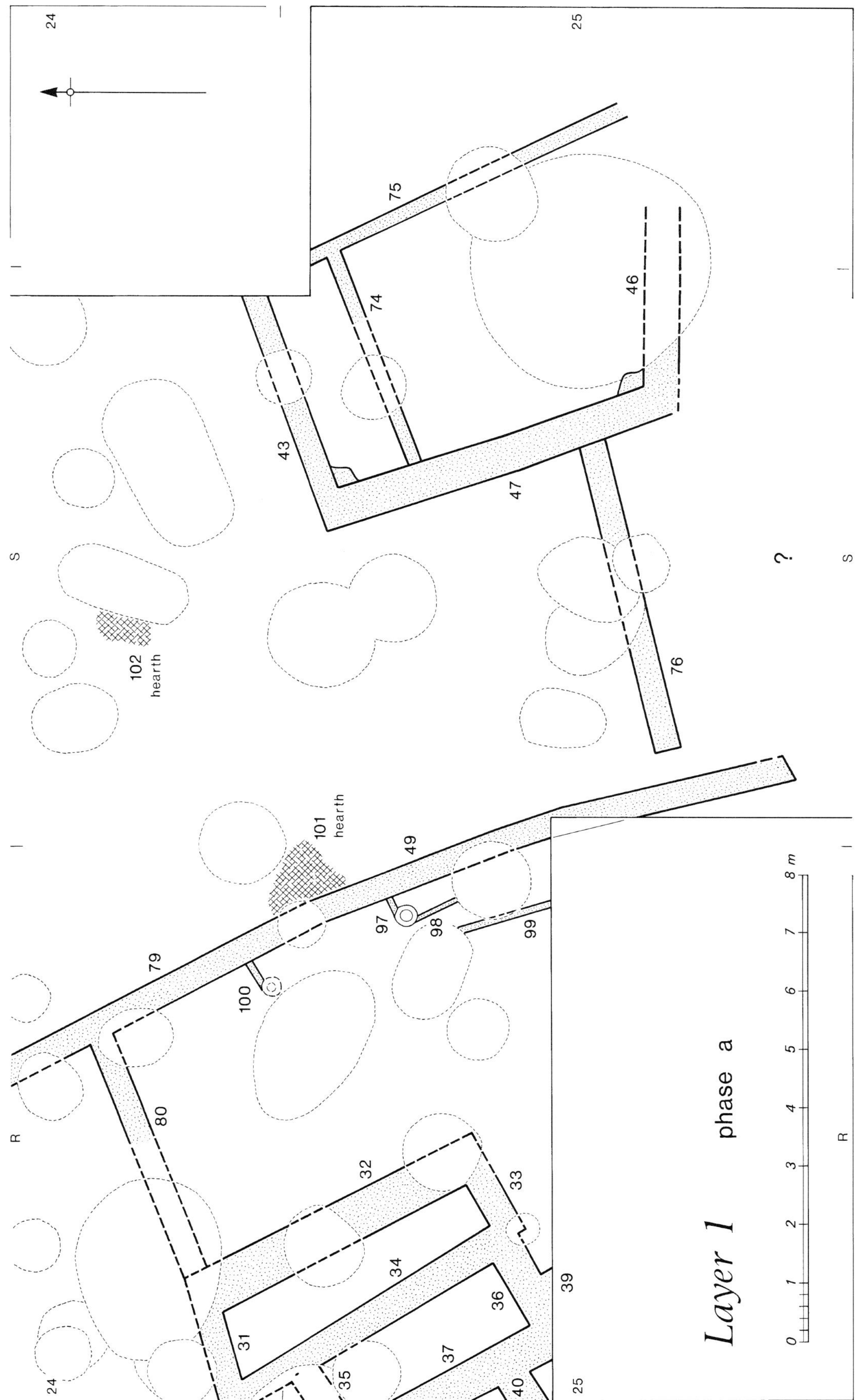

Fig. 28. Plan of Layer 1, S trenches: phase a (1:100); key on p. 54

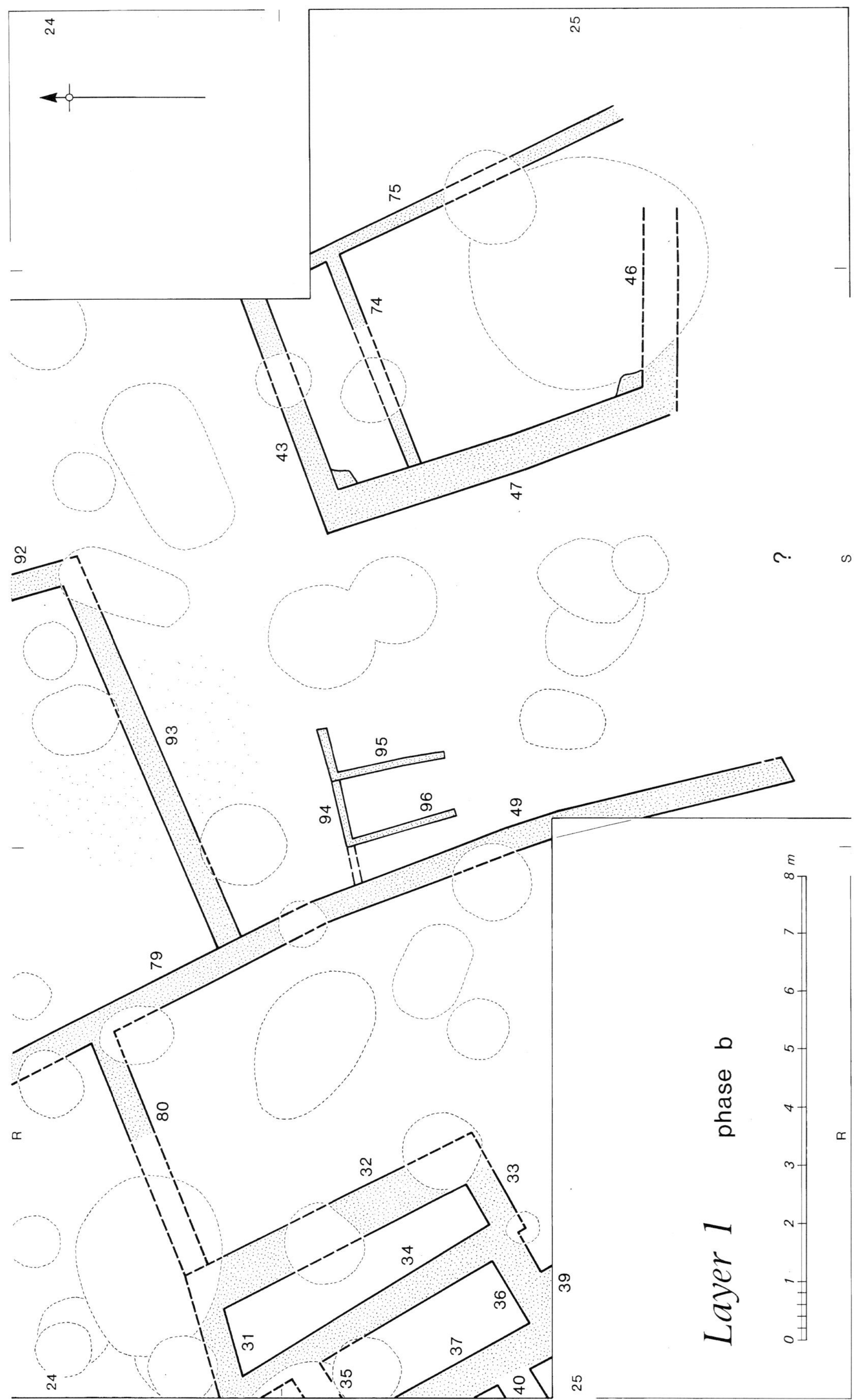

Fig. 29. Plan of Layer 1, S trenches: phase b (1:100); key on p. 54

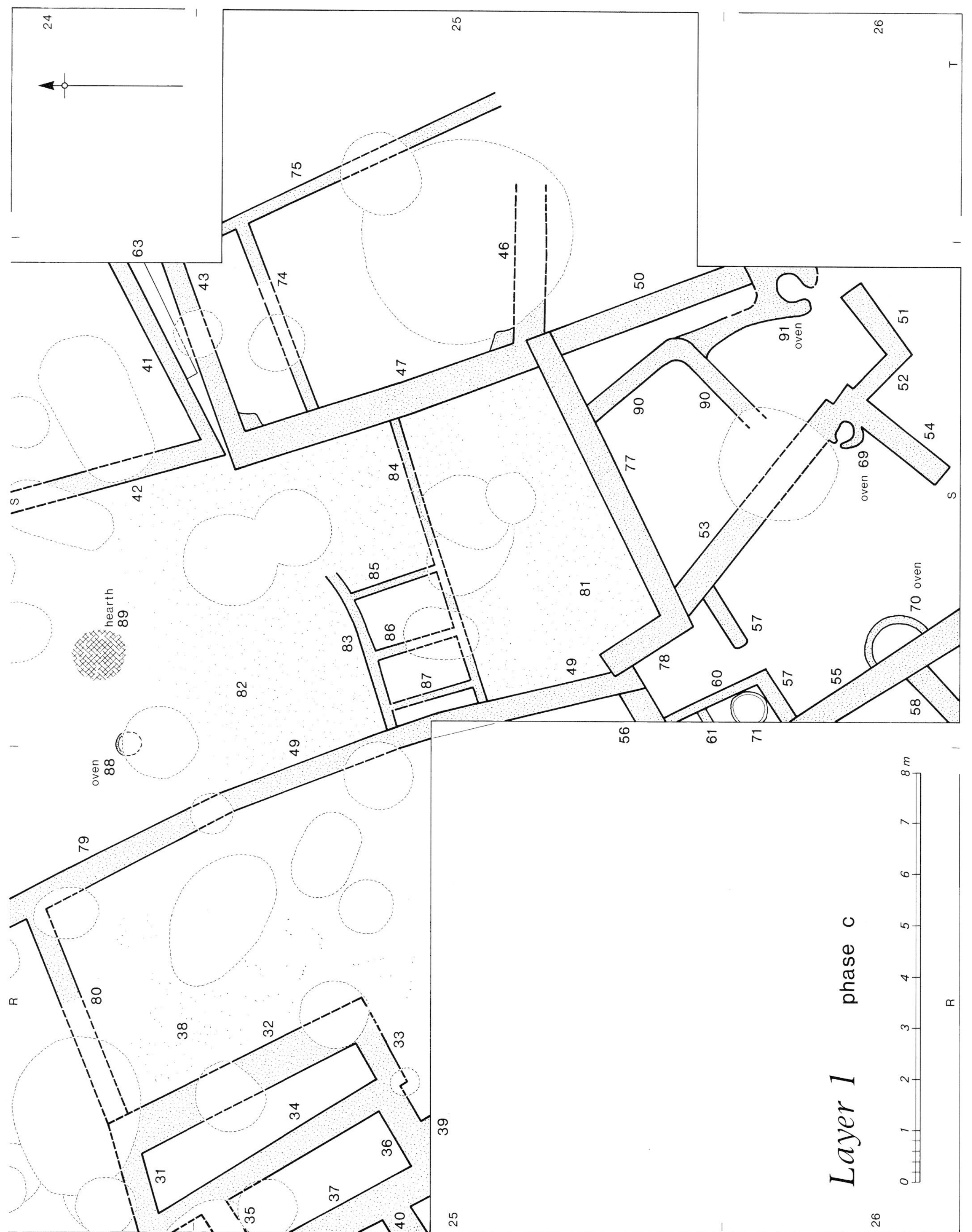

Fig. 30. Plan of Layer 1, S trenches: phase c (1:100); key on p. 54

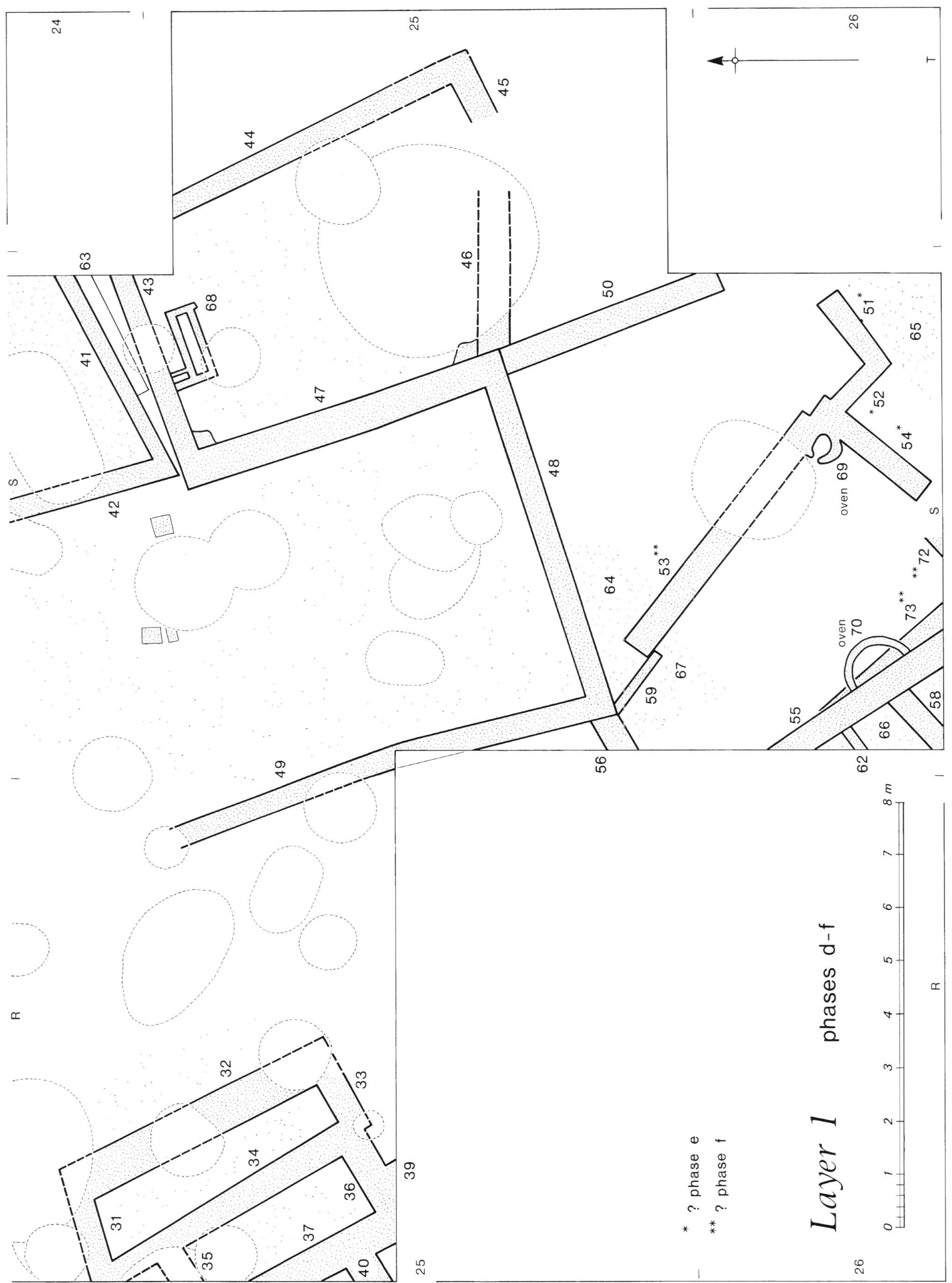

Fig. 31. Plan of Layer 1, S trenches: phases d-f) (1:100); key on p. 54

The Phases e–f of Layer 1 have been added to the plan (Fig. 31) of phase d. The earliest phase (f) is indicated by three walls (nos 72, 73 and 75 on the plan, Fig. 31) and the next phase (e) by three walls (nos 51, 52 and 54) and an oven (no. 69; photograph, Pl. 8.2).

For illustrations of the Layer 1 structures in the southern trenches (S25a&b, S26a&b), see the photographs, Pl. 9.1,2.

Trenches R21a and b (excavated in 1965): "In squares R21a and b we found no structures or buildings although there was a small quantity of sherds of Late Chalcolithic type. There was also a large, deep pit in the northeast corner of R21a." (French 1966b: 113)

Not recorded in the first reports is the presence of abundant sherds of Layer 1 in the area of the Canhasan dig-house. The material came to light in 1964 during the preparation of foundations for the house and the courtyard wall.

2.7 Post-Chalcolithic Periods

The Post-Chalcolithic material includes the Iron Age, the Classical period, the Roman/Late Roman period and the Early Byzantine period. Only the Early Byzantine period was represented by a structure. The other periods are known from pottery found in pits or are represented only by scattered sherds and coins.

Post-Chalcolithic 5.—Iron Age

1961 Season: 'Black on Red pottery. Stray sherds.' (French 1962b: 34)

1962 Season: 'This layer ... includes Iron Age ... material. The material ... (entirely sherds) is found only in the surface dust and in numerous pits which, on all parts of the site, intruded into the earlier layers. There are as yet no buildings of these later periods.' (French 1963b: 30)

1963 Season: "Much later still, in the Iron Age and Classical periods, the area" [sc. R24c–d, S24c–d, R25a–b, S25a–b] "was again occupied; the evidence for this occupation comes from pits, of which there are a great number, and very occasionally from 'floors'." "The area excavated this year was scattered with numerous pits. In one of them (square S24d, pit 1) was found a fairly well preserved jug painted in the Black on Red technique which in Cilicia and South-West Anatolia is called 'Iron Age'. ... There are as yet no building levels of this period." (French 1964b: 125)

1964 Season: 'A large number of pits was found in all parts of the excavated area. All are of recent date, i.e. Iron Age or succeeding periods. There are as yet no buildings associated with these pits. Sherds of a jar of Phrygian Grey ware from pits 2 and 3 in square S25d are the first certain pieces of this type found at Can Hasan' (French 1965b: 87)

Post-Chalcolithic 4.—Classical

A Black-Gloss ('Black Glaze') sherd of excellent quality (?Attic), from a kylix.

Post-Chalcolithic 3.—Hellenistic

Sherds of mould-made relief ware ('MMRW').

Post-Chalcolithic 2.—Roman/late Roman

1961 Season: "... several pits of the Roman or Early Byzantine period have cut into walls and associated debris" [sc. Layer 2B] '...' (French 1962b: 30) 'Work-floors.' (ibid. 34)

1962 Season: "This layer ... includes Roman ... material. The material ... (entirely sherds) is found only in the surface dust and in numerous pits which, on all parts of the site, intruded into the earlier layers. There are as yet no buildings of these later periods." (French 1963b: 30)

1963 Season: "Much later still, in the Iron Age and Classical periods, the area" [sc. R24c–d, S24c–d, R25a–b, S25a–b] "was again occupied; the evidence for this occupation comes from pits, of which there are a great number, and very occasionally from 'floors'." (French 1964b: 125)

1964 Season: "A large number of pits was found in all parts of the excavated area. All are of recent date, i.e. Iron Age or succeeding periods. There are as yet no buildings associated with these pits." (French 1965b: 87) In 1961 we were shown a bronze coin of Septimius Severus, said to have been found in the area of the village cemetery.

Post-Chalcolithic 1.—Byzantine

Trench R21b (excavated in 1965).

Illustrations: plan, Fig. 32; sections, Figs 37, 38, 40–43, 50.1.

"Most of a structure probably belonging to the Byzantine period came to light in the uppermost stratum in square R21b. Mud brick walls, fairly well preserved, about 0.50 m. high and laid on stone foundations, were found just below the surface. On the uppermost of the floors which were associated with the walls lay a single small jar. There were no other finds." (French 1966b: 113)

The walls are constructed of mud-brick (dimensions: 0.47 × 0.25 × 0.11 m.) set on stones—in complete contrast to the general practise of the Chalcolithic period.

The plan of this structure, as it is preserved in Trench R21b and Baulk R21b/d, is illustrated here (Fig. 32).

A worn Byzantine coin of the Anonymous Bronze series (10–11th cent. AD) was found on the excavation dump in 1964 (Inv.no. Can/64/649).

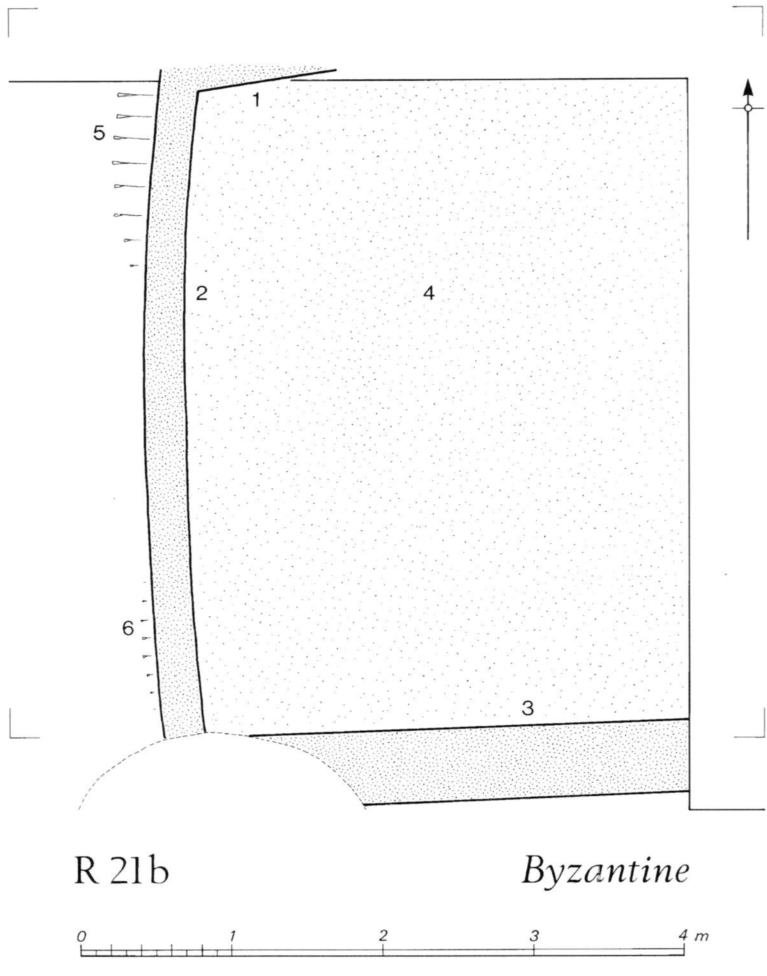

Fig. 32. Plan of Byzantine Layer: R21b (1:50)

Cf. Sections, Figs 38, 41–43

1 (129) Wall: E–W; Mud-brick (dimensions 0.47 × 0.25 × 0.11) on stone Foundation; one Mud-brick thick (i.e. 0.25)

2 (129, 130) Wall: N–S; same

3 Wall: E–W; Mud-brick on stone Foundation; two Mud-bricks thick, laid side-by-side (i.e. 0.50)

4 (131) Floor: grey mud

5 (127) Foundation-cut

6 (128) Foundation-cut

Note: The (?SE) corner of a late structure was found in R22d (06/x/61). It survived as a course of stones c. 0.10 m. below the surface, and a surface of white ash c. 0.50 m. below the surface. A stone quern was located on this surface. At the time the stones were interpreted as a stone-lined pit: they may, however, have been part of the Byzantine structure in R21b.

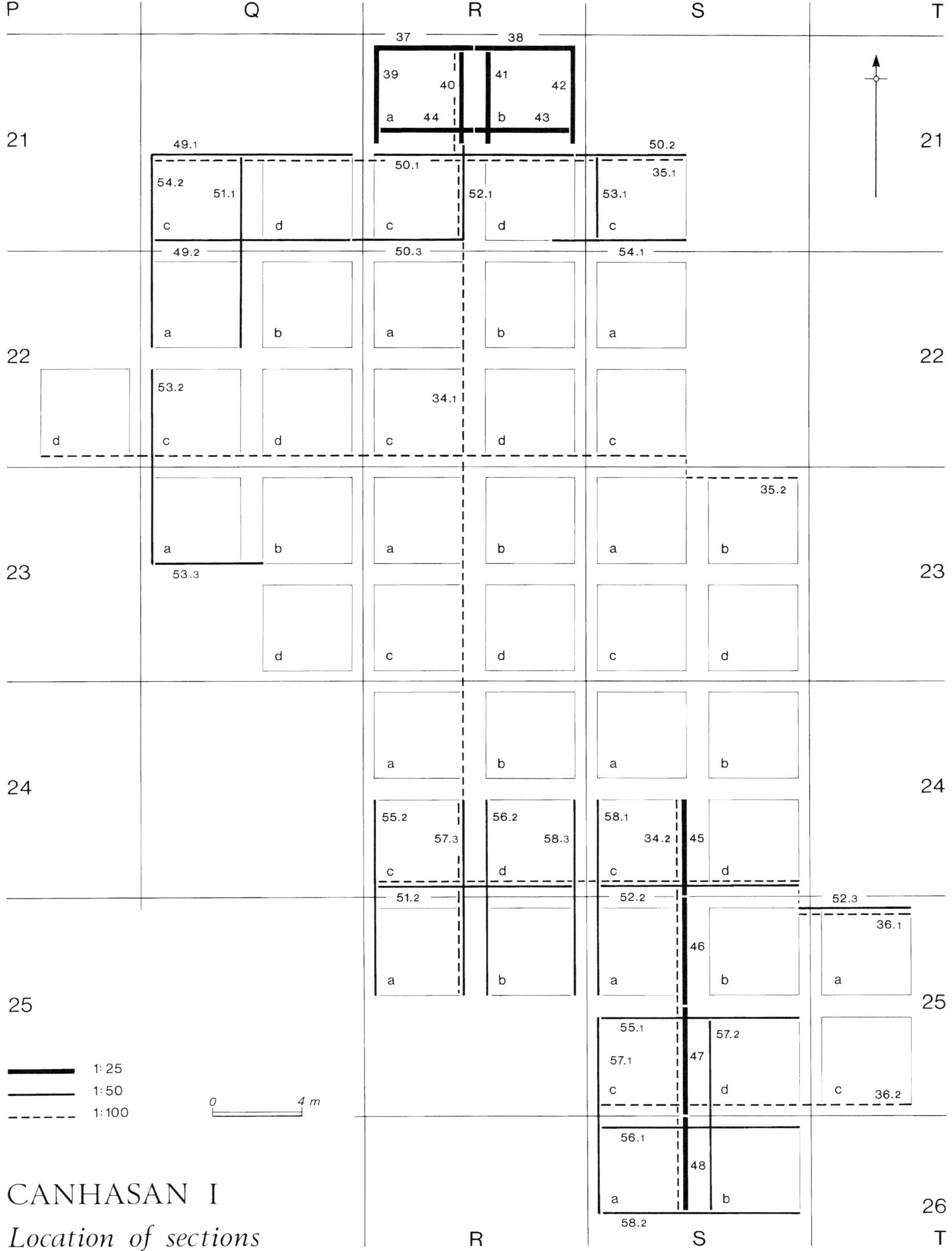

Fig. 33. Plan showing location of illustrated sections (1:250)

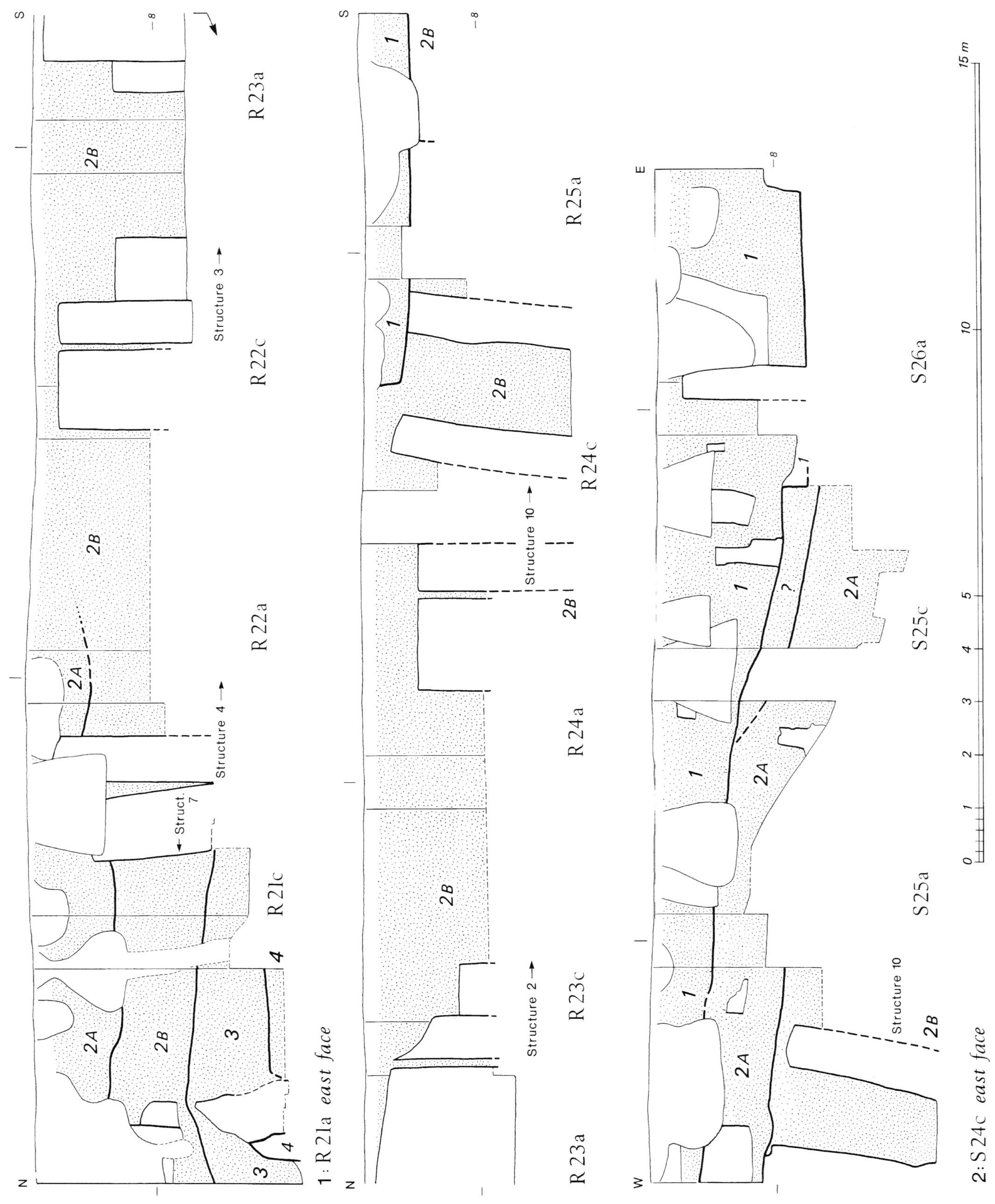

Fig. 34. Simplified N–S section (1:100)

Fig. 35. Simplified E–W section (1:100)

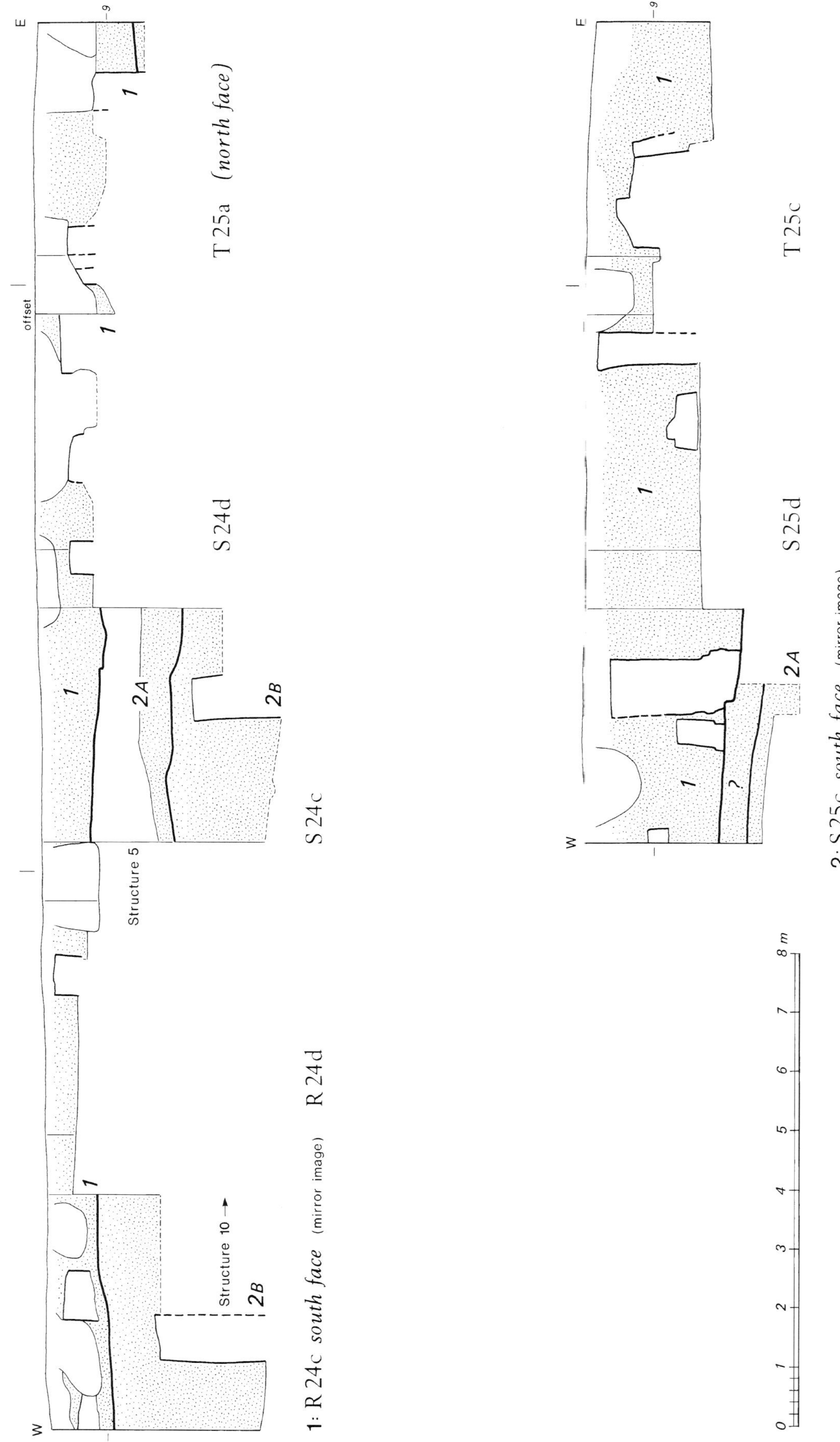

Fig. 36. Simplified E–W section (1:100)

3. Notes

3.1 Stratigraphic sequence

The aims of the excavation were not entirely achieved.

It was impossible, without serious damage to Layer 2B structures, to carry out a stratigraphic sondage through the earlier layers or to excavate a wide area. A broad, horizontal exposure of Layer 3, for example, was not permissible.

No one trench provides a complete, unbroken stratified sequence of all the structural levels known at Canhasan. Moreover the form and nature of the strata did not allow for uncomplicated excavation and record (cp. the N sections of trenches R21a and b, Figs 37, 38). The longest and most complete sequence was found in trench R21b: Layers 7 to 2A. Indeed Layers 7 to 4 are known only from trenches R21a and b. There the structures of each level were seen to be, to a considerable degree, superimposed, one above the other, but it was also observed, especially in Layers 7–4, that there were frequent re-modellings of the walls and floors. The sequence is by no means straightforward.

With the exception of Layer 2B, there was apparently never an attempt, by the ancient occupants of the Canhasan site, to prepare a more-or-less level surface on top of the earlier structures.

Layer 3 was observed immediately under structures of Layer 2B in other trenches (R21c and d) but excavation was hindered by the overlying walls.

The transition from Layer 3 to Layer 2B is direct. For the new structures of Layer 2B the older layer was flattened (but cf. R21b, E section, Fig. 42) and on this prepared surface each new structure of Layer 2B was laid out, apparently, in co-ordination with its neighbours. There is some evidence (N face, R21c, Fig. 50.1, Layer 2B Wall [no. 9] cut into Layer 3 Wall [no. 1]) for an awareness of pre-existing structures.

In trenches R21a and b Layer 2A was not represented by any structure. For Layer 2A structures, though poorly preserved, in stratigraphic association with Layer 2B, one must turn to the NW trenches, Q21c and d, and Q22a and to the S trenches, S24c and S25a. Elsewhere, especially in the core or heart of Layer 2B occupation (Structures 1–6), there is no evidence for structural re-use, in Layer 2A, of an area occupied in Layer 2B, although inside and over the top of Layer 2B walls there are soil-deposits (over Structures 1, 6 and 7) full of domestic refuse (sherds, animal bone, broken objects) representing occupation of Layer 2A elsewhere on the site.

The transition, therefore, was not abrupt. The transition from Layer 2B to Layer 2A, however, was made obscure by the inability, at the time of excavation, to recognize the occurrence of two features: (1) 'insertion', which results in the near-exact, horizontal mimicry of an earlier structural plan by a structure of the immediately succeeding level, and (2) deep terracing from the side of the mound into the core of an older structure. The two features are described above (p. 46). The failure to recognize 'insertion' has been mitigated, however, by the almost total absence, in the Layer 2A structures, of finds in situ, i.e. small objects and whole and complete pots. Nevertheless, the transition could perhaps have been better understood if there had been greater understanding of the stratigraphic significance of 'insertion' and of deep terracing.

In the NW and S trenches, therefore, there is evidence, in the form of Layer 2A structures 'inserted' into and onto (or perhaps terraced into and against) structures of Layer 2B, for a direct transition from Layer 2B to Layer 2A.

Stratigraphically there is a clearly visible distinction between Layer 2A and Layer 1: Layer 1 walls and floors lie directly over structures of Layer 2A. Nevertheless the transition may not have been immediate. The evidence for an interval can be observed in trenches S25c (W Face, Fig. 57.1, and N Face, Fig. 55.1). The soil-deposit (no. 3 on the section, Fig. 57.1, and no. 11 on the section, Fig. 55.1) which may represent this interval is a soft, dark, unstructured earth, of (?)humic origin, not unlike the surface dust of the modern mound. The soil has not been tested.

For composite profiles drawn along the major axes (N–S along a central line, W–E along the latitudinal lines at the N, central and S sides of the excavated area), see the plan and sections, Figs 33–36. The profiles are intended to illustrate the vertical relationships, as they occur at different points of the excavated area, between layers (e.g. the influence of Layer 3 on the vertical configuration of Layer 2B or the result of later, Layer 2A terracing/insertion) and between structures in each layer (e.g. in the dense agglomeration of Layer 2B).

3.2 Structural sequence

Probably from the time of the earliest level excavated at Canhasan I, certainly from Layer 5 onwards until the innovations of Layer 1, the stratigraphic sequence and development of structures on the site is lineal. There are, it seems, no major vertical discontinuities resulting, for instance, from the re-location of structures away from the preceding area of occupation. This hypothesis can be demonstrated from:

(1) the unchanging orientation of the walls from level to level,
(2) the use of wall-stumps (of Layer 5) in re-building (Layer 4),
(3) the introduction (in Layer 3) and adoption (in Layer 2B) of standard-size mud-bricks and
(4) the introduction (?in Layer 4) and adoption of internal wall-buttresses.

If one accepts this hypothesis, the structural history of Canhasan may be described as an explanation of the adoption, abandonment, adaptation and development of six basic characteristics which have been noted in the earliest excavated layer, as follows:

(1) structural orientation,
(2) compact, cellular agglomeration of structures,
(3) square or rectangular plans (i.e. structures with right-angled corners),
(4) small, single-storey structures,
(5) the use of a small, (?)hand-formed mud-brick,
(6) the lack of stone-foundations for the mud-brick walls.

Layers 7–6

It is assumed that all these characteristics were inherited from earlier levels on the site and that they were transmitted to Layer 7 and then to Layer 6. Both, however, were represented by no more than an area of a few square metres at the bottom of trench R21b.

Layer 5

The six, basic characteristics, (1)–(6) (as above), are transmitted from the previous Layers to Layer 5.

In addition, there is now evidence, namely, storage-bins and stone-querns, for internal arrangements and activities; this same evidence may perhaps confirm that the structures were single-storied, on the grounds that the activity implied by the presence of a grinding-stone requires light (not available on the lower or ground floor of a two-storied structure which has no peripheral space such as a courtyard). There is some evidence for the limited use of twigs/branches in the construction of the walls.

Layer 4

The characteristics (1)–(6) (as above) are accepted from the previous layer. The limited use of twigs/branches was noted in one wall of this layer.

Layer 3

Characteristics (1)–(3) and (6) are accepted from the previous layer but there is now a change of scale.

Characteristic (4), the tradition of small, single-storied structures, is abandoned (at least on that part of the site which was excavated).

(5) The small, (?)hand-formed mud-brick is abandoned in favour of a large, standard-size, mould-made mud-brick, the use of which leads to a significant change of scale. Walls are no longer narrow but massive. The increased width of the walls undoubtedly facilitated the construction of an upper storey.

Layer 2B

Characteristics (1)–(3), (5) (as developed in Layer 3) and (6) are accepted from the previous layer.

There is now clear evidence (in Structure 10) for the construction of an upper storey and for the partial decoration of some surfaces, such as (?)door- and window-surrounds, (?)niches, within the upper storey.

Evidence for areas of domestic activity is not clear but it can be assumed, from the position (near the tops, as preserved, of the surviving walls) of pottery and other objects, that living space was available on the upper storey, while storage of movables such as tools, small objects and grain was possible on the ground-floor to which, of course, access was limited to members of the household. Pottery was not found on the floor of the ground-storey. The safe-keeping of animals was evidently not a function of the Layer 2B structures.

Layer 2A

Earlier characteristics, (1)–(3), (5) and (6), continue.

There is evidence (in the structure-plans of the NW and SW trenches) for the adaptation of pre-existing structures. In some cases (Structures 2 and 5) the re-use takes the form of 'insertion' and/or terracing (Structures 3, 4). In other cases (Structure 6) the new building ignores the orientation of the Layer 2B structures but retains the internal features, e.g. opposing buttresses.

Layer 1

There is a clear distinction, best observed in plan, shape and form, between structures of Layer 1 and those of an earlier layer (Layer 2B).

The major characteristics of Layer 2B do not continue, although there is still no regular use of stone-foundations for mud-brick walls. The plan of a Layer 1 structure (in-so-far-as this can be restored) is irregular, the shape is no longer uniformally square or rectangular (i.e. corners are not right-angles) and the form represents a free-standing structure surrounded by open areas such as court-

For ease of reference, comparison and contrast, a table of comparative mud-brick sizes is given here.

Layer	*Mud-brick*	*Mud-brick sizes (m.)*	*Source*
7–4	irregular, hand-made	c.0.50 × 0.30 × 0.08	[1]Q21c: Structure 2
3	(?)mould-made	0.80 × 0.40 × 0.10	[2]same, Buttresses 2.8 and 9
2B	mould-made	same	[3]see p. 46
2A	irregular (1) early	0.80 × 0.40 × 0.10[1]	[4]Q22a: Structure 6, earliest phase
		slightly smaller[2]	[5]Q22a: Structure 6, middle phase
		0.66 × 0.20 × 0.10[3]	[6]S24c: fallen bricks in S24c
	(2) late	0.65 × 0.30 × 0.08[4]	[7]S24c: Wall 93
		0.60 × 0.30 × 0.08[5]	[8]Q22a: Walls 5 and 6
		0.35 × 0.20 × 0.12[6]	[9]Q22c: fallen bricks
		0.30 × 0.23 × 0.07[6]	[10]Wall 53
		0.28 × 0.28 × 0.06[6]	[11]Wall 51
1	irregular	0.54 × 0.28 × (?)[7]	[12]Wall 76
		0.53 × 0.22 × 0.09–10[8]	[13]Wall 55
		0.52 × 0.25 × 0.10[8]	[14]French 1964b: 126; see p. 53
		0.51 × 0.22 × 0.125–15[9]	[15]see p. 59
		0.51 × 0.10 × 0.125[9]	
		0.52–3 × 0.15 × 0.10–2[10]	
		0.49 × 0.26 × 0.12[11]	
		0.46 × 0.27 × 0.10[12]	
		0.45 × 0.16 × 0.10[12]	
		0.42–5 × 0.26 × (?)[13]	
		0.30 × 0.18 × 0.12[14]	
Byzantine		0.47 × 0.25 × 0.11[15]	
17th cent. Karaman	mould-made	0.27 × 0.27 × 0.10	
		0.14 × 0.27 × 0.10	
Alaçatı	mould-made (old)	0.25 × 0.25 × 0.12	
		0.25 × 0.115 × 0.12	
	(new)	0.25 × 0.25 × 0.10	
		0.25 × 0.115 × 0.10	

yards. Unlike earlier structures, those of Layer 1 provide fuller evidence for areas of domestic activity, such as hearths and ovens. In Layer 1 there is now space inside or beside the structure for the safe-keeping of animals, cp. the remarks here on Layer 2B.

3.3 The internal development and history of the site

For this report the structural sequence has been arranged and described (above, Chapter 2.2–6) according to a descriptive tradition familiar in Anatolian archaeology. It is based on pottery, as follows (for the pre-Bronze Age):

Neolithic	—	Early
		Late
Chalcolithic	—	Early
		Middle
		Late

These descriptive terms, however, conceal the continuities (and discontinuities) and transitions that are demonstrable in the pottery sequences and it has been noted that the structural development and internal history of Canhasan I do not entirely conform to this ceramic outline (to be published in Canhasan I, 2. The Pottery).

There are 9 stages in the development of the site in the periods described as Neolithic and Chalcolithic:

(1) The first occupational layers on the site could not, of course, be excavated. One may assume, perhaps, a series of occupations in the post-aceramic period, i.e. in the Early Neolithic (as defined at Çatal Hüyük, Eastern mound).
(2) Occupation (Layers 7–4) continued as an (?)agglomeration of small structures, i.e. closely grouped, without change, it seems, to form and methods of construction.
(3) The first changes in the development of the site took place between Layer 4 and Layer 3. There is a change of scale in the dimensions (horizontal and vertical) of structures (but not necessarily of the site). Structures probably became two-storied. The close grouping of structures does not change.

(4) The site is levelled and re-built but Layer 2B is essentially a continuation of the preceding layer. It is, however, better preserved. Structures were certainly two-storied. It was largely destroyed by fire.
(5) On the evidence of the 'inserted' structures Layer 2A is also a continuation of the preceding layer (Layer 2B), at least in the early stages.
(6) In later stages of Layer 2A, however, there is evidence (1) for the partial, if not complete, abandonment of Layer 2B orientations and structures, (2) a scattered occupation on the periphery of the Layer 2B core and (3) an open space at the high point of the site over the top of the central, Layer 2B structures nos 1–5.
(7) The end of Layer 2A occupation is not clearly understood. On present evidence the settlement was abandoned and deserted when the final occupation came to an end (if indeed it did) over the whole site.
(8) After an interval (of unknown length) the site was levelled and re-occupied (Layer 1).
(9) When Layer 1 occupation ceased, the site was totally abandoned and thereafter re-occupied only intermittently (as in the IA and Byzantine periods).

3.4 Nature of the site

The comparative size of each successive layer cannot be reconstructed. Nor is there any evidence for defensive requirements (perimeter wall and gates), if any were necessary.

In Layers 7–4 nothing is known of the spatial arrangements of the site, e.g. access to individual structures, open areas (if any), streets.

In Layer 3 there is the possibility of a narrow access street between two adjacent structures. In Layer 3 (probably) and in Layer 2B (certainly) it must be assumed that by communal agreement access to individual structures was possible by use of neighbouring roofs. On the other hand, the disposal of rubbish must have taken place outside the area of the structures. There are no pits inside the structures. Any gap between the walls was probably covered by roofing/ceiling arrangements. Moreover, the space between walls is far too narrow for anything but drainage. The only instance of rubbish accumulating between walls occurs in Trench R21c, between Layer 2B Structure 7 (Wall 7.4) and Structure 4 (Wall 4.1) (see above, p. 37; consult the sections, E Face, R21c, Figs 34 and 52.1). The accumulation of rubbish clearly occurred *after* Structure 7 had fallen into disuse and *before* Structure 4 was replaced by Layer 2A Structure 2 (formerly Layer 2B 'House 8').

On the basis of the evidence from Structures 6 and 10 it can be assumed that roof-occupation was a normal feature of the Canhasan site during the time-span of Layer 2B structures. It is possible that the roof-occupation was seasonal and that the lower storey was used, according to necessity, for storage or for residence.

"Again, like certain houses in modern Canhasan, Houses 2, 3" [and others, nos 1, 4–7 and 10] "were two-storeyed. Probably the upper storey occupied about half the total roof space and the remaining half was used for work purposes, possibly cooking, certainly for drying and storage. In modern Canhasan wheat and maize are dried on the roofs as well as such vegetables as peppers.

That there was a second storey and that it, and not the ground floor, was used for living purposes is clearly shown by the position of fallen debris. Pottery and wall plaster both overlay ceiling material in Houses 2, 3 and 5. The ground floor was therefore presumably used for storage purposes. It was on the benches of House 3, for example, that we found samples of burnt grain. Benches, however, were not a regular feature of every house, as can be seen from the plan (Fig. 4) ... There were no hearths on the ground floor." (French 1962b: 31)

For a hypothetical reconstruction of the area given to upper-storey occupation (1) in Layer 2B Structure 10, see the plan, Fig. 21, and (2) over the Layer 2B site as excavated, see the plan, Fig. 12. Dr Geoffery Summers points out to me that in the upper storey plan as reconstructed not only do the units face away from each other, e.g. 7 faces to N, 3 and 6 to E, 10 to SW, 4 to S and E, but there appears also to be no specific orientation, i.e. to the sun or to the prevailing winds: the SW (which brings rain and snow) or the NE (which brings cool or cold, dry air).

For imaginary views of the Layer 2B structures and of the roof arrangements, see the reconstructions (drawn by Ian James Walls), Front Cover and Figs 59, 60.

Because of an insufficiency of comparative data, the plan of the site and the use of space may be studied and contrasted only in two layers: 2B and 1. In neither is there self-evident isolation: no structure takes a pre-eminence which could suggest a social stratification. In Layer 2B some structures are small, but none are dominantly large or differently planned and oriented. There is a certain uniformity of plan, though not of scale. Indeed the arrangement of structures and the intricate dove-tailing of walls and corners appears to have been the result of social cohesion, if not of community planning.

The tight organization of space in Layer 2B is in sharp contrast with the irregular positioning of Layer 1 structures. Again in contrast with Layer 2B, there are, in Layer 1, open areas where domestic activities were located outside a structure but in close relationship to it. The movement away from a close agglomeration to an loose distribution of structures seems, therefore, to have taken place before Layer 1, i.e. at some time within the period represented, at Canhasan, by Layer 2A.

3.5 Summary of occupation at Canhasan I

The summaries given above (3.1–4), when combined with the evidence for the presence, at Canhasan, of post-Bronze Age periods, may be set down in tabular form, as follows:

Stage	*Layer*	*Structures* etc.	*Plan*	*Pottery*
(1)	(?)	(?)small	(?)close agglomeration	Early Neol.
(2)	(7–4)	small	close agglomeration	Late Neol.
		---------- Change in scale ----------		
(3)	3	large, 2-storey	close agglomeration	Early Chalc.
(4)	2B	large, 2-storey	close agglomeration	Transitional (ECh/MCh)
		---------- Layer 2B destroyed by fire ----------		
(5)	2A (early)	rubbish deposits over Layer 2B; insertions into Layer 2B		Middle Chalc.
(6)	2A (late)	irregular building on edge of Layer 2B core		Middle Chalc.
(7)		---------- End of Layer 2A not understood ----------		
		---------- Interval of unknown length; site (?)deserted until Layer 1 ----------		
(8)	1	irregular, small	open distribution	Late Chalc.
(9)		---------- Site abandoned ----------		
		scattered presence; sherds		Iron Age
		scattered presence; sherds		Classical
		scattered presence; sherds		Hellenistic
		scattered presence; sherds, coin		Roman
		scattered occupation; coin		Byzantine

Key to conventions used in Figs 37–58

The keys to the numbers used in each section are to be found on pp. 92–101.

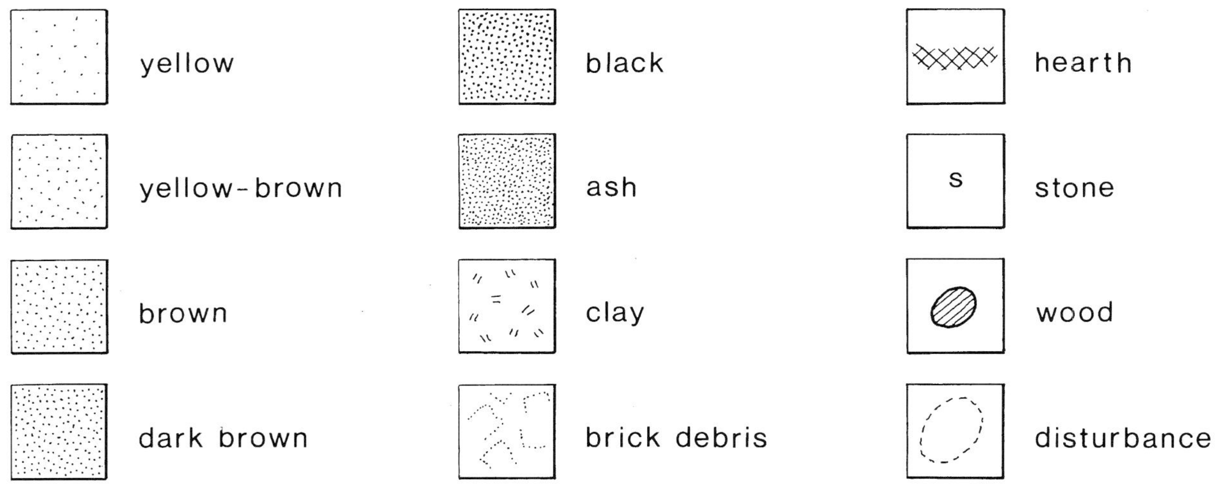

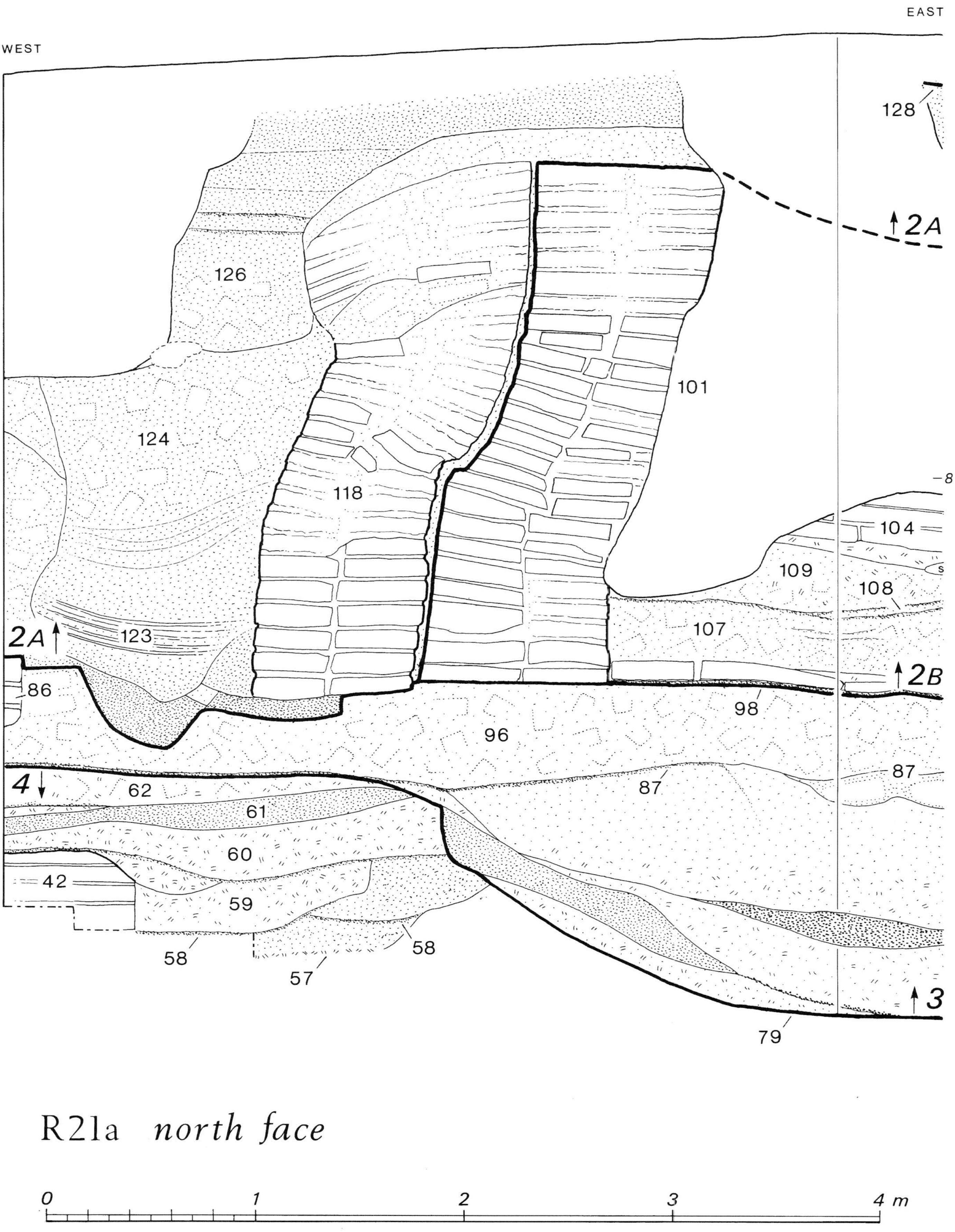

R21a *north face*

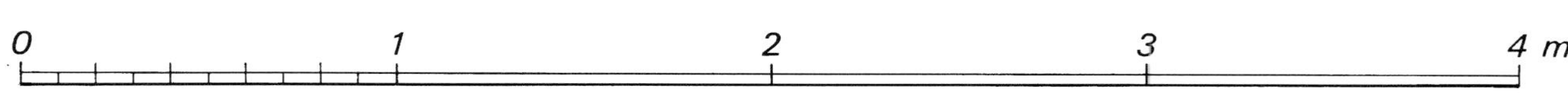

Fig. 37. Trench R21a, N Face (1:25); key on pp. 92–93

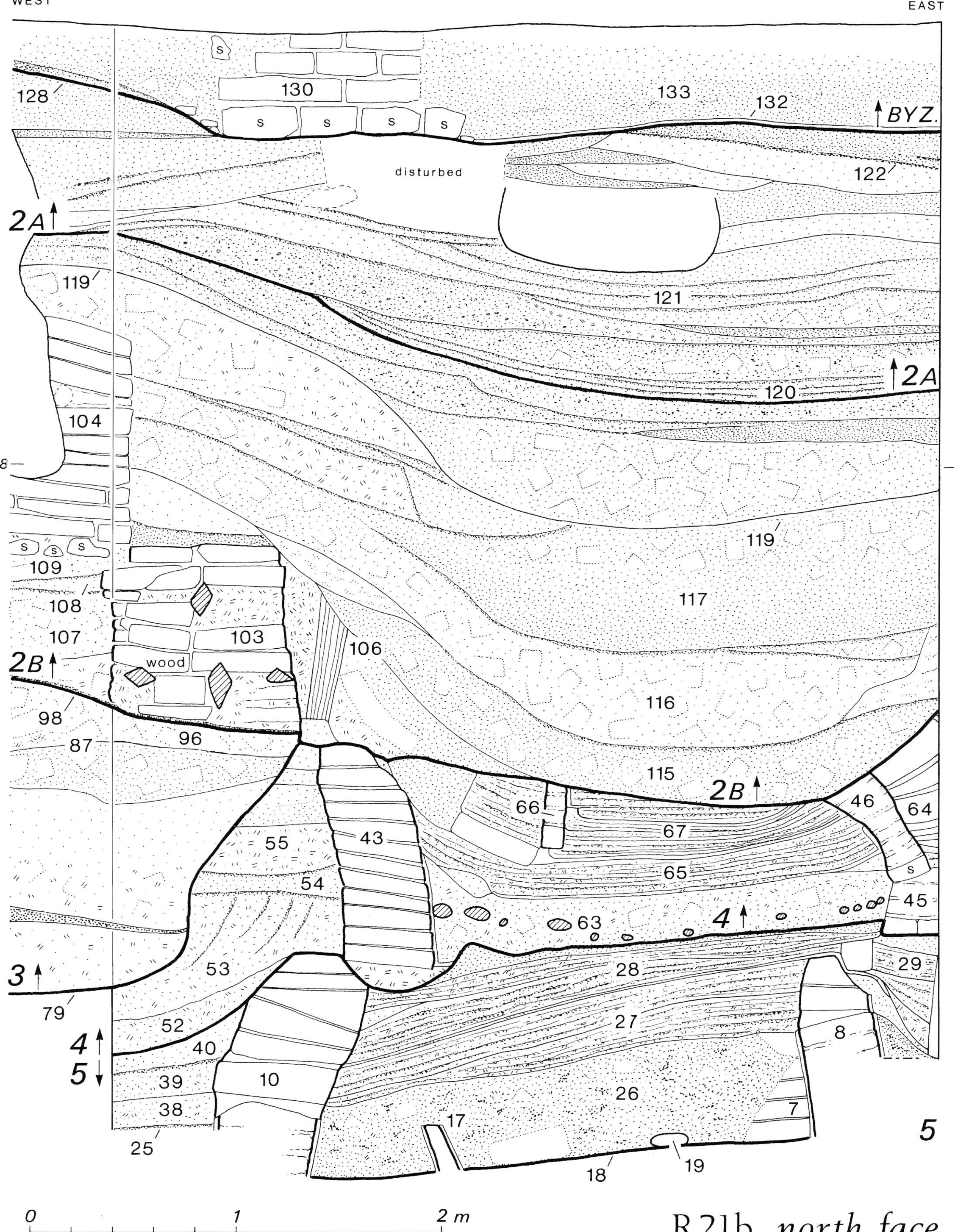

Fig. 38. Trench R21b, N Face (1:25); key on pp. 92–93

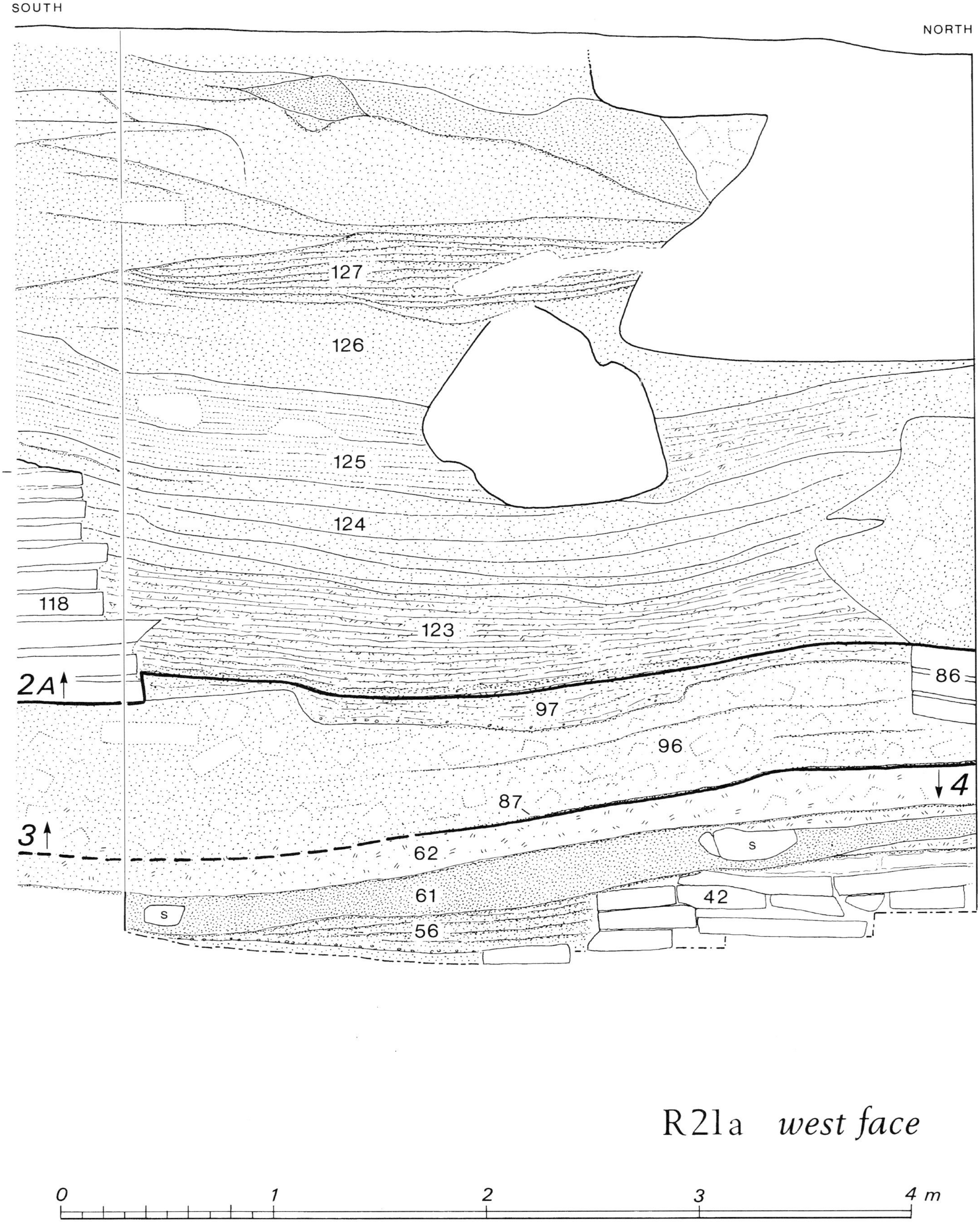

SOUTH
NORTH
127
126
125
124
118
123
2A
86
97
96
87
4
3
62
S
61
42
S
56
R21a west face
0
1
2
3
4 m

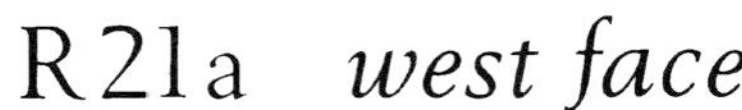

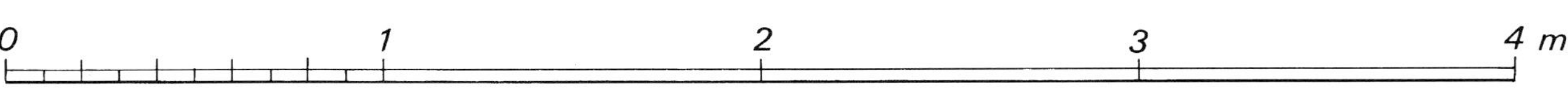

Fig. 39. Trench R21a, W Face (1:25); key on pp. 92–93

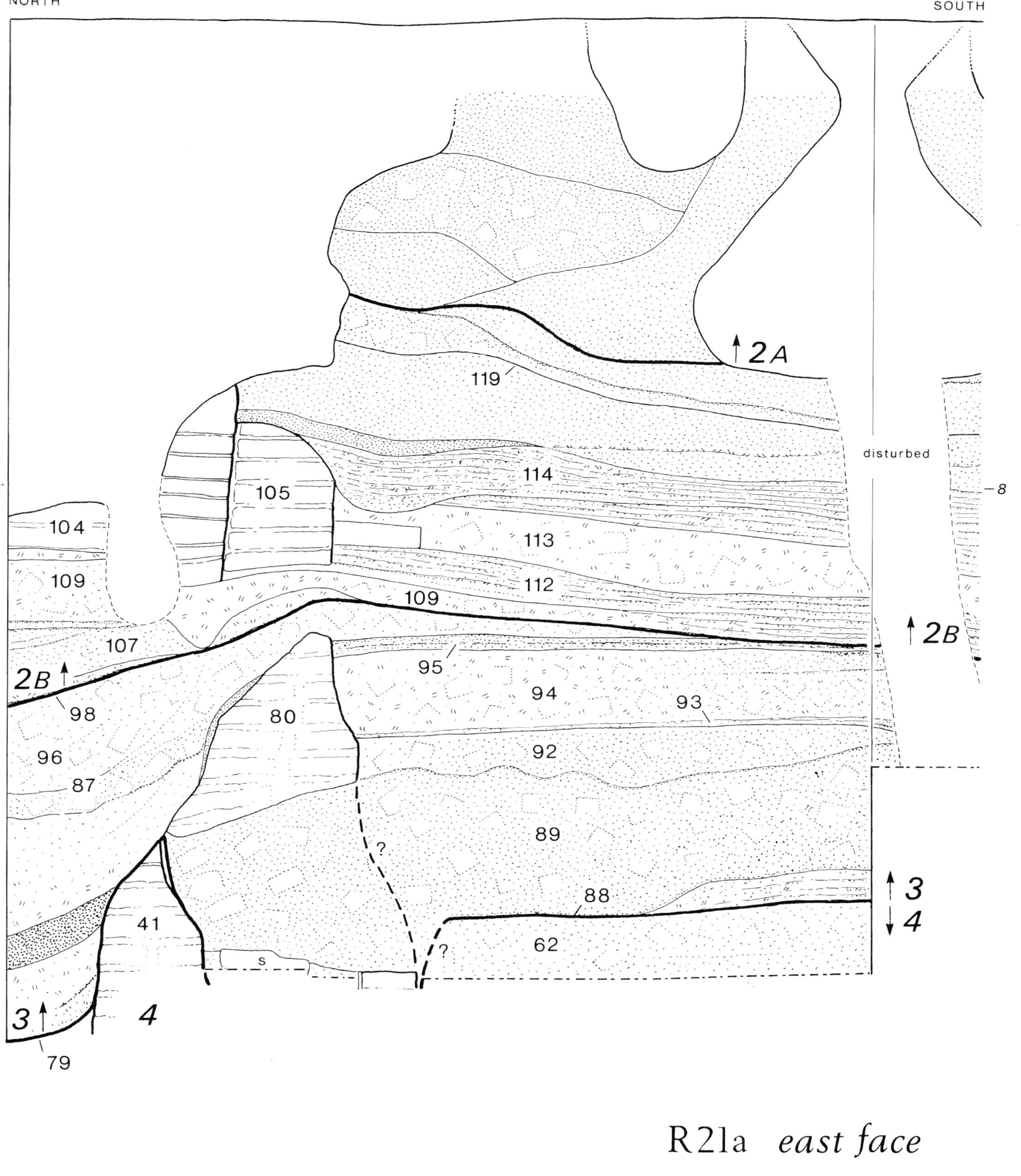

0 1 2 3 4 m

Fig. 40. Trench R21a, E Face (1:25); key on pp. 92–93

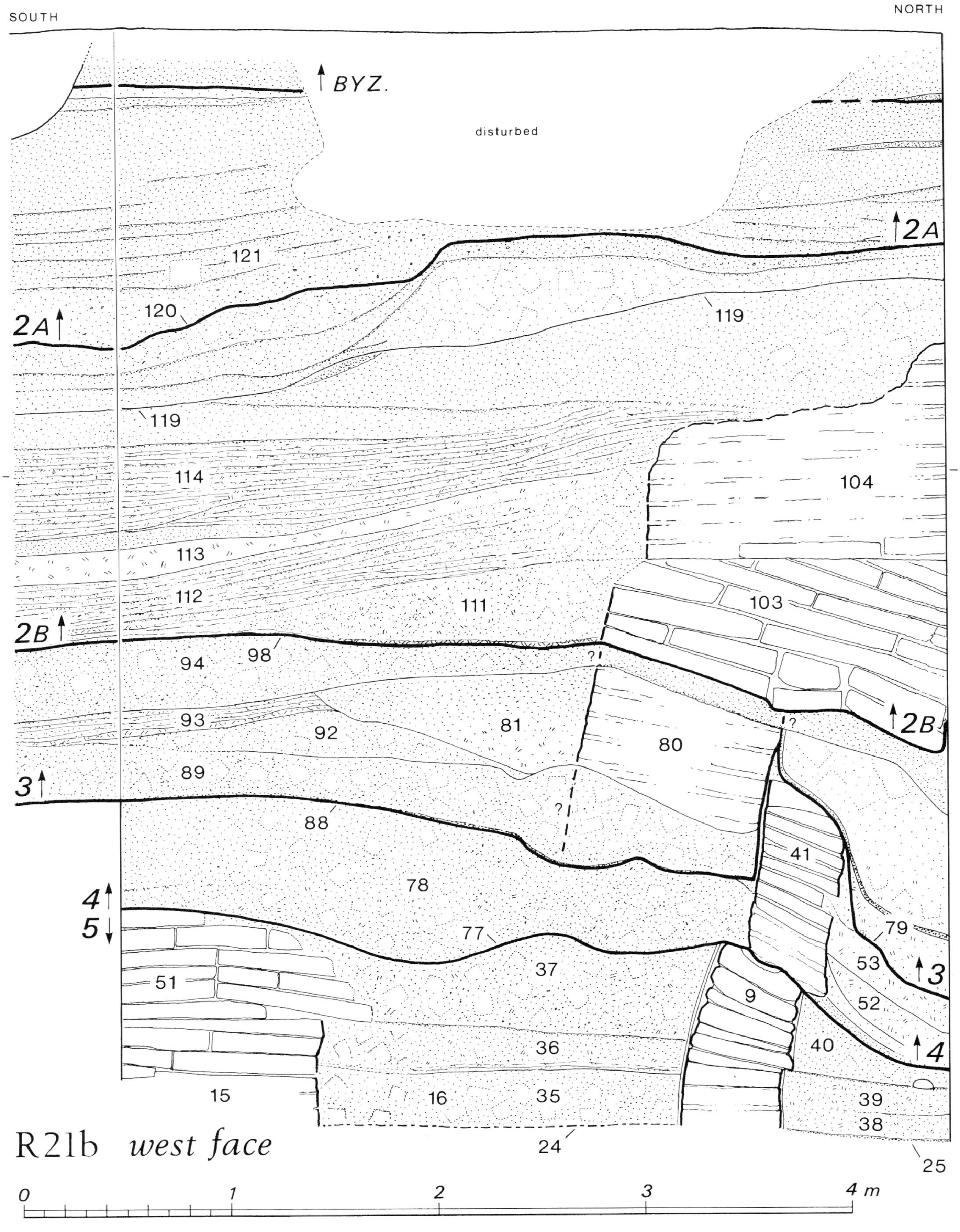

R21b *west face*

Fig. 41. Trench R21b, W Face (1:25); key on pp. 92–93

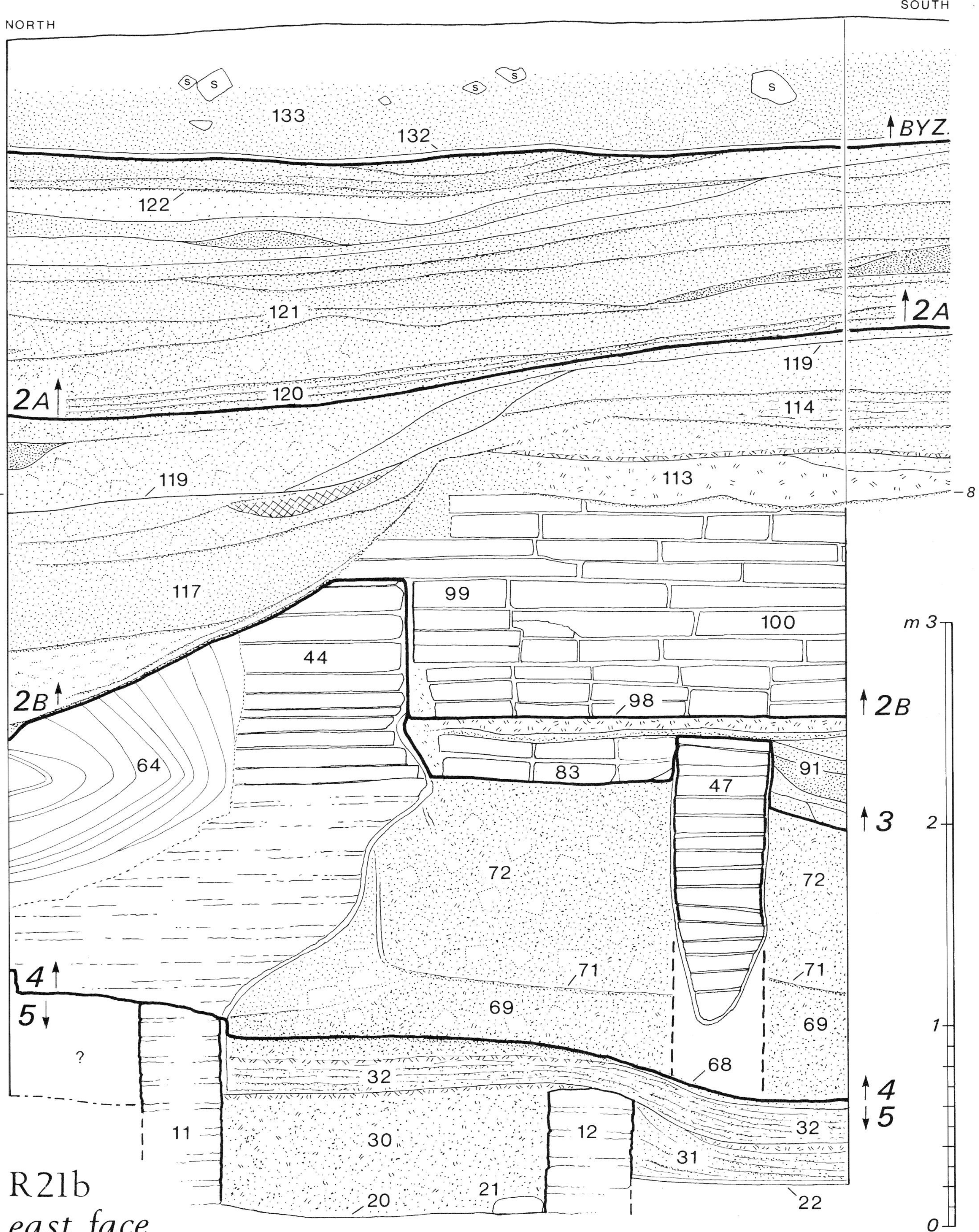

Fig. 42. Trench R21b, E Face (1:25); key on pp. 92–93

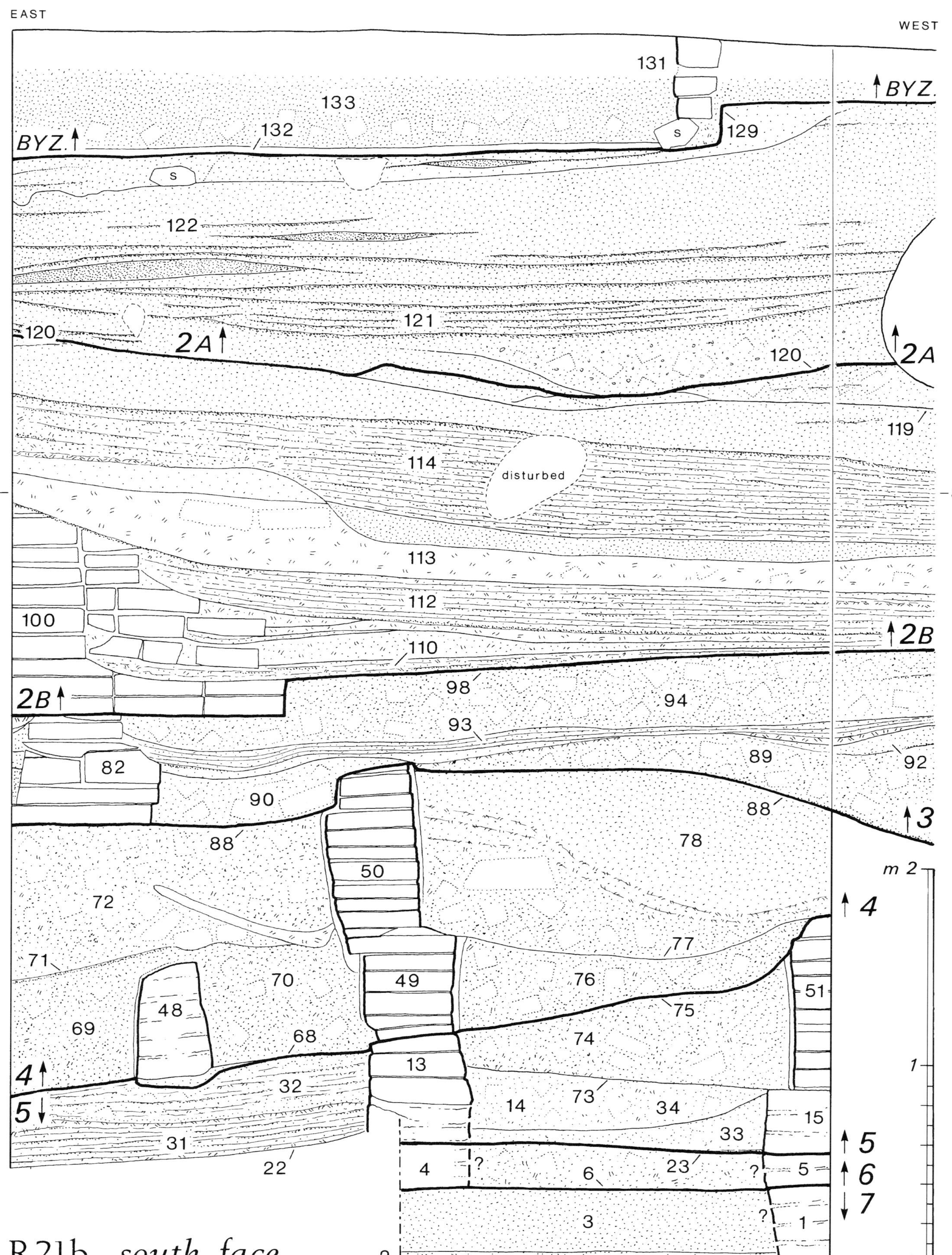

Fig. 43. Trench R21b, S Face (1:25); key on pp. 92–93

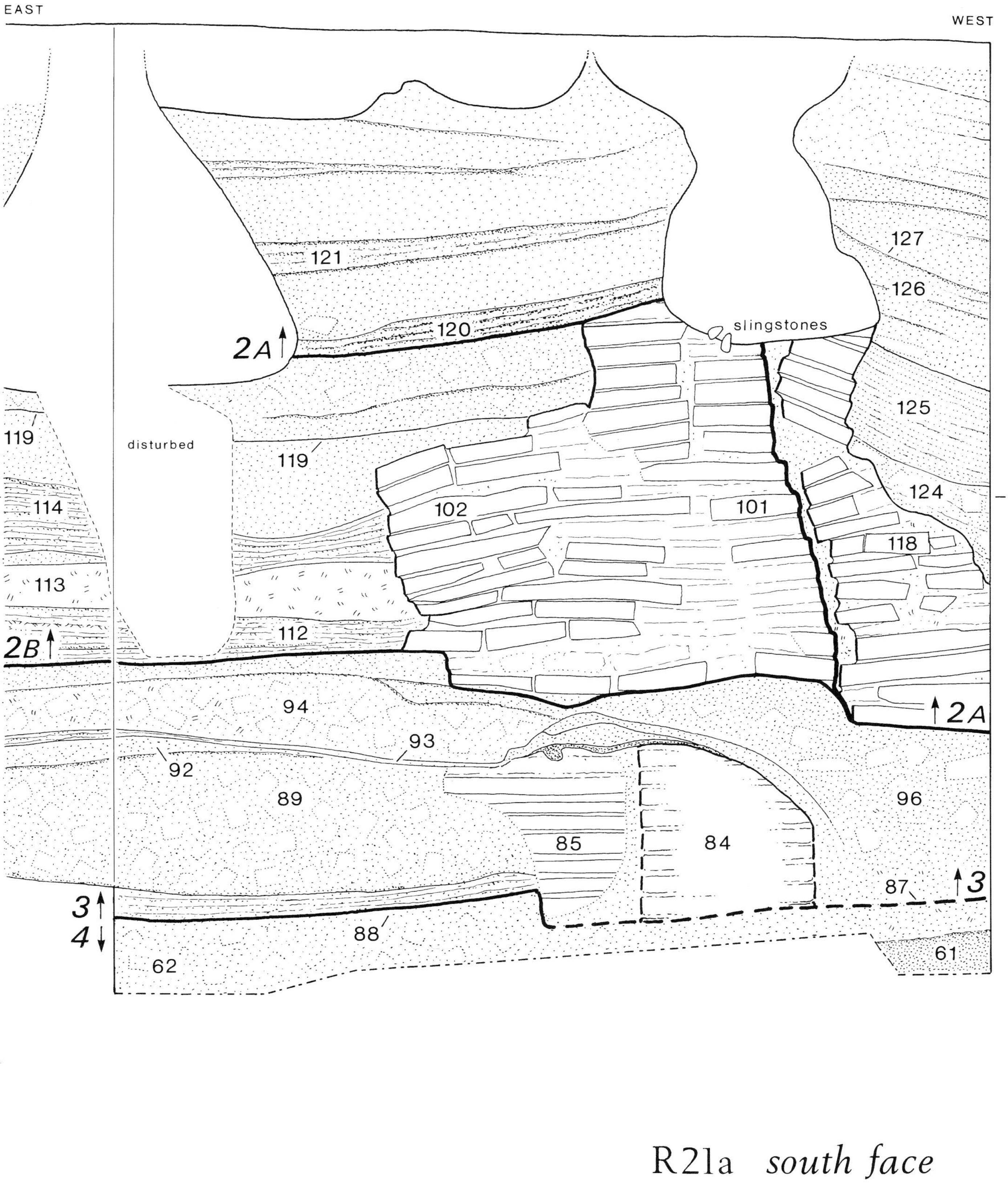

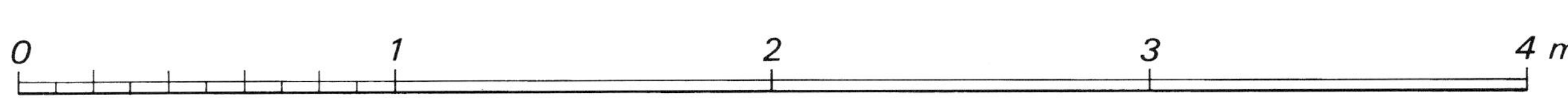

Fig. 44. Trench R21a, S Face (1:25); key on pp. 92–93

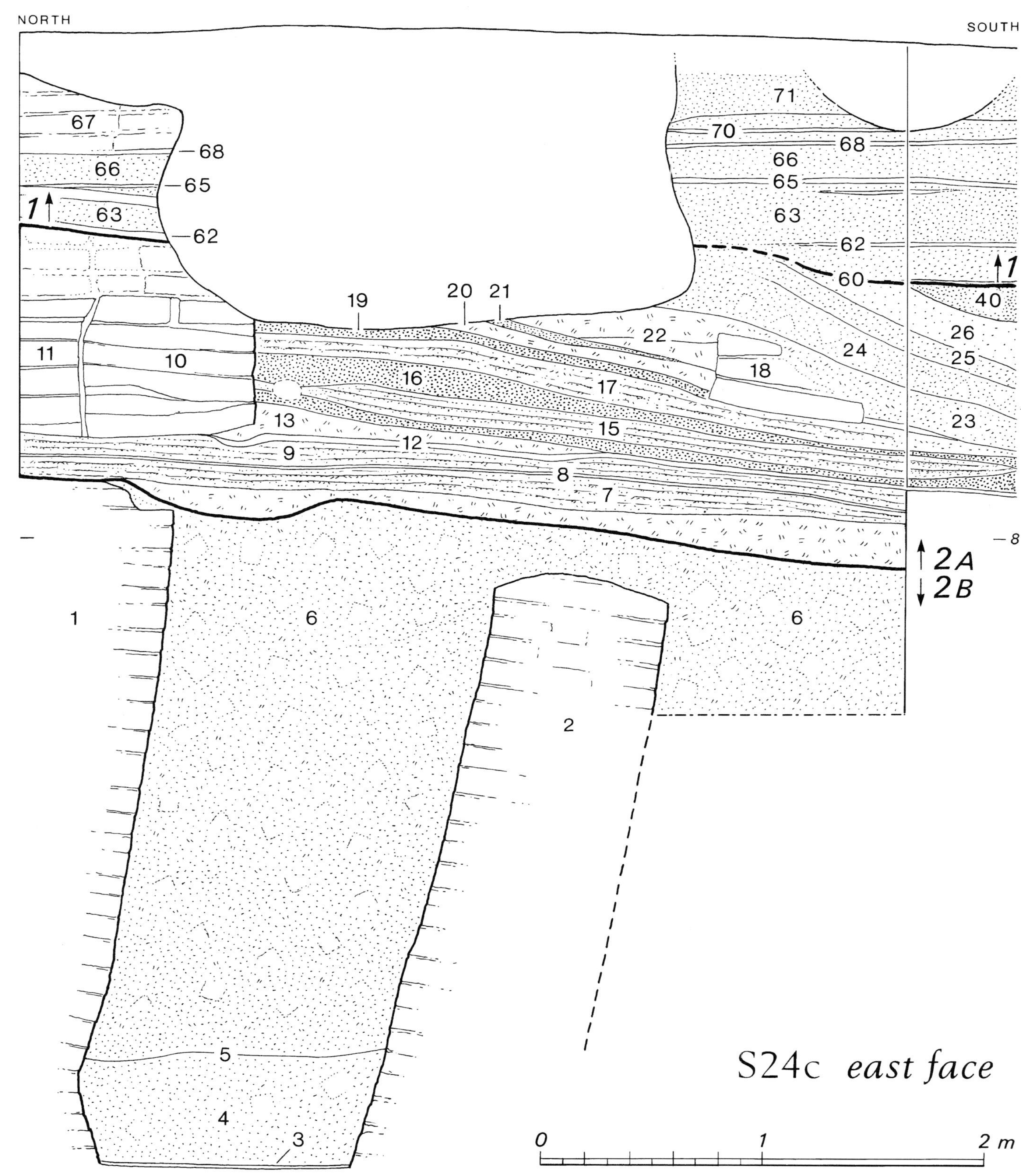

Fig. 45. Trench S24c, E Face (1:25); key on p. 93–94

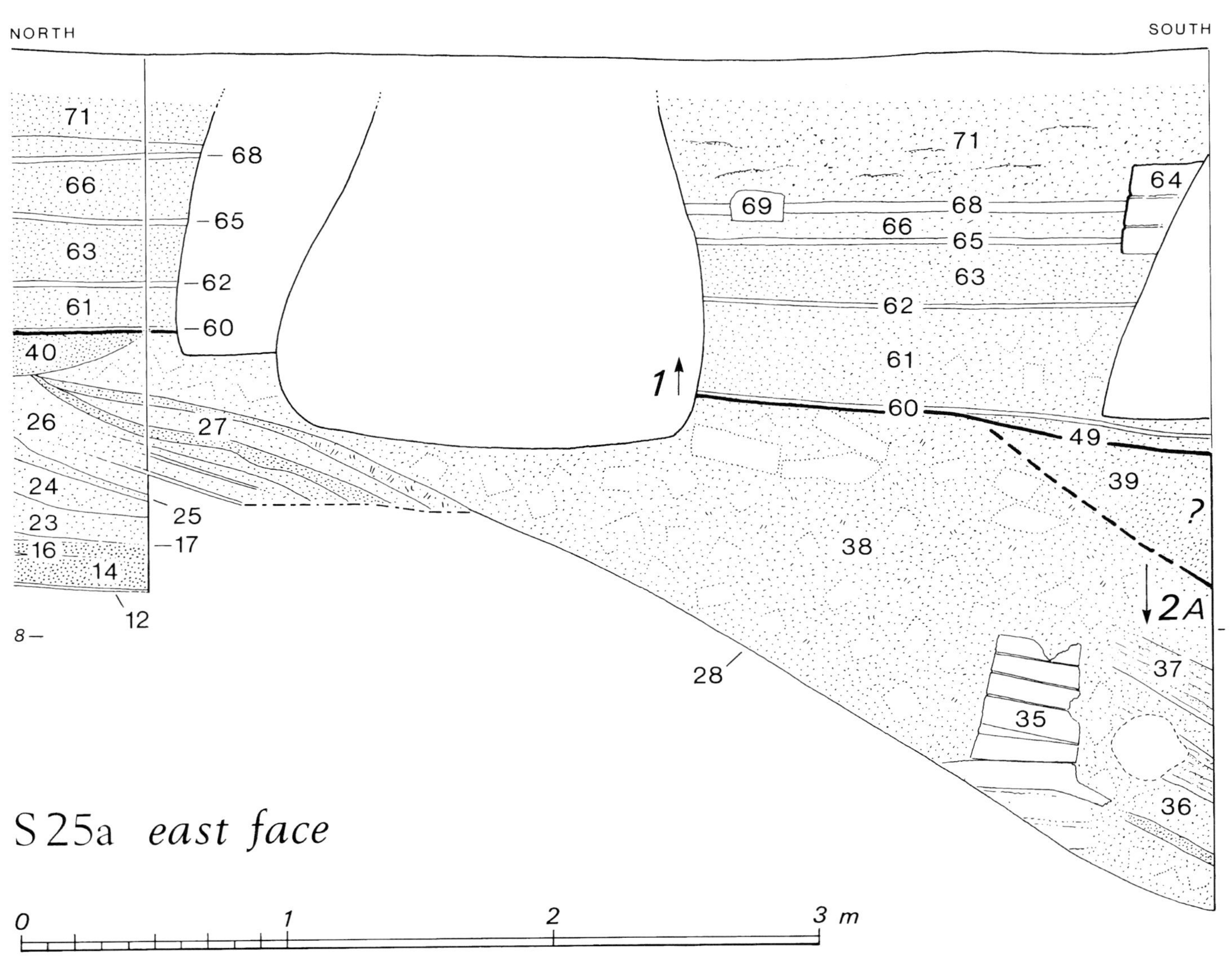

Fig. 46. Trench S25a, E Face (1:25); key on p. 93–94

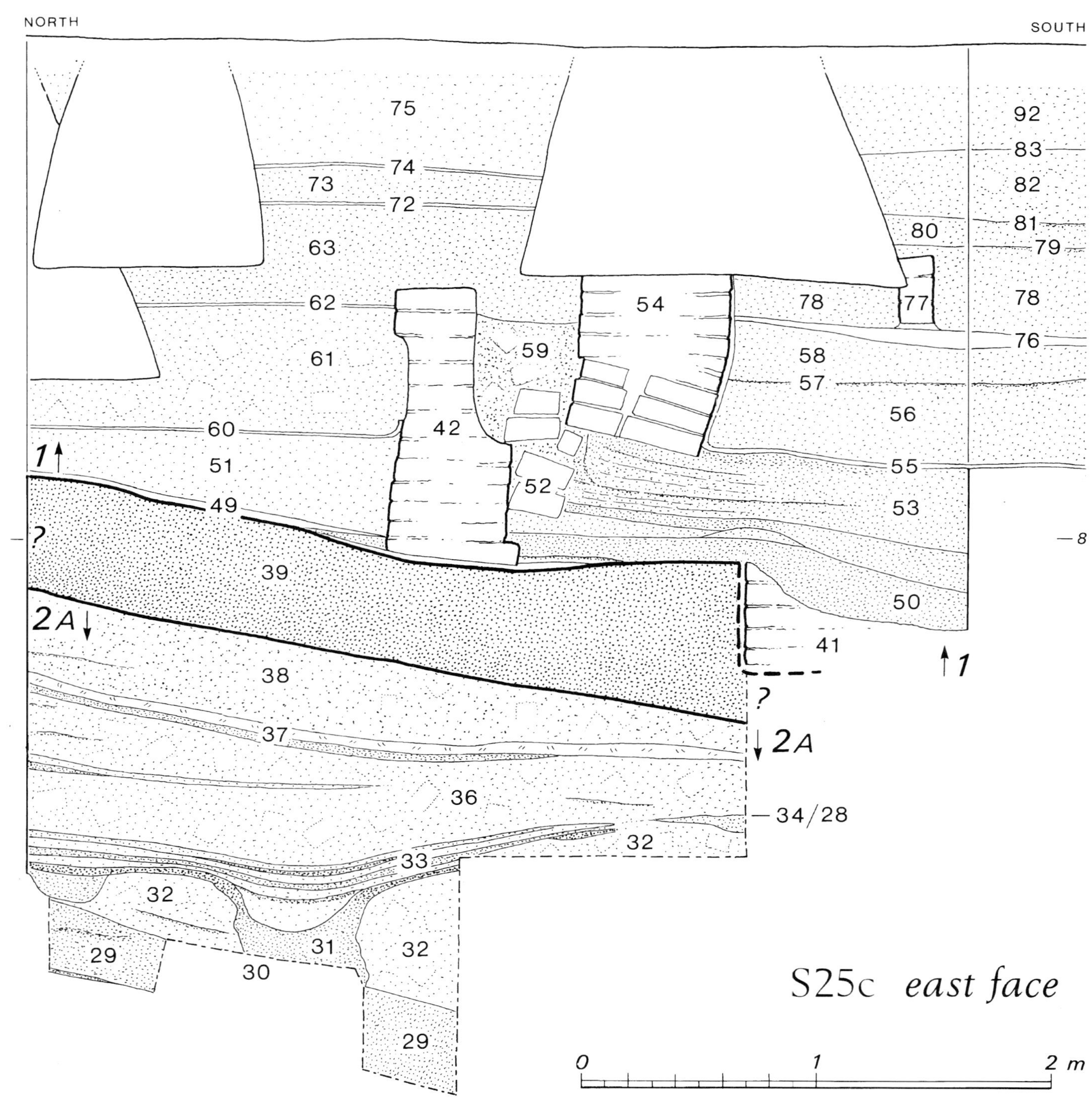

Fig. 47. Trench S25c, E Face (1:25); key on p. 93–94

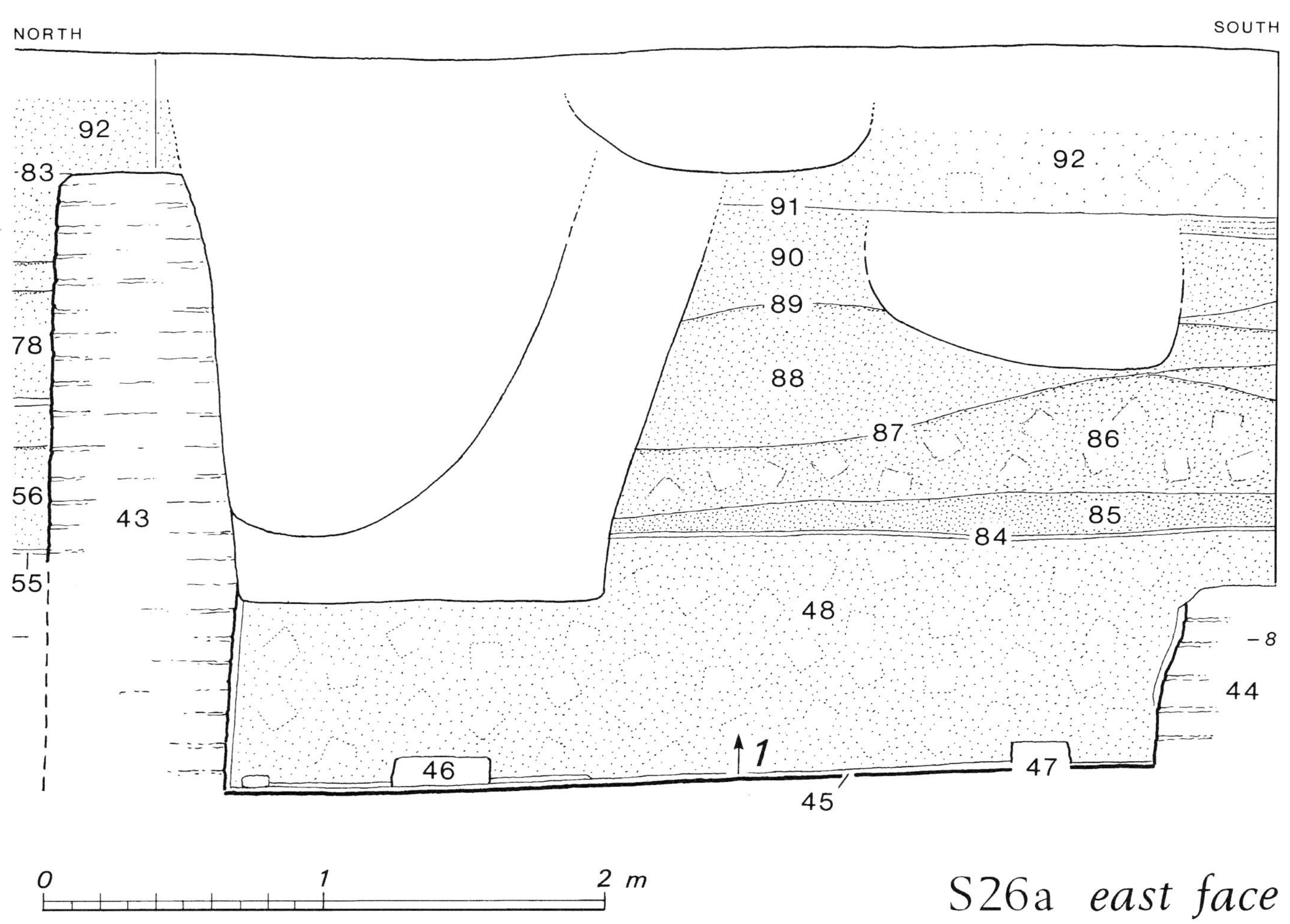

Fig. 48. Trench S26a, E Face (1:25); key on p. 93–94

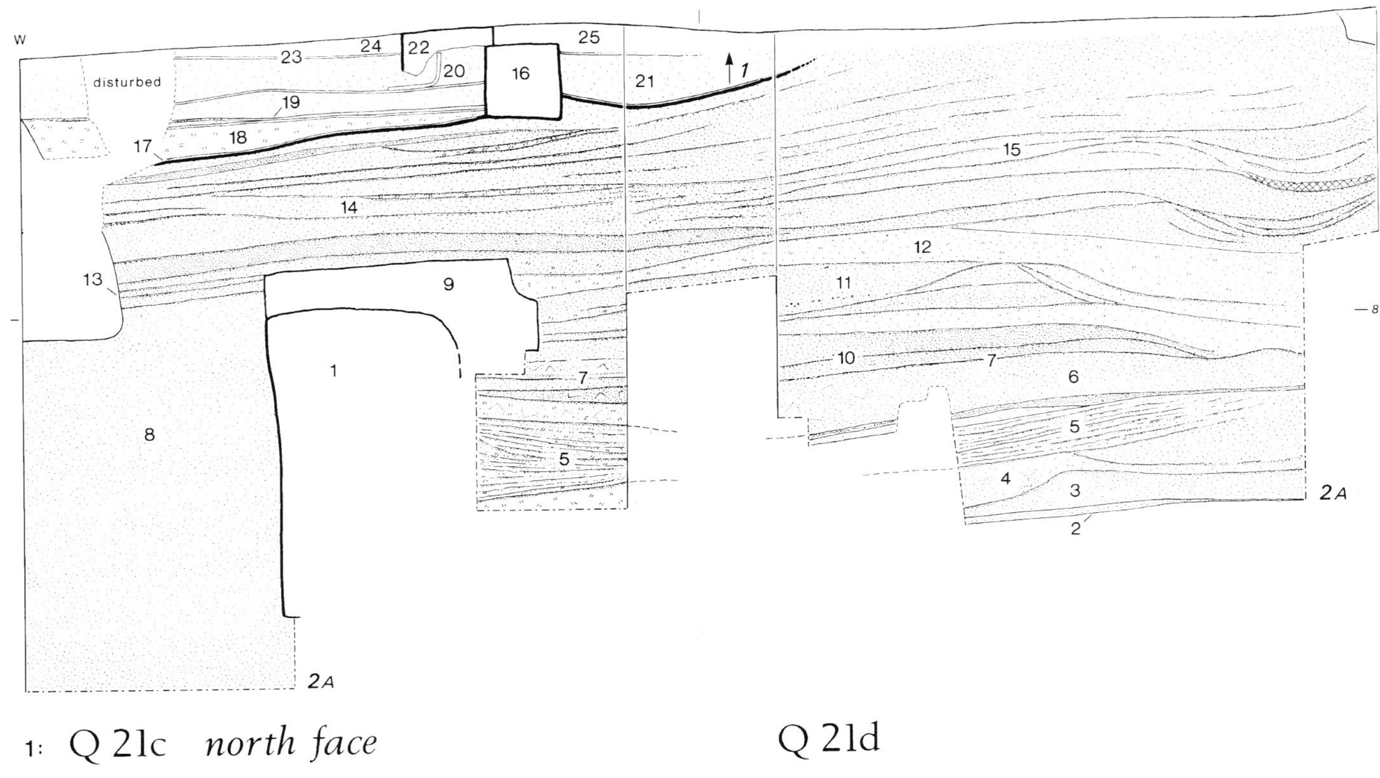

1: Q 21c *north face* Q 21d

2: Q 21c *south face* (mirror image) Q 21d

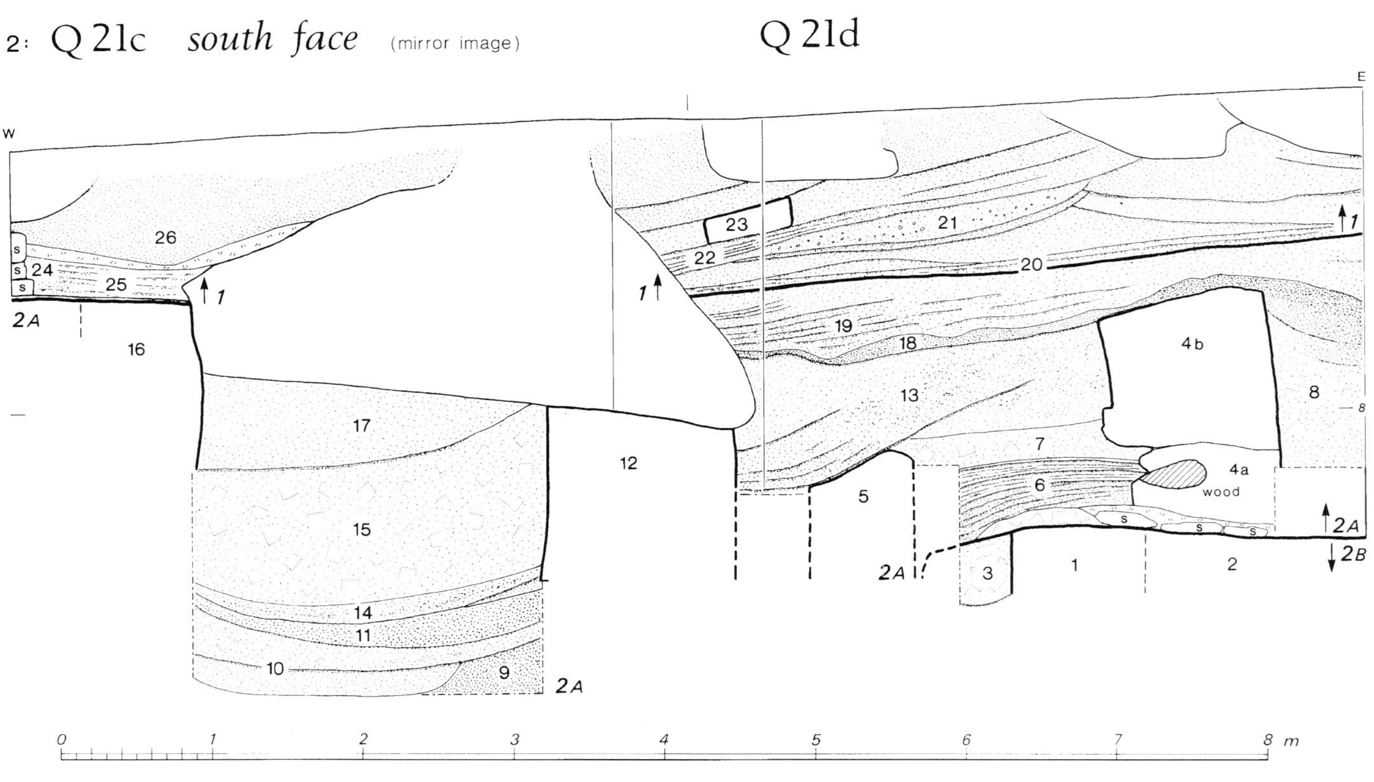

Fig. 49. Trenches Q21c & d, N Face; Q21c & d, S Face (1:50); key on p. 94–95

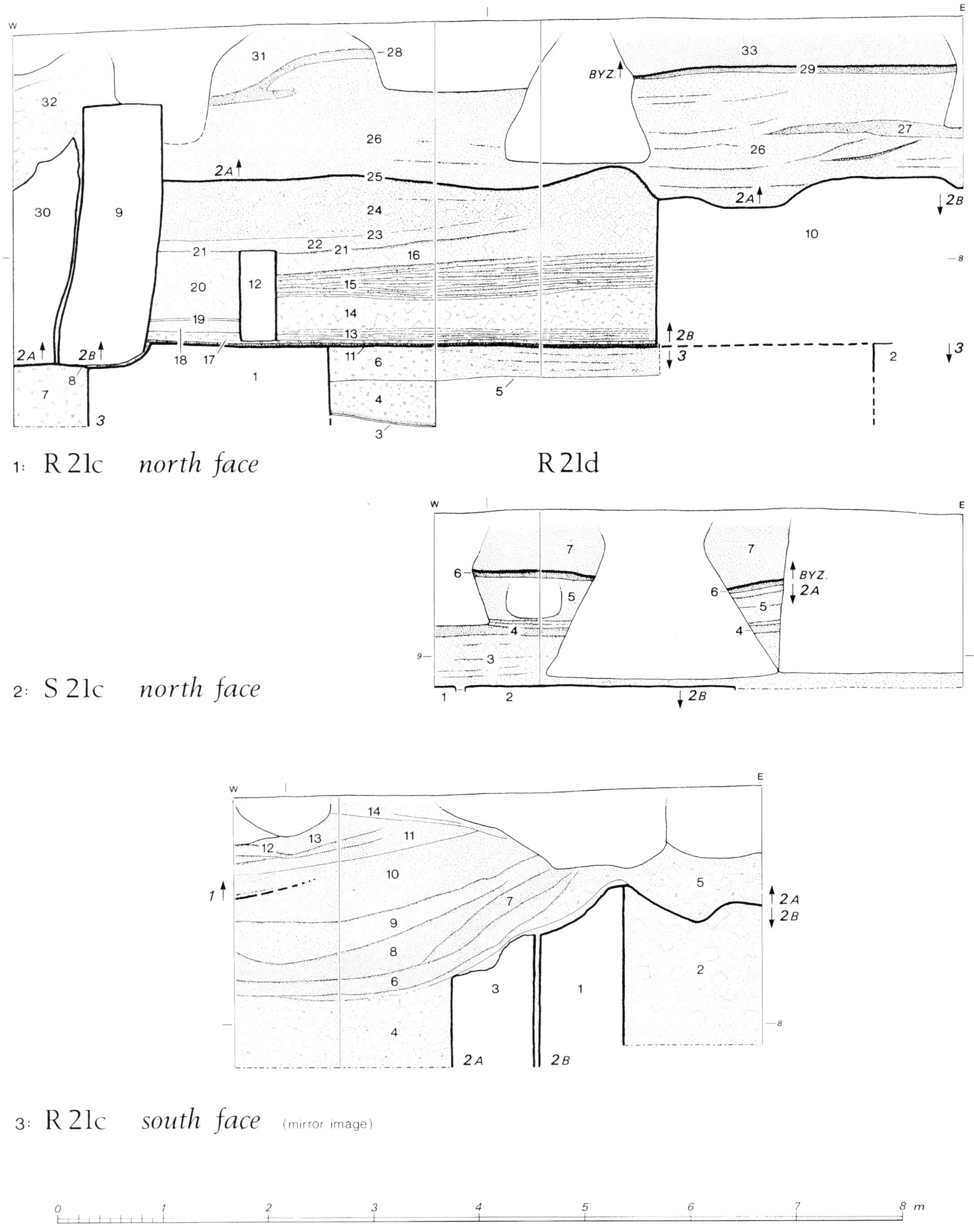

Fig. 50. Trenches R21c & d, N Face; S21c, N Face; R21c, S Face (1:50); key on p. 95–96

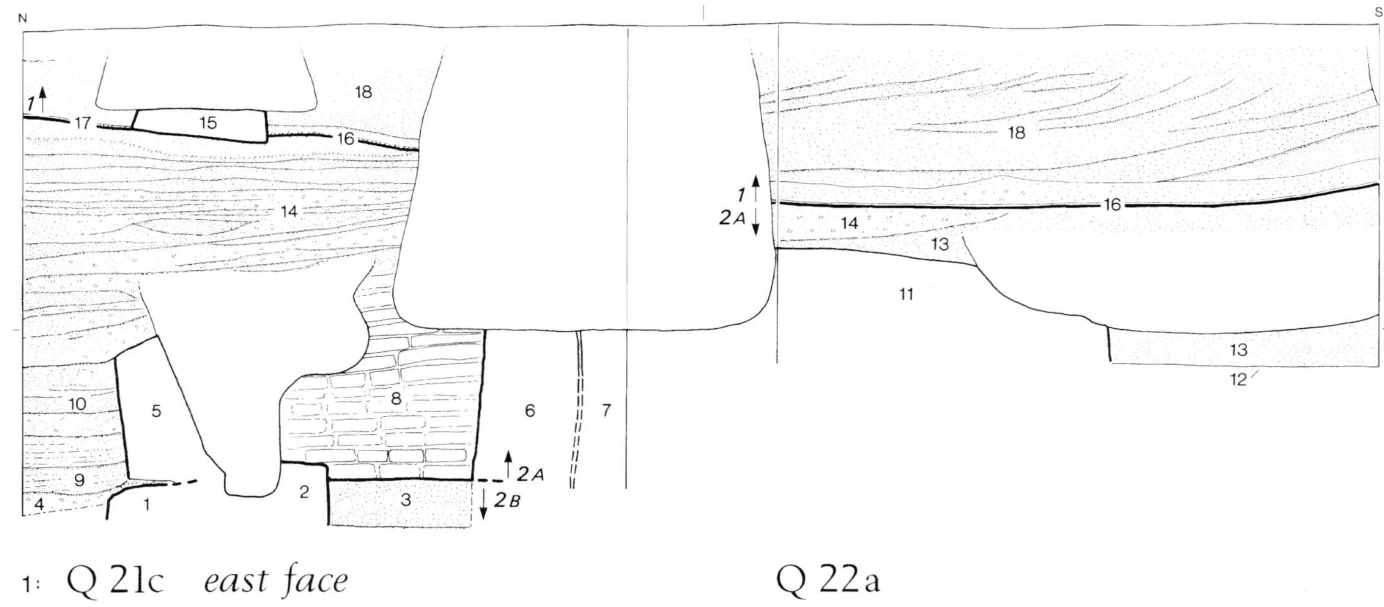

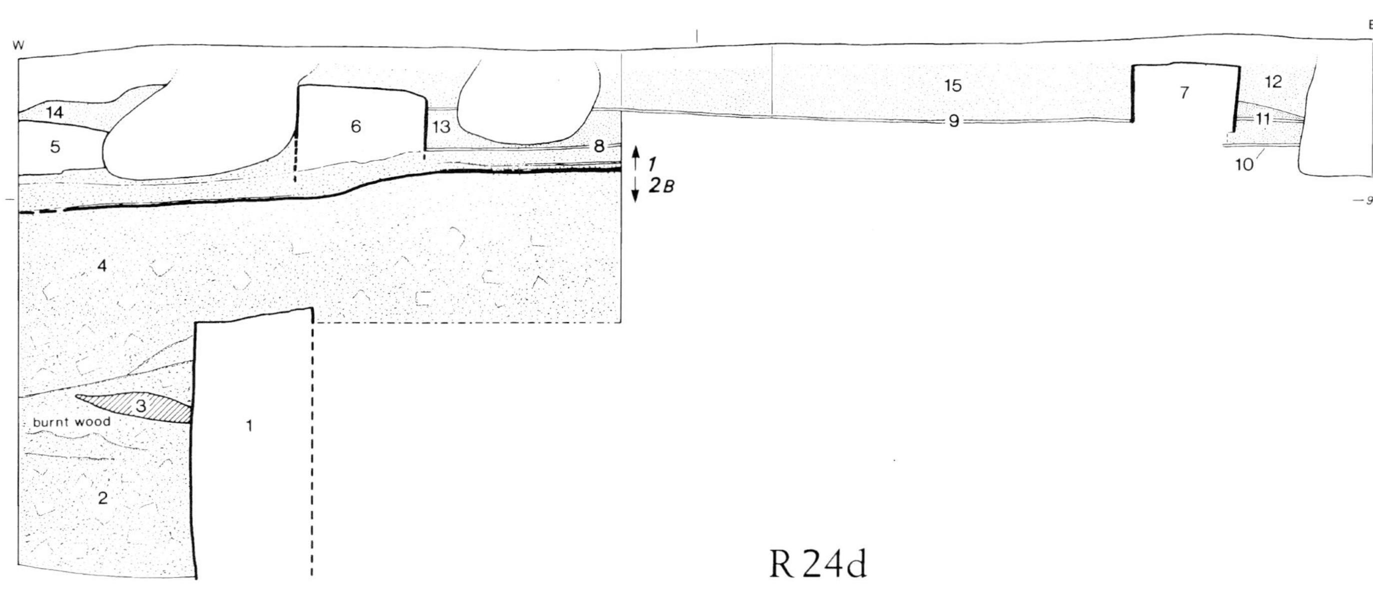

2: R 24c south face (mirror image)

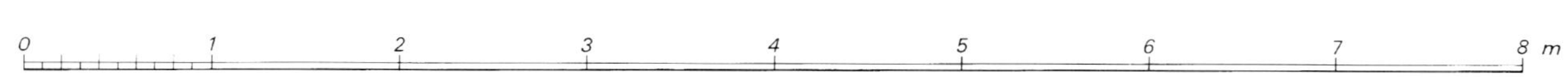

Fig. 51. Trenches Q21c and 22a, E Face; R24c & d, S Face (1:50); key on p. 96

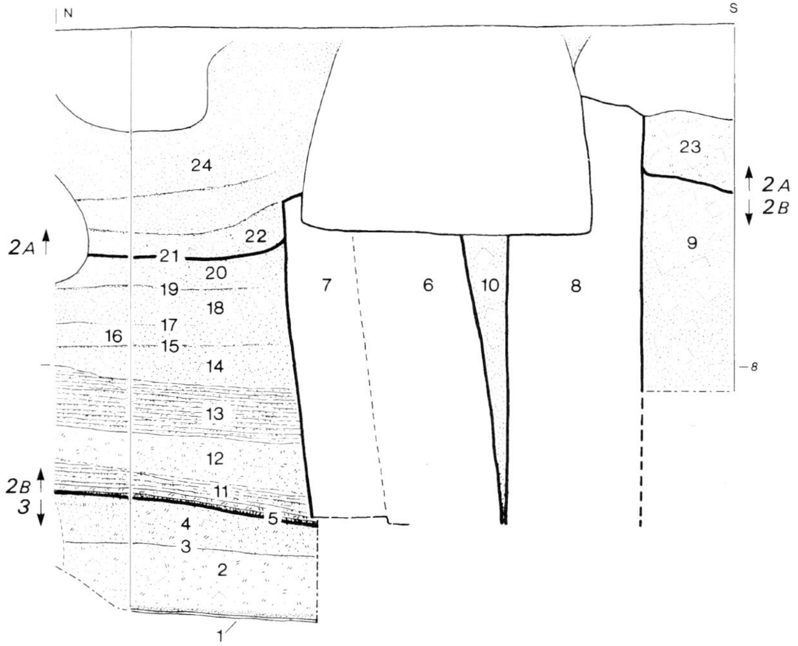

1: R21c *east face*

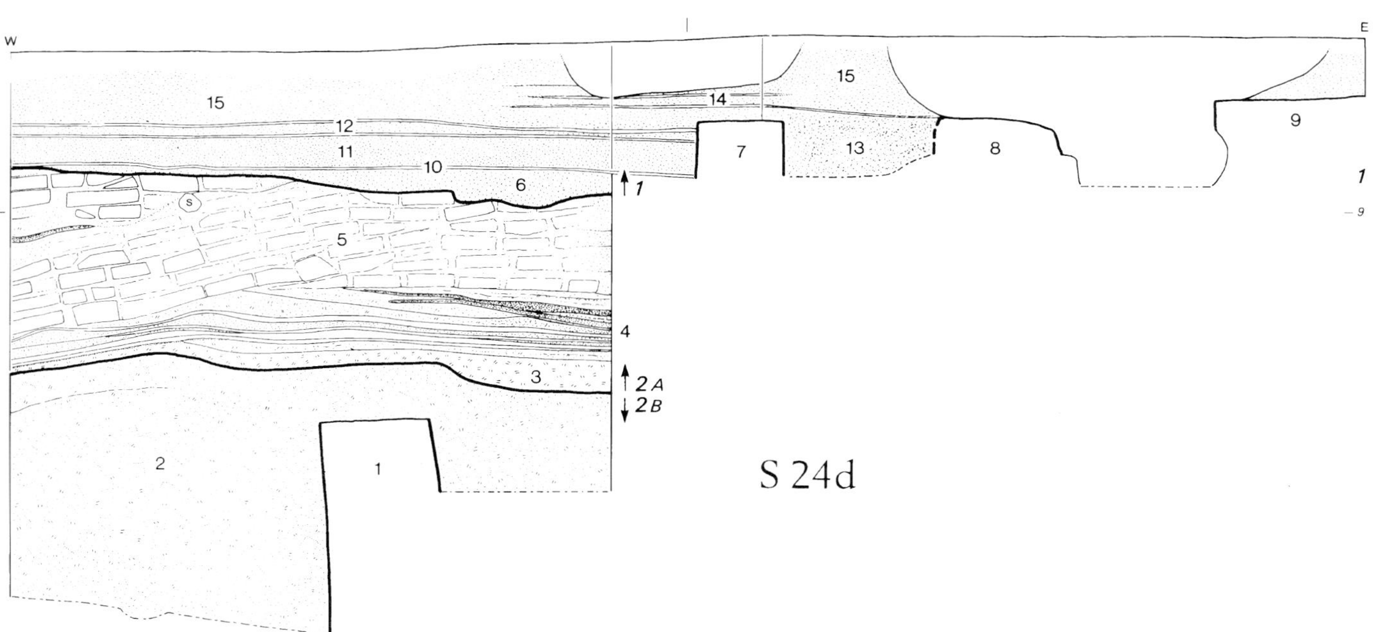

2: S 24c *south face* (mirror image)

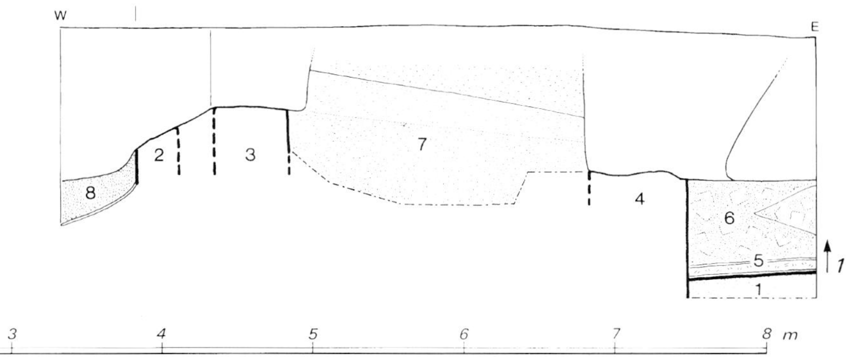

3: T 25a *north face*

0 1 2 3 4 5 6 7 8 m

Fig. 52. Trenches R21c, E Face; S24c & d, S Face; T25a, N Face (1:50); key on p. 96–97

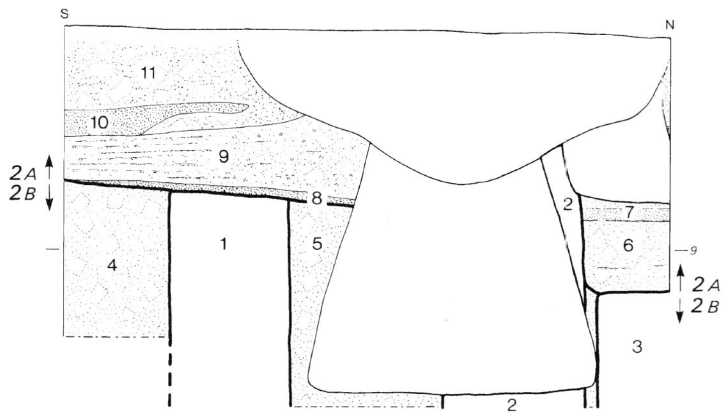

1: S 21c *west face*

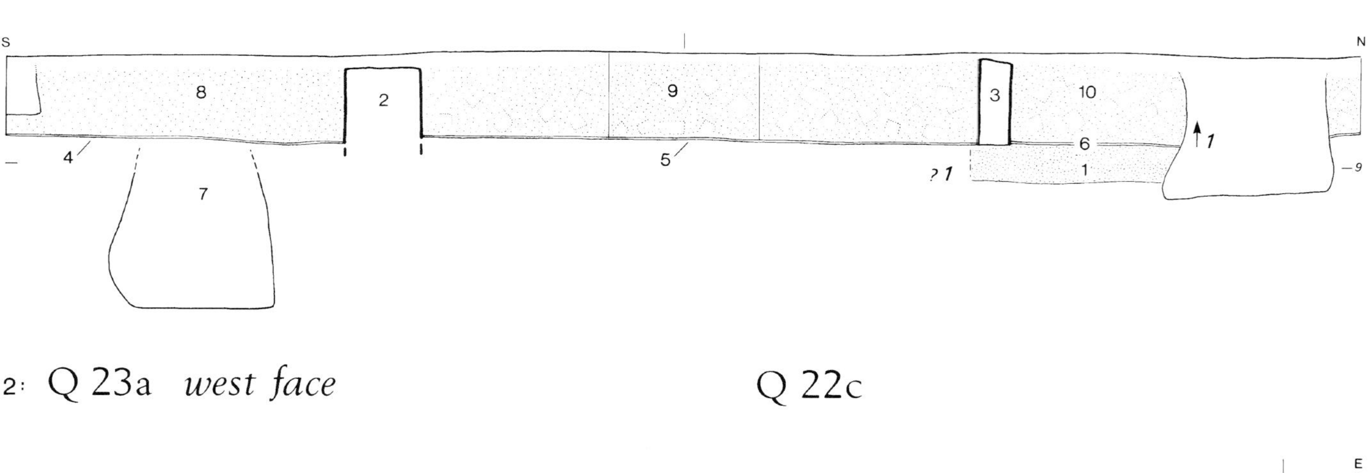

2: Q 23a *west face* Q 22c

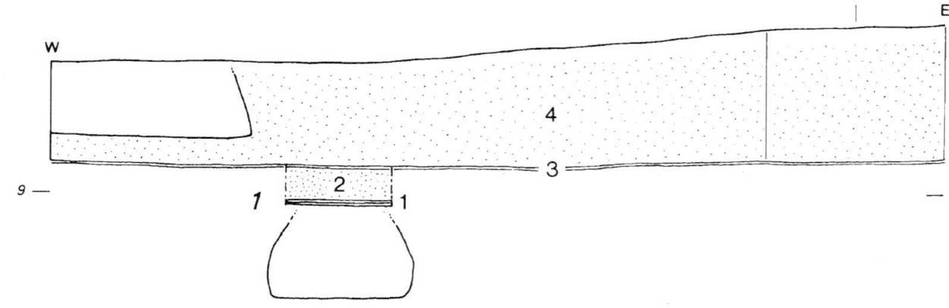

3: Q 23a *south face* (mirror image)

Fig. 53. Trenches S21c, W Face; Q23a and 22c, W Face; Q23a, S Face (1:50); key on p. 97

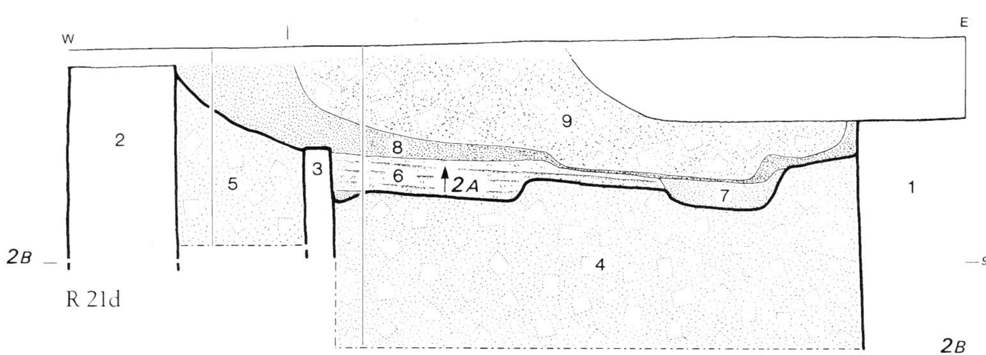

1: S 21c *south face* (mirror image)

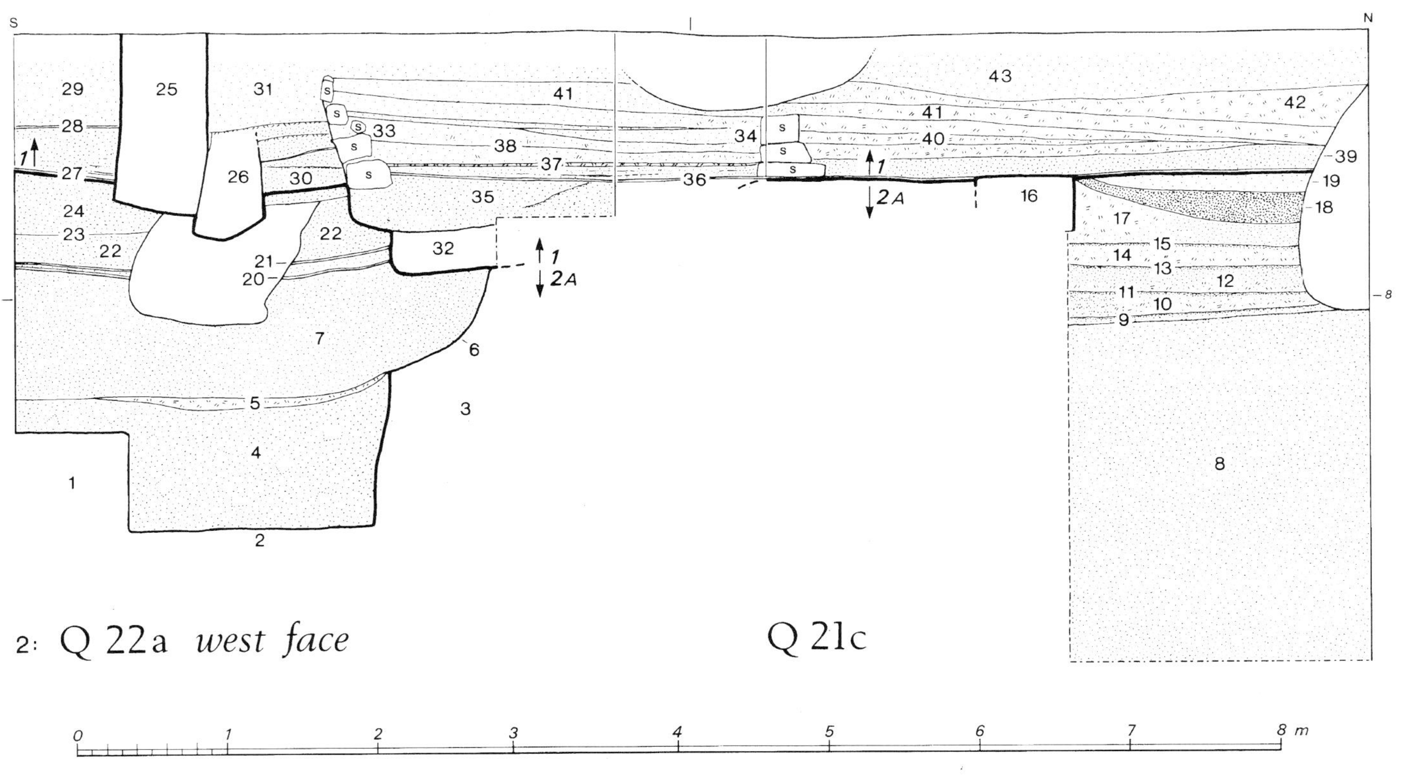

Fig. 54. Trenches S21c, S Face; Q22a and 21c, W Face (1:50); key on p. 97–98

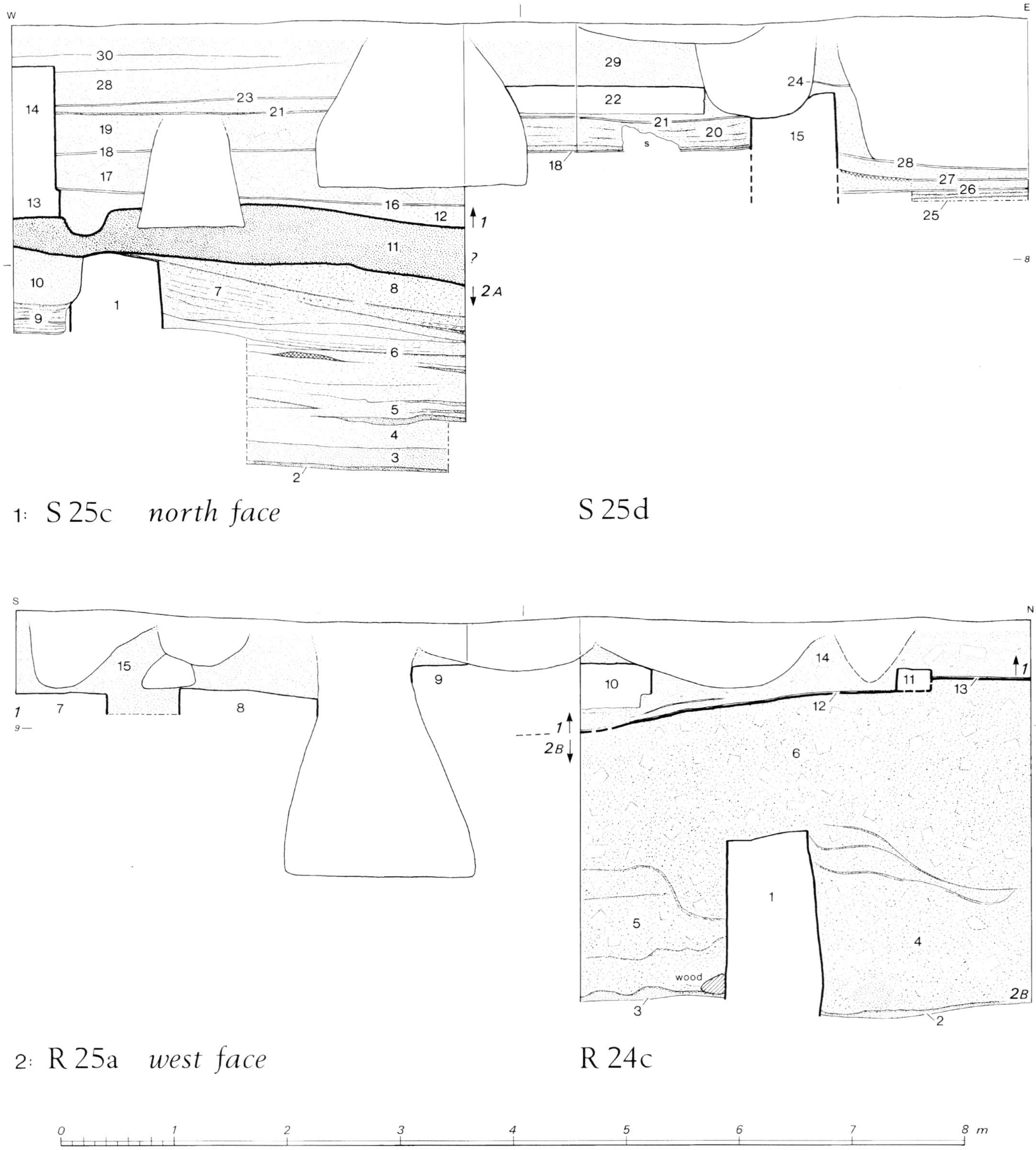

W E

30 28 14 23 21 19 18 17 13 16 12 11 10 1 7 8 9 6 5 4 3 2 29 22 21 20 s 18 24 15 28 27 26 25

1: S 25c *north face* S 25d

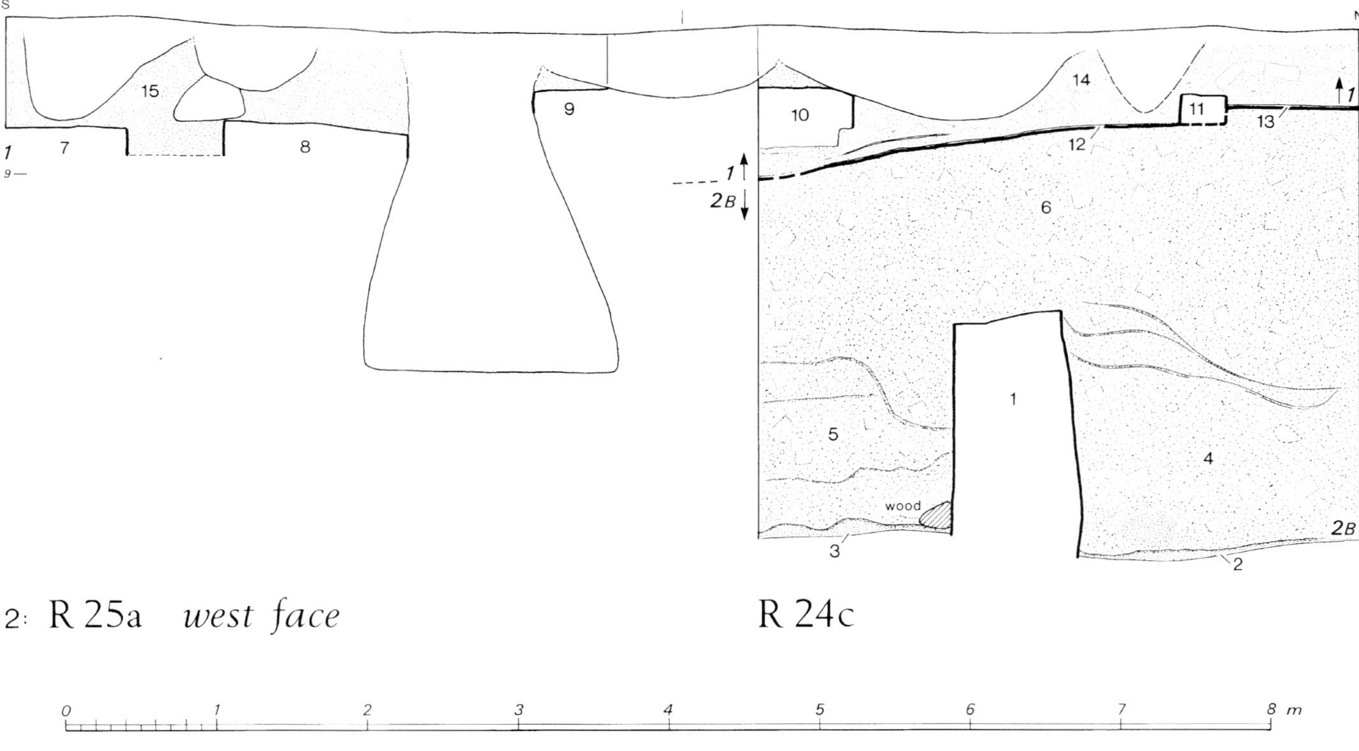

Fig. 55. Trenches S25c & d, N Face; R25a and 24c, W Face (1:50); key on p. 98

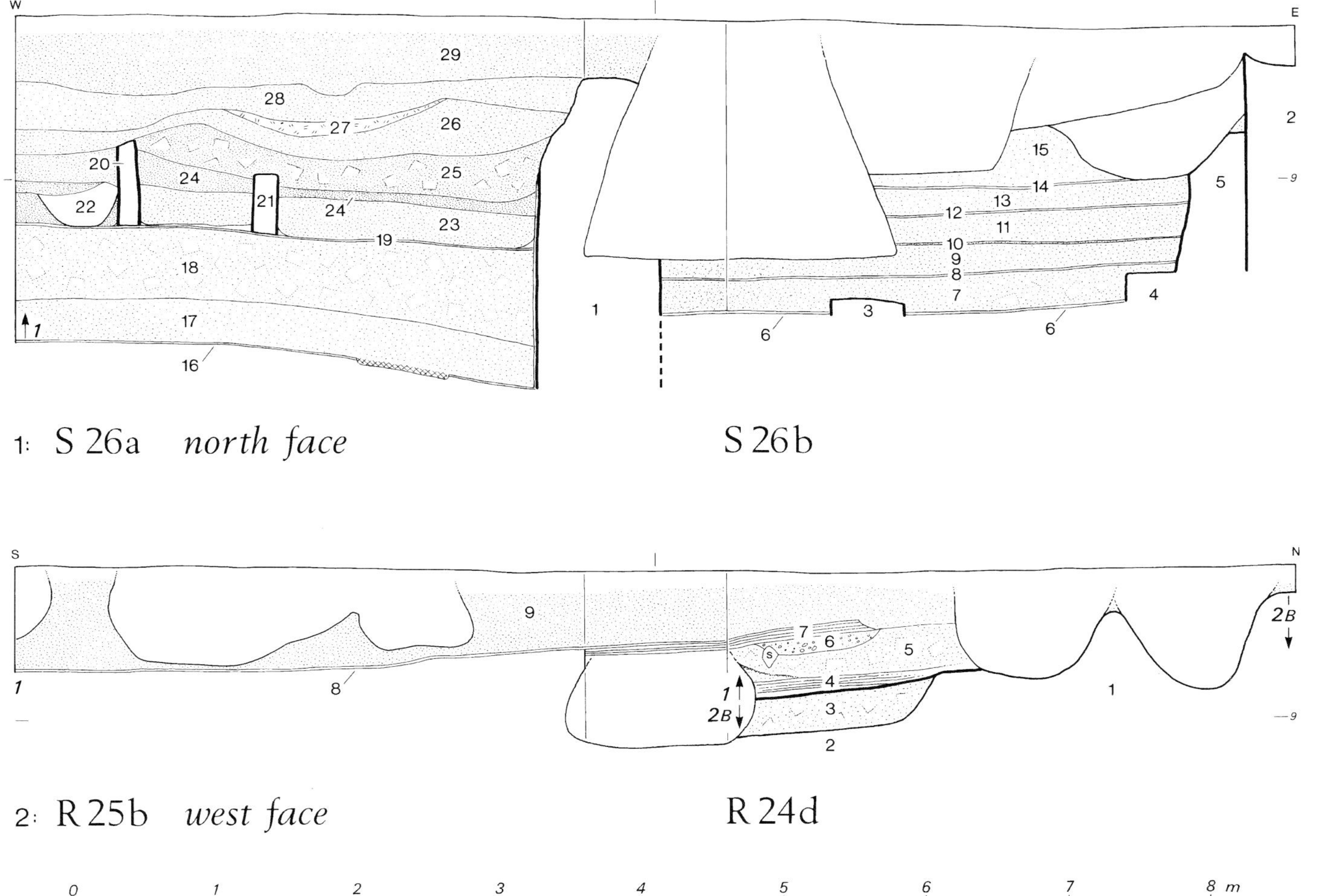

Fig. 56. Trenches S26a & b, N Face; R25b and 24d, W Face (1:50); key on p. 98–99

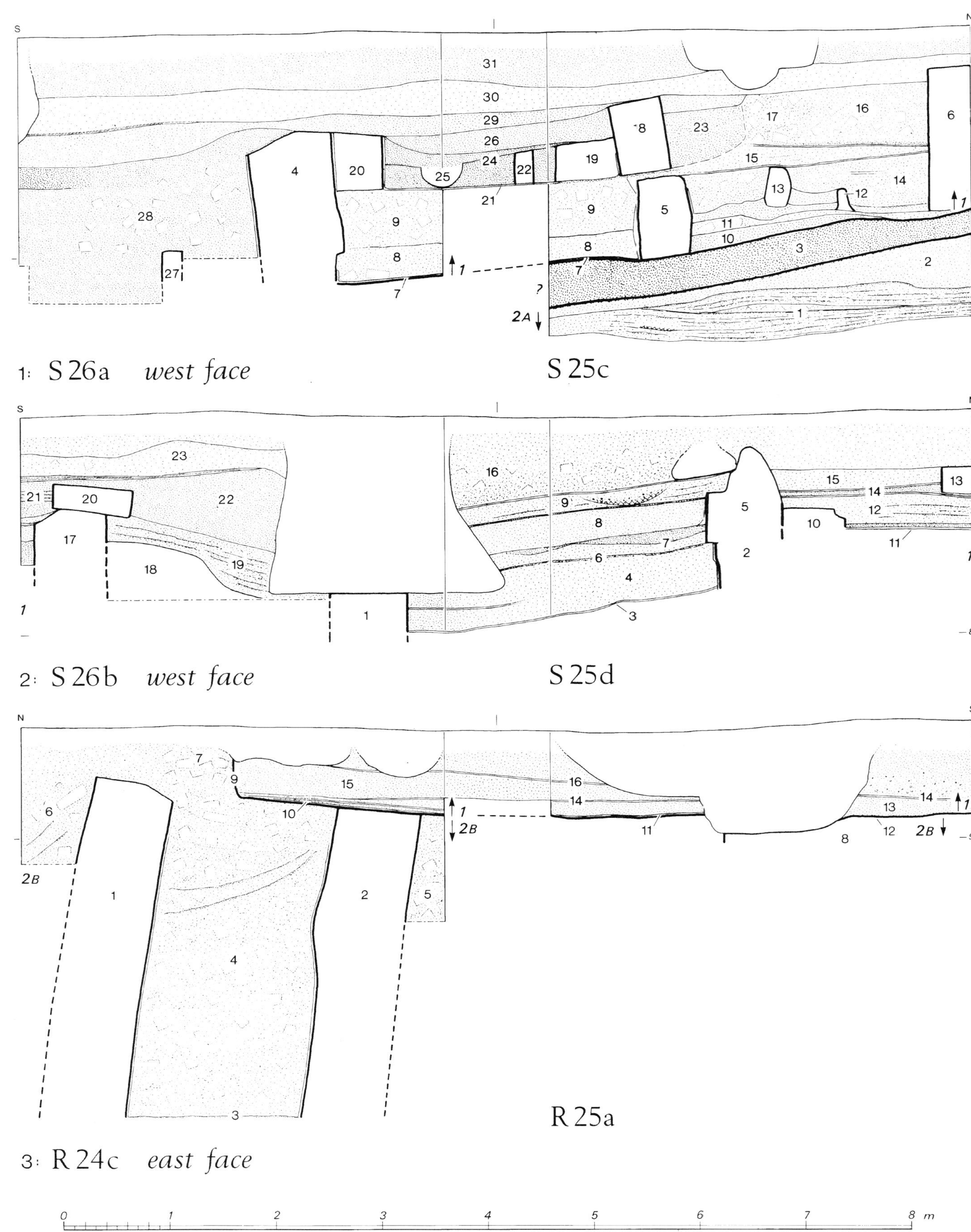

Fig. 57. Trenches S26a and 25c, W Face; S26b and 25d, W Face; R24c and 25a, E Face (1:50); key on p. 99–100

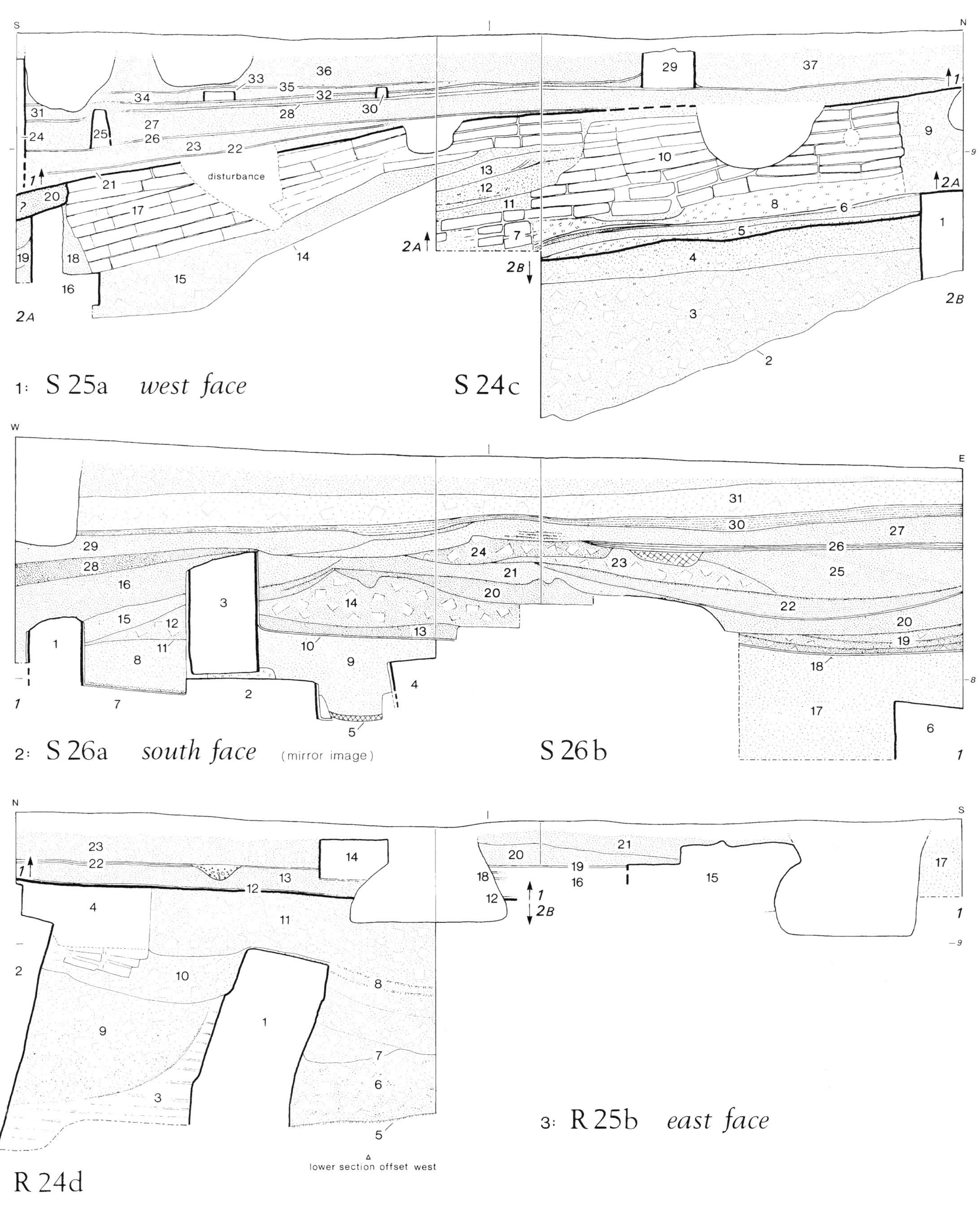

Fig. 58. Trenches S25a and 24c, W Face; S26a and b, S Face; R24d and 25b, E Face (1:50); key on p. 100–101

Key to Figs 37–44: Sections of Trenches R21a & b

Note: In the keys to all sections the figures in brackets identify the same features in the relevant plans.

Layer 7 (R21b, SE Quadrant only)

1 Wall (probable); yellow Mud-brick
2 Surfaces: mixed grey
3 Fill: yellow-brown

Layer 6 (R21b, SE Quadrant only)

4 Wall (probable)
5 Wall (probable)
6 Surface: ash on a burnt fill; below yellow-brown Mud-brick debris

Layer 5 (R21b only) (Plan, Fig. 08)

7 (1) Wall: E–W; white clay Plaster on S face
8 (2) Wall: N–S; same on W face and on N end of E face
9 (3) Wall: E–W; same on N face
10 (4) Wall: N–S; same on E and W faces
11 (5) Wall: E–W; same on N face
12 (6) Wall: E–W
13 (7) Wall: N–S; re-used in Layer 4
14 (8) Wall: E–W; (?)dividing-wall, inserted between Walls 7 & 9; on the drawing (Fig. 43) the number 14 indicates the point where Wall 8 almost touches the section
15 (9) Wall: N–S; red Mud-brick
16 (10) Wall: N–S ; white clay plaster on all faces; on the drawing (Fig. 41) the number 16 indicates the point where Wall 10 almost touches the section
17 (11) Partition: for one Bin; on Floor 15 and against Wall 3; white clay Plaster on Mud-brick
18 (15) Floor: white clay; against Walls 1–4
19 (16) Quern (stone): on Floor 15
20 (18) Floor: against Walls 2, 5 & 6
21 (19) Quern (stone): on Floor 18
22 (20) Floor: white clay; against Wall 6 & 7
23 (21) Floor and burnt Hearth: against S face of Wall 8 and E face of Wall 9
24 (24) Floor: white clay; against Walls 3 & 10; imperfectly excavated
25 (25) Floor: same; against Walls 3 & 4; imperfectly excavated
26 Fill: mixed debris and burning
27 Floors: Surfaces and ashy lines
28 Floors: same
29 Floors: same
30 Fill: mixed debris and burning
31 Floors: Surfaces and ashy lines
32 Floors: same
33 Fill: yellow-brown Mud-brick debris
34 Fill: same
35 Fill: same; above Floor 24
36 Fill: same; above a burnt Surface
37 Fill: same: above an ashy line
38 Fill: same; above Floor 25
39 Fill: same
40 Fill: same

Layer 4 (Plan, Fig. 09)

41 (1) Wall: E–W
42 (7) Wall: N–S
43 (9) Wall: E–W
44 (11) Wall: N–S; corner with Wall 10; white clay coat on a thick, yellow clay Plaster
45 (14) Facing: Mud-brick against W face of Walls 10 & 11
46 (14) Facing: Mud-brick on a stone Foundation
47 (12) Wall: E–W; perhaps a buttress or a Wall divided by a Door
48 (13) Wall: N–S
49 (2) Wall: N–S ; (?)re-built on the stump of Wall 13 (Layer 5)
50 (2) Wall: N–S; re-built on the stump of Wall 49 (Layer 4–5)
51 (3) Wall: N–S; re-use of Wall 15 (built in Layer 5)
52 Fill: yellow-brown above an ashy Surface
53 Fill: yellow-brown Mud-brick debris
54 (15) Floor: same above an ashy Surface
55 Fill: brown clay above an ashy Surface and below a dark brown and yellow, bricky fill
56 Surfaces: ashy; above a pebbly Floor; against Wall 42
57 Floor(s): brown clay
58 Surface: ashy; below Fill 59 and a brown, mixed Fill (not numbered)
59 Fill: yellow-brown Mud-brick debris
60 Fill: yellow-brown and grey on an ashy line
61 Fill: ashy
62 Fill: yellow-brown Mud-brick debris
63 Fill: yellow-brown and grey Mud-brick debris on a brown clay Surface; horizontal, N–S beams
64 Plaster: thick, red and yellow clay on Floor and face of Wall
65 (16) Surfaces: on a yellow clay
66 Facing: yellow Mud-brick
67 Floors: grey, red and yellow clay (= bottom of 66)
68 Floor: yellow clay; runs below Walls 47 & 48
69 Fill: yellow-brown Mud-brick debris
70 Fill: same
71 Floor: white and yellow clay on an ash-line
72 Fill: yellow-brown Mud-brick debris
73 Floor: yellow clay

74 Fill: yellow-brown Mud-brick debris
75 Surface: ashy
76 Fill: yellow-brown Mud-brick debris
77 Surface: ashy
78 Fill: yellow-brown Mud-brick debris

Layer 3 (Plan, Fig. 10)

79 (11) Cut
80 Walls 1 (R21a) and 2 (R21b)
81 (7) Buttress: N–S; yellow Mud-brick, partly oxydised to a bright red colour by an open fire/hearth
82 (3) Wall: N–S
83 (3) Wall: N–S
84 (5) Wall: N–S
85 (9) (?)Facing: against N face of Buttress 7; not recorded in the trench
86 (10) (?)Wall: (?)fallen Mud-brick or E face of Wall 10
87 Surface: ashy
88 Wall: same
89 Fill: yellow-brown Mud-brick debris
90 Fill: same; above Surface 88 and against W face of Wall 82
91 Fill: same; against E face of Wall 82
92 Fill: same
93 Floors: brown clay and ash
94 Fill: yellow-brown Mud-brick debris
95 Floors: grey clay and ash
96 Fill: yellow-brown Mud-brick debris
97 Fill: gravel and ash-lines

Layer 2B (Plans, Figs 11, 19)

98 Surface: dark brown clay, ash and sand
99 (7.1) Wall: E–W
100 (7.2) Wall: N–S
101 (7.5) Wall: N–S
102 (7.10) Buttress: E–W
103 (7.7) Wall: N–S
104 (7.6) Wall: E–W; (?)correctly to be assigned to Layer 2A
105 (?)Bench or Facing, against Wall 104; not illustrated on the plan, Fig. 19
106 Plaster: red
107 Fill: yellow-brown Mud-brick debris
108 Line: ash
109 Fill: yellow-brown Mud-brick debris
110 Floors: brown clay and ash
111 Fill: yellow-brown, ash and Mud-brick debris, against Wall 7.6
112 Floors: yellow clay and ash
113 Fill: yellow clay
114 Floors: greyish brown clay with ash, and white clay
115 Fill: grey Mud-brick debris, sherds and animal bones
116 Fill: yellow Mud-brick debris on a line of blue sand and ash
117 Fill: yellow-brown and grey Mud-brick debris on a line of sherds and ash

Layer 2A (Plans, Figs 23, 24)

118 (1.1) Wall: N–S
119 Line: ash below yellow-brown, ash and Mud-brick debris
120 Lines and fill: ash-lines and ash-lenses, Mud-brick debris, gravel and sand, below a sandy line
121 Lines: ash
122 Lines and fill: ash-lenses, Mud-brick debris, gravel and brown earth, above a sandy line
123 Floors: ashy
124 Fill: green Mud-brick debris
125 Fill: yellow and red clay, and sandy lines
126 Fill: yellow-brown
127 Lines: ash-lines in yellow-brown

Byzantine Layer (Plan, Fig. 32)

128 (5) Cut
129 (6) Cut
130 (1) Wall: E–W; Mud-brick on a stone Foundation
131 (2) Wall: N–S; same
132 (4) Floor: grey clay
133 Fill: soft, ashy, grey with Mud-brick and grey, chunky debris

Key to Figs 45–48: E Face of Trenches S24c, 25a & c, 26a,

Layer 2B (Plans, Figs 11, 20)

1 (10.2) Wall: E–W
2 (10.21) Wall: E–W
3 Surface (?= Floor)
4 Mud-brick debris
5 Surface (?= Floor)
6 Mud-brick debris

Layer 2A (Plans, Figs 23, 25)

7 Floors and Surfaces: above a fill of yellow-brown clay
8 Floor: thin white clay
9 Floors and Surfaces
10 (5.5) Buttress
11 (5.1) Wall: E–W
12 Floor: yellow clay
13 Packing: brown clay
14 Ash: black
15 Surfaces: brown and white clay
16 Ash: black
17 Surfaces: clay and ash
18 Mud-brick (?= Wall)

19 Ash: grey
20 Fill: yellow-brown
21 Ash: grey
22 Fill: olive-grey clay
23 Fill: same
24 Fill: Mud-brick debris
25 Fill: greyellow-brownrown
26 Fill: yellow-brown and ash-lines
27 Fill: yellow-brown above grey ash
28 Line: greyish clay
29 Fill: yellow-brown, grey, dense white ash
30 Excavators' pedestal below bone-pile
31 Bone-pile: in dark ash and yellow-brown
32 Fill: yellow-brown and Mud-brick debris
33 Lines: ash, yellow clay, greyellow-brownrown
34 Line (= 28): greyish clay
35 Mud-brick (?= Wall)
36 Fill and Surfaces: yellow-brown debris, multiple Surfaces, ash-lines
37 Lines and Surfaces: multiple Surfaces and ash-lines
38 Fill: yellow-brown and Mud-brick debris

Layer (?)

39 (?): soft, black earth, 'dead', i.e. featureless and unstructured; (?)organic, humic origin; cp. Figs 55.1(11) & 57.1(3)
40 'Scoop': ashy above a white ash-line

Layer 1 (Plans, Figs 26, 28–31)

41 Wall: (?)foundation-cut not observed in the trench; not on the Plan (Fig. 31)
42 (48) Wall
43 (53) Wall
44 (72) Wall
45 (65) Floor: white clay
46 Mud-brick
47 Mud-brick
48 Fill: yellow-brown and Mud-brick debris
49 Floor: reddish clay overlying a hard-packed earth
50 Fill: yellow-brown, dusty, 'dead'
51 Fill: brown, ashy
52 Mud-brick
53 Ash-lines and ashy fill: above a thin Floor
54 (77) Wall
55 Floor: white clay
56 Fill: yellow-brown and Mud-brick debris
57 Floor: underlying black ash
58 Fill: yellow-brown and Mud-brick debris
59 Fill: yellow-brown, Mud-brick debris and ash
60 Floor: white clay
61 Fill: yellow-brown and Mud-brick debris
62 Floor: red clay
63 Fill: yellow-brown
64 (84) Partition
65 Floor: white clay
66 Fill: yellow-brown
67 (42) Wall and Plaster
68 Floor: white clay
69 Mud-brick
70 Floor: white clay
71 Fill: grey with ash-line
72 Floor: white clay
73 Fill; yellow-brown
74 Floor: white ash on red
75 Fill: yellow-brown
76 Floor: white clay
77 Mud-brick or Mud-brick Partition: not on the Plan (Fig. 30)
78 Fill: yellow-brown
79 Floor: black ash on white clay
80 Fill; yellow-brown
81 Floor: black ash on white and yellow clay
82 Fill: yellow-brown and brown
83 Line: ashy
84 Floor: white clay
85 Fill: ashy
86 Fill: yellow-brown and Mud-brick debris
87 Line: ashy
88 Fill: yellow-brown and ashy
89 Line: ashy
90 Fill: yellow-brown
91 Line: ashy
92 Fill: yellow-brown

Key to Fig. 49.1: Sections of Trenches Q21c & d, N Face

Layer 2A (Plans, Figs 23, 24)

1 (2.16) Wall
2 Floor: hard, brown clay
3 Fill: yellow-brown
4 Fill: yellow-brown and ash
5 Floors: grey and brown clay below yellow clay and ash
6 Fill: yellow-brown below a line of ash and gravel
7 Line: ash
8 Fill: yellow-brown (?)Mud-brick, 'dead', i.e. featureless and unstructured
9 (2.17) Wall
10 Lines and ashy fill
11 Fill: yellow-brown and ash-lines
12 Fill: yellow-brown
13 Lines: ash
14 Lines: ash with red Mud-brick debris
15 Lines: ash and yellow-brown

Layer 1 (Plans, Figs 26, 27)

16 (1) Wall
17 Floor: white clay

18 Fill: yellow clay
19 Floor: white clay
20 Floor and Wall-plaster: yellow clay
21 Fill: yellow-brown
22 Wall: discovered by brushing the surface dust; not illustrated on the Plan, Fig. 27
23 Floor: white clay
24 Fill: red, burnt
25 Fill: same

Key to Fig. 49.2: S Face of Trenches Q21c & d (mirror image)

Layer 2B (Plans, Figs 11, 16)

1 (4.5) Wall
2 (4.14) Buttress
3 Fill: yellow-brown Mud-brick debris

Layer 2A (Plans, Figs 23, 24)

4 (2.5) Wall
5 (2.13) Wall
6 Lines: ash
7 Fill: yellow-brown and Mud-brick debris
8 Fill: same
9 Fill
10 Fill: yellow-brown and ash
11 Fill: ashy
12 (2.14) Wall
13 Fill: yellow-brown and reddish
14 Fill: yellow-brown and ash
15 Fill: yellow-brown and Mud-brick debris
16 (?)Wall: see plan, Fig. 24
17 Fill: yellow-brown
18 Fill: ash
19 Fill: yellow-brown and ash

Layer 1 (Plans, Figs 26, 27)

20 Lines: ash and burning
21 Fill: red, greyish, yellow-brown with red pebbly
22 Lines: ash
23 Mud-brick
24 Facing or Lining (stone)
25 Floors: clay lines
26 Fill: soft, greyish brown

Key to Fig. 50.1: N Face of Trenches R21c & d

Layer 3 (Plan, Fig. 10)

1 (5)(8) Wall and Buttress
2 (3) Wall
3 Floor: black ash on red
4 Fill: yellow-brown
5 Line: yellow clay and soft, brown
6 Fill: yellow clay
7 Fill: yellow-brown Mud-brick debris

Layer 2B (Plans, Figs 11, 19)

8 Cut
9 (7.5) Wall
10 (7.3, 8) Wall
11 Surfaces: yellow clay on red clay
12 (7.11) Partition
13 Floors: grey, ashy
14 Fill: yellow-brown and Mud-brick debris
15 Floors: yellow and grey, ashy
16 Fill: yellow-brown
17 Surface: yellow clay
18 Fill: yellow
19 Floor: white clay
20 Fill: yellow-brown and Mud-brick debris
21 Line: ash
22 Fill: yellow-brown
23 Line: ash
24 Fill: yellow-brown and red Mud-brick debris

Layer 2A (Plans, Figs 23, 24)

25 Line: ash
26 Fill: yellow-brown
27 Ash
28 Ash
29 Ash
30 (1.1) Wall
31 Fill: yellow
32 Fill: yellow-brown and Mud-brick debris

Byzantine Layer (Plan, Fig. 32)

33 Fill: grey, ashy above a grey clay floor

Key to Fig. 50.2: N Face of Trench S21c

Layer 2B (Plans, Figs 11, 18, 19)

1 (7.2) Wall
2 (8.1, 2) Wall

Layer 2A

3 Fill: red and red Mud-brick debris, and ash-line
4 Fill: grey, ashy and ash-lines
5 Fill: yellow-brown and ash-lines
6 Ash

Byzantine Layer (Plan, Fig. 32)

7 Fill: yellow-brown and reddish

Key to Fig. 50.3: S Face of Trench R21c (mirror image)

Layer 2B (Plans, Figs 11, 16)

1 (4.6) Wall
2 Fill: yellow-brown Mud-brick debris

Layer 2A (Plans, Figs 23, 24)

3 (2.2) Wall
4 Fill: Mud-brick debris
5 Fill: ashy grey
6 Fill: same
7 Fill: same
8 Fill: same
9 Fill: same
10 Fill: yellow-brown and ash-lines

Layer 1

11 Fill: yellow-brown and ash-lines
12 Line: grey-green clay
13 Fill: dark red
14 Line: hard, yellowish clay

Key to Fig. 51.1: E Face of Trenches Q21c and 22a

Layer 2B (Plan, Fig. 11)

1 (11.-) Wall
2 (11.-) Wall
3 Fill: yellow-brown and Mud-brick debris
4 Fill: same

Layer 2A (Plans, Figs 23, 24)

5 (2.18) Wall
6 (2.15) Wall
7 (2.12, 14) Wall
8 (2.14) Wall
9 Lines: ash
10 Fill: yellow-brown and Mud-brick debris between ash-lines
11 (6.6, 11) Wall
12 Brown clay: (?)Floor or Wall (6.8)
13 Fill: yellow-brown and Mud-brick
14 Fill: yellow with multiple ash-lines

Layer 1 (Plans, Figs 26, 27)

15 (1) Wall
16 (18) Floor: white clay
17 Floor: same
18 Fill: yellow with multiple ash-lines

Key to Fig. 51.2: S Face of Trenches R24c & d

Layer 2B (Plans, Figs 11, 20)

1 (10.15) Wall
2 Fill: Mud-brick debris with chunks of fallen Floor
3 Beam: burnt
4 Fill: Mud-brick debris

Layer 1 (Plans, Figs 26, 29–31)

5 (34) Wall
6 (32) Wall
7 (79) Wall
8 Floor
9 Floor: white clay
10 Floor: red clay
11 Floor
12 Fill: brown with ash-line
13 Fill: yellow-brown
14 Fill: brown
15 Fill: yellow-brown

Key to Fig. 52.1: Sections of Trench R21c, E Face

Layer 3 (Plan, Fig. 10)

1 Floor: black ash on red clay
2 Fill: yellow clay
3 Line: ash
4 Fill: yellow-brown Mud-brick debris
5 Line

Layer 2B (Plans, Figs 11, 16, 19)

6 (7.4) Wall
7 (7.9) Buttress
8 (4.1) Wall
9 Fill: brick-red, Mud-brick debris
10 Fill: same
11 Floors: yellow clay and ash-lines
12 Fill: burnt, brick-red, Mud-brick debris
13 Floors
14 Fill: yellow-brown Mud-brick debris
15 Line: ash
16 Fill: yellow-brown and Mud-brick debris
17 Line: ash
18 Fill: yellow-brown and Mud-brick debris
19 Line: ash
20 Fill: yellow-brown and Mud-brick debris

Layer 2A (Plan, Fig. 23)

21 Line: ash
22 Fill: yellow-brown and Mud-brick debris
23 Fill: yellow-brown and Mud-brick debris above an ash-line
24 Fill: yellow-brown and ash-line

Key to Fig. 52.2: S Face of Trenches S24c & d (mirror image)

Layer 2B (Plans, Figs 11, 20)
1 (10.22) Wall
2 Fill: yellow-brown and Mud-brick debris

Layer 2A (Plans, Figs 23, 25)
3 Floor make-up: grey-green clay
4 Floors
5 (5.2) Wall

Layer 1 (Plans, Figs 26, 28–31)
6 Fill
7 (42) Wall
8 (63) Bench
9 (43) Wall
10 Floor: red clay
11 Fill: yellow-brown
12 Floors (two): white clay
13 Fill: burnt, red, with ash and carbon
14 Floors
15 Fill: brown

Key to Fig. 52.3: N Face of Trench T25a

Layer (?2A)
1 Fill: hard, brown

Layer 1 (Plans, Figs 26, 28–31)
2 (75) Wall
3 (44) Wall
4 (?): indeterminate phase
5 Floors: hard, red clay between two white clay floors
6 Fill: Mud-brick debris and ash
7 Fill or Pit: light brown
8 Fill: ashy

Key to Fig. 53.1: W face of Trench S21c

Layer 2B (Plans, Figs 11, 18)
1 (6.11) Buttress
2 (6.1) Wall
3 (8.1) Wall
4 Fill: yellow-brown and Mud-brick debris
5 Fill: same

Layer 2A
6 Fill: orange-red and Mud-brick debris
7 Ash
8 Ash
9 Lines: grey clay and ash
10 Carbon and black ash
11 Fill: yellow-brown and Mud-brick debris

Fig. 53.2: W Face of Trenches Q23a and 22c

Layer (?)1
1 Fill: soft brown; (?)above a floor

Layer 1 (Plans, Figs 26, 27)
2 (9) Wall
3 (13) Partition
4 (28) Floor: white clay
5 (25) Floor: same
6 Floor: same
7 Pit: stone-lined
8 Fill: yellow
9 Fill: same but with Mud-brick debris
10 Fill: same as 9

Key to Fig. 53.3: S Face of Trench Q23a

Layer 1 (Plans, Figs 26, 27)
1 Floor: white clay
2 Fill: yellow-brown
3 (28) Floor: white clay
4 Fill: yellow-brown

Key to Fig. 54.1: S Face of Trench S21c (mirror image)

Layer 2B (Plans, Figs 11, 18)
1 (6.7) Buttress
2 (6.4) Wall
3 (6.12) Partition
4 Fill: black and red, burnt Mud-brick debris
5 Fill: same

Layer 2A (Plan, Fig. 23)
6 Floors: clay with ash-lines
7 Ash
8 Ash: carbon chunks
9 Fill: black and red, burnt, Mud-brick debris

Key to Fig. 54.2: W Face of Trenches Q22a and 21c

Layer 2A (Plans, Figs 23, 24)
1 (6.5) Wall
2 Line
3 (6.3,10) Wall
4 Fill: yellow-brown Mud-brick debris, masking Wall 6.1
5 Line: yellowish clay
6 Cut
7 Fill: yellow-brown
8 Fill: yellow-brown Mud-brick debris
9 Lines: ash

10 Fill: yellow clay
11 Line: ash
12 Fill: yellow-brown
13 Line: ash
14 Fill: yellow clay
15 Line: ash
16 Wall: orientation not determined
17 Fill: yellow-brown
18 Ash: black; burnt material
19 Fill: yellow clay
20 Floor: white clay below yellow-brown
21 Floor: yellow clay
22 Fill: yellow-brown
23 Fill: yellow-brown above yellow and white clay floors (= 20, 21)
24 Fill: yellow-brown

Layer 1 (Plans, Figs 26, 27)

25 (5) Wall
26 (16) (?)Bench
27 (25) Floors
28 Floors
29 Fill: yellow-brown
30 Lines: ash
31 Fill: yellow-brown
32 (?)Robber-trench
33 (22) Lining or Facing (stone)
34 (21) (?)Post-pad (stone)
35 Fill: yellow-brown
36 (20) Floor: white clay
37 Line: clay below yellow-brown
38 Line: brown clay below yellow-brown
39 Fill: brown
40 Fill: yellow-brown
41 Fill: same
42 Fill: same
43 Fill; same

Key to Fig. 55.1: N Face of Trenches S25c & d

Layer 2A (Plans, Figs 23, 25)

1 (5.9) Wall
2 Surface: grey, ashy
3 Fill: dark reddish brown, mixed with Mud-brick
4 Fill: yellow-brown mixed with Mud-brick
5 Fill: ash-lenses and lines, and yellow-brown and reddish brown
6 Fill: same
7 Surfaces: yellow and grey
8 Fill: yellow-brown
9 Surfaces: ash-lines on (above) a yellow clay floor and (below) a white clay floor, against a white clay Wall-plaster
10 Fill: yellow-brown
11 Fill: soft black, 'dead' i.e. featureless and unstructured; (?)organic, humic origin; cp. no. 3 on Fig. 57.1 and no. 39 on Figs 46, 47

Layer 1 (Plans, Figs 26, 28–31)

12 Fill: yellow-brown, dusty, 'dead'
13 (49) Wall: (?)foundation bricks
14 (49) Wall
15 (47) Wall
16 Floor: white clay
17 Fill: yellow-brown with Mud-brick debris
18 (81) Floor: red clay
19 Fill: yellow-brown
20 Fill: yellow-brown with ash-lines
21 Floor: grey, ashy
22 (76) Wall
23 Floor: white clay
24 Floor: burnt
25 Surfaces: ashy
26 Floor: white clay
27 Floor: ashy, with Hearth (against Wall)
28 Fill: yellow-brown and soft black
29 Fill: soft dark
30 Line: ashy

Key to Fig. 55.2: W Face of Trenches R25a and 24c

Layer 2B (Plans, Figs 11, 20)

1 (10.12) Wall
2 Surface: burnt surface below ash, burnt debris and carbon chunks
3 Surface: same
4 Fill: yellow-brown with ash, burnt debris including Mud-brick and plaster, and carbon chunks
5 Fill: same
6 Fill: same

Layer 1 (Plans, Figs 26, 28–31)

7 (40) Wall
8 (37) Wall
9 (35) Wall
10 (31) Wall
11 (?)Wall, (?)Mud-brick: indeterminate phase
12 Floor: white clay
13 Floor: same
14 Fill: yellow-brown with Mud-brick debris
15 Fill: brown with Mud-brick debris

Key to Fig. 56.1 N Face of Trenches S26a & b

Layer 1 (Plans, Figs 26, 28–31)

1 (53) Wall: white clay Plaster on W Face

2 (50) Wall
3 (90) Partition
4 (91) Oven
5 (91) Oven: clay surround for a circular Oven
6 Floor: hard, white clay
7 Fill: yellow-brown with Mud-brick debris
8 Floor: red, burnt
9 Floor: ashy
10 Floor: red, burnt
11 Floor: yellow clay and ash
12 Floor: yellow clay
13 Fill: yellow-brown
14 Floor
15 Fill: yellow
16 Floor with Oven or Hearth
17 Fill: yellow-brown
18 Fill: yellow-brown with Mud-brick debris and Plaster
19 Floor: white clay
20 (60) Partition
21 (57) Partition
22 (71) Pot
23 Fill: hard, brown or yellow-brown
24 Fill: ash
25 Fill: yellow-brown with Mud-brick debris and ash
26 Fill: loose, brown earth
27 Fill: clay
28 Fill: hard, brown
29 Fill: brownish

Key to Fig. 56.2: W Face of Trenches R25b and 24d

Layer 2B (Plans, Figs 11, 20)

1 (10.7) Wall
2 (10.7) Wall
3 Fill: Mud-brick debris

Layer 1 (Plans, Figs 26, 28–31)

4 Floors
5 Fill: yellow-brown with Mud-brick debris
6 Pebbles
7 Floors: hard, white clay
8 Floor: hard, white clay
9 Fill: brown

Key to Fig. 57.1: W Face of Trenches S26a and 25c

Layer 2A (Plan, Fig. 23)

1 Surfaces: yellow and red clay, and ash
2 Fill: yellow-brown

Layer (?)

3 Fill: soft, black, 'dead' i.e. featureless and unstructured; (?)organic, humic origin; cp. no. 11 on Fig. 55.1

Layer 1 (Plans, Figs 26, 28–31)

4 (55) Wall
5 (56) Wall
6 (49) Wall
7 Floor: white clay
8 Fill: yellow-brown
9 Fill: yellow-brown with Mud-brick debris and Plaster fragments
10 Fill: dark brown
11 Mud-brick
12 Mud-brick: (?)Partition
13 Partition: (?)same
14 Fill: grey, greyish brown, with ash and Mud-brick debris
15 Fill: yellow-brown above a red line
16 Fill: yellow-brown and Mud-brick debris
17 Mud-brick
18 (56) Wall: continuation of Wall 56
19 (60) Partition: Mud-brick plastered with white clay
20 (57) Partition: same
21 Floor: white clay
22 (61) Partition: Mud-brick
23 Fill: soft, grey ash
24 Fill: grey, ashy
25 (71) Pot segment
26 Fill: grey, ashy
27 (62) Partition
28 Fill: greyish brown with Mud-brick debris
29 Fill: brown
30 Fill: yellow
31 Fill: dark brown

Key to Fig. 57.2: W Face of Trenches S26b and 25d

Layer 1 (Plans, Figs 26, 28–31)

1 (53) Wall
2 (77) Wall
3 Floor: white clay
4 Fill: grey, ashy
5 (77) Wall: continuation of Wall 2
6 Surface: ashy
7 Fill: grey, ashy
8 Fill: yellow-brown
9 Fill: dark; gravel in 'scoop', (?)= a surface
10 (?)Bench: not on Plan, Fig. 30
11 Floors: ash on red clay
12 Fill: ashy
13 (76) Wall
14 Floors: ash on white clay

15 Fill: yellow-brown
16 Fill; yellow-brown with Mud-brick debris
17 (54) Wall
18 (?): Mud-brick
19 Lines: ash
20 (?)Mud-brick
21 Lines: ash-lines above a soft, brown fill
22 Fill: dark grey
23 Fill: grey

Key to Fig. 57.3: E Face of Trenches R24c and 25a

Layer 2B (Plans, Figs 11, 20)

1 (10.7) Wall
2 (10.11) Wall
3 Floors: ashy
4 Fill: yellow-brown and red, with burnt Mud-brick debris
5 Fill: same
6 Fill: same
7 Fill: same
8 (10.8) Buttress

Layer 1 (Plans, Figs 26, 28–31)

9 Cut
10 Floors: white clay
11 (?)Floor
12 Floor
13 Fill: fine, soft, brown
14 Floor
15 Fill: brown
16 Floor

Key to Fig. 58.1: W Face of Trenches S25a and 24c

Layer 2B (Plans, Figs 11, 20)

1 (10.2, 3) Wall
2 Line: blue sand
3 Fill: green clay and Mud-brick debris
4 Fill: yellow-brown and Mud-brick debris

Layer 2A (Plans, Figs 23, 26)

5 Lines (?Floors): green clay
6 Surface: white clay
7 (5.2) Wall
8 Packing: hard, yellow clay
9 Mud-brick: (?)= Wall 5.1 or Mud-brick rubble/ debris
10 (5.3) Wall
11 Fill: yellow-brown and ash
12 Fill: yellow-brown, yellow clay, ash and charcoal
13 Fill: yellow-brown
14 Line: yellow-brown
15 Fill: reddish and Mud-brick debris
16 (5.8) Wall
17 (5.7) Wall
18 Fill: brown
19 Fill: brown
20 Fill: soft, ashy (?= S25c Fill: soft black [3])

Layer 1 (Plans, Figs 26, 28–31)

21 Fill: yellow
22 Floor: white clay
23 Fill: soft, yellow-brown
24 (49) Wall
25 (83) Partition
26 Floor: red clay
27 Fill: dark brown
28 Floor: white clay
29 (93) Wall
30 (94) Partition
31 Fill: brown
32 Floor: white clay
33 Partition
34 Fill: brown
35 Floor: white clay
36 Fill: brown
37 Fill: brown

Key to Fig. 58.2: S Face of Trenches S26a & b (mirror image)

Layer 1 (Plans, Figs 26, 28–31)

1 (58) Wall
2 (73) Wall
3 (55) Wall
4 (72) Wall
5 Floor
6 (?)Wall: not on the Plan, Fig. 31
7 Floor: black ash above white clay
8 Fill: yellow-brown
9 Fill: same
10 Floor
11 Floor: ashy
12 Fill: pale grey ash and Mud-brick debris
13 Fill: ashy
14 Fill: yellow-brown with Mud-brick debris and ash
15 Fill: yellow-brown
16 Fill: pale grey, ashy
17 Fill: yellow-brown
18 Floor: white ashy
19 Floors: ashy with Mud-brick debris
20 Fill: ashy
21 Fill: same
22 Fill: same
23 Fill: yellow-brown Mud-brick debris

24 (?)Mud-brick: in yellow-brown Mud-brick debris
25 Fill: hard, grey
26 Floors: hard clay
27 Fill: hard, grey
28 Fill: dark grey with Mud-brick debris
29 Fill: grey
30 Floors: hard clay
31 Fill: yellow-brown

Key to Fig. 58.3: E Face of Trenches R24d and 25b

Layer 2B (Plans, Figs 11, 20)

1 (10.18) Buttress
2 (10.2) Wall
3 Mud-bricks: Face of Wall 10.3
4 Mud-bricks: white clay Plaster on Face of Wall 10.3
5 Floor: clay
6 Fill: yellow and grey Mud-brick debris, with patches of charcoal
7 Ash
8 Fill: red Mud-brick debris, ash and clay lines
9 Fill: red Mud-brick debris
10 Fill: same; (?)fallen Mud-brick at N end against Wall 10.3
11 Fill: red Mud-brick debris

Layer 1 (Plans, Figs 26, 28–31)

12 Floor: red clay 13 Fill: brown
14 (93) Wall
15 (49) Wall
16 Fill
17 Fill
18 Floors
19 Floor: white clay
20 Fill: brown
21 Fill: grey
22 Floors: white clay
23 Fill: yellow-brown

Fig. 59. Reconstructed view of layer 2B from a rooftop, looking towards Karadağ

Fig. 60. Reconstructed view of layer 2B, upper storey, looking towards Karadağ

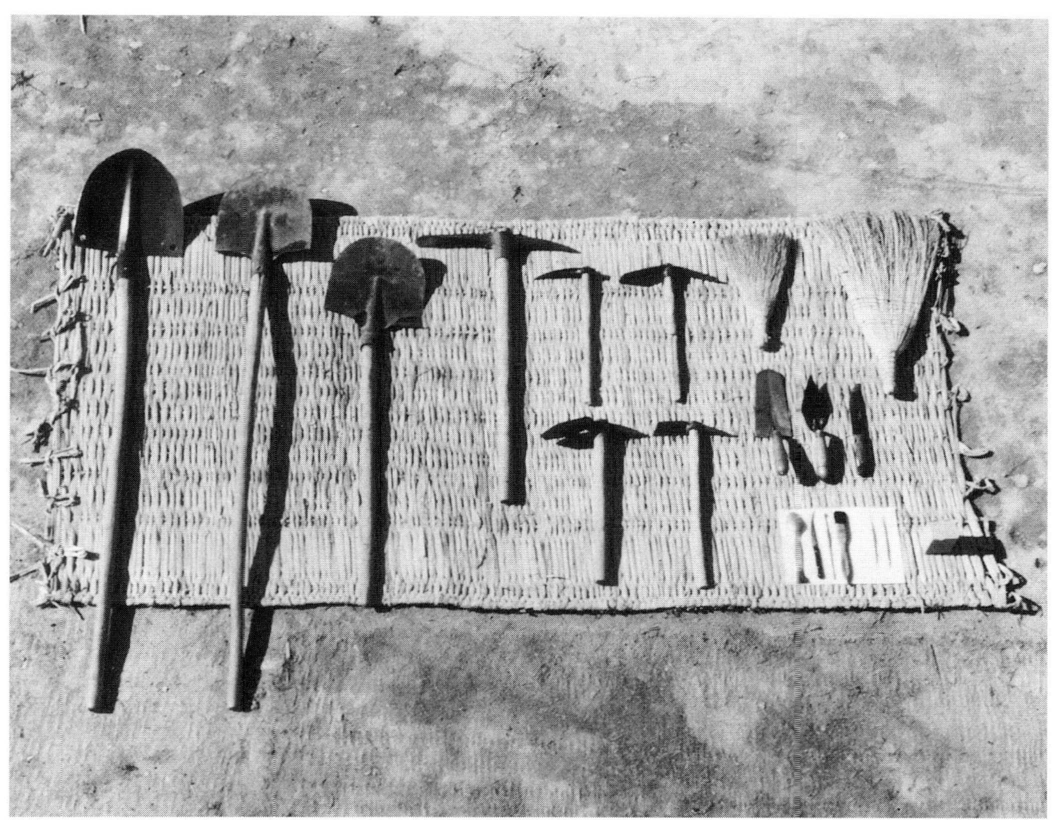

1 Canhasan: dig tools (1965) (see pp. 8–9)

2 Canhasan: dig house, plain and Karadağ (autumn 1964) (see pp. 13, 17)

2 Layer 5: R21b, from E (1967) (see p. 23)

1 Alaçatı: wooden mould for mud-bricks (see pp. 21, 67)

1 Layer 5: reed and/or twig impressions in Wall 3, from E (1967). Scale division = 10 cm. (see p. 23)

2 Layer 5: same, detail. Scale division = 10 cm.

1 Layer 4: beam impressions in and against Wall 1, from N (1967). Scale division = 1 cm. (see p. 25)

2 Layer 4: burial of two dogs under threshold, from S (1967). Scale division = 10 cm. (see p. 25)

1 Layer 4: burial of two dogs under threshold, from S (1967). Scale division = 1 cm. (see p. 25)

2 Layer 2B: Structure 3, E room, from S (1961). Scale division = 20 cm. (see p. 32)

1 Layer 2B: same, from E (1961). Scale division = 20 cm. (see p. 32)

2 Layer 2B: Structure 10, E wall (1967). Scale division = 50 cm. (see p. 38)

1 Layer 2B: Structure 10, E wall (1967). Scale division = 50 cm. (see p. 38)

2 Layer 2A: mud-brick features in Q21d, from N (1966). Scale division = 50 cm. (see p. 47)

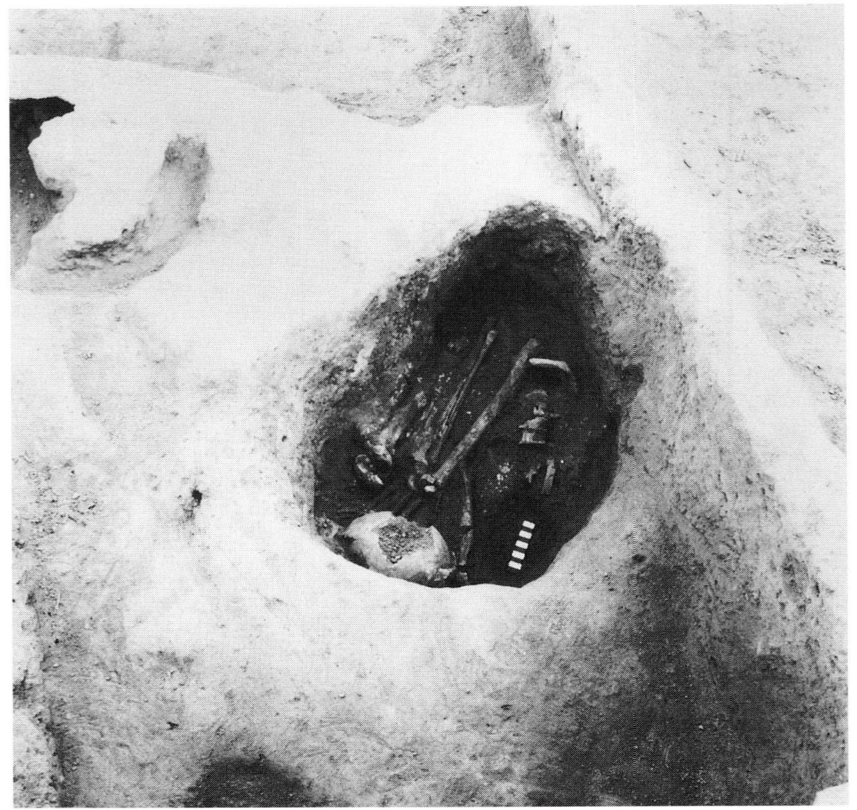

1 Layer 2A: infant burial in baulk S24c/25a, from W (1967). Scale division = 1 cm. (see p. 49)

2 Layer 1: oven (plan 29 no.69) in S26b (1964). Scale division = 10 cm. (see p. 59)

1 Layer 1: the southern trenches, from W (1964) (see pp. 50, 59)

2 Layer 1: same (see pp. 50, 59)